FIRST SETTLERS
of the
REPUBLIC OF TEXAS

Volume II
Headright Land Grants Which Were Reported as Genuine and Legal by the Traveling Commissioners January 1840

Carolyn R. Ericson
and
Frances T. Ingmire

Heritage Books
2024

HERITAGE BOOKS

AN IMPRINT OF HERITAGE BOOKS, INC.

Books, CDs, and more—Worldwide

For our listing of thousands of titles see our website
at
www.HeritageBooks.com

A Facsimile Reprint
Published 2024 by
HERITAGE BOOKS, INC.
Publishing Division
5810 Ruatan Street
Berwyn Heights, MD 20740

— Publisher's Notice —
In reprints such as this, it is often not possible to remove blemishes from the original. We feel the contents of this book warrant its reissue despite these blemishes and hope you will agree and read it with pleasure.

International Standard Book Number
Paperbound: 978-0-7884-8598-5

TABLE OF CONTENTS

JEFFERSON COUNTY

No.	Names	Lgs.	Lbr.	Acres	Date	Remarks
37	Allen, Hannah	1	1			
28	Allen, Elisha	1/3				
62	Allen, George		1			
88	Arthur, Barnabas C.	1	1			
27	Allen, William; dec'd.	1	1			
1	Balinger, John	1	1			
2	Balinger, Peter	1/3				
3	Balinger, Lewis	1/3				
4	Balinger, John, Jr.	1/3				
21	Bowton, Nathan	1	1			
39	Bulrerease, J.B.	1	1			
50	Booth, Robert E.	1	1			
52	Beach, Clarke	1	1			
95	Brenam, Thos. H.	1	1			
99	Barrett, David	1	1			
100	Blackman, Bennett		1			
101	Blackman, Josiah	1/3				
106	Blann, Peyton	1/3				
121	Bumstead, Morad W.	1/3				
125	Brake, Michael J.	1/3				Wm.H. Iron, Admr.
128	Balew, Richard		1			
155	Bland, John		1			
167	Bland, Peyton	2/3	1			
41	Bulrease, Mary C.	1	1			
117	Burwell, Nancy	1	1			Robin Burwell Admr.
23	Cole, Solomon	1/3				
25	Cole, David	1/3				
67	Cole, John	1	1			
68	Cole, James	1	1			
101	Clark, John	1/3				
121	Clark, William		1			
157	Cole, David	2/3	1			
159	Cottle, Mary Ann		1			
162	Court, Thomas	1	1			
163	Cottle, Lorenzo D.	1/3				
40	Carruthers, John	1	1			
107	Carr, William	1	1			
36	Coles, James, Sr. Dec'd.	1	1			Geo.A. Patillo, cur.
71	Disboe, Valentine E.	1/3				
73	Dyson, Jesse	1	1			
108	Dyches, Wm. C.	1	1			
115	Dyches, Lucinda	1	1			
117	Dyches, Josiah	1	1			
10	Doom, Ralph C.	1	1			
70	Dooling, John	1	1			Heirs of.

No.	Names	Lgs.	Lbr.	Acres	Date	Remarks
51	Forsyth, John H.	1/3				Jos. P. Pul-siter, Admr.
22	Gibson, Uriah	1	1			
35	Green, Michael	1	1			
42	Garner, David	1/3				
47	Garner, Jacob H.	1/3				
85	Gray, Sarah	1	1			
97	Garner, Isaac	1/3				
105	Gray, James	1/3				
123	Gray, Absalom	1	1			
126	Griffith, Henry		1			
130	Graner, Bradley, Sr.	1	1			
141	Grigsby, Joseph		1			
144	Grigsby, Nathaniel			369		
145	Grigsby, Enoch	1/3				
2	Garner, Jacob	2/3	1			
15	Hodges, Wm. H.		1			
24	Harmon, John					5,922,250 square varus.
32	Harmon, David	1	1			
34	Hayes, William	1	1			
46	Harris, Uriah	1/3				
72	Hatton, Wm. T.	1	1			
74	Hatton, Wm. E.	1/3				
75	Hatton, Marmaducke S.	1/3				
116	Harper, Benjamin J.		1			
119	Hillibrent, Christian		1			
129	Halbert, Nathan	1/3				
153	Hanks, Samuel G.	1	1			
42	Higdore, Ezekiel	1	1			
18	Iron, Wm. H.	1	1			
7	Johnson, John	1	1			
38	Jett, Absalom	1	1			
45	Johnson, Benjamin	1/3				
84	Jett, James	1	1			
118	Jackson, Stephen		1			
149	Jett, Sarah		1			
152	Johnson, Elizabeth		1			
166	Johnson, Benjamin	2/3				
70	Jett, John		1			
51	Kerr, Lucius H.	1/3				
90	Lejoice, Charles, Dec'd.	1	1			John C. Read, Admr.
30	Lewis, Thomas H.	1	1			
76	Labode, Franswar	1/3				

No.	Name	Lgs.	Lbr.	Acres	Date	Remarks
93	Longly, Henry B.	1/3				
8	McFaden, James		1			
19	McFaden, William	1	1			
31	Millard, Henry	1	1			
33	McDonald, William	1	1			
36	Myers, Charles	1	1			
37	McFaden, William, Sr.		1			
56	McFerron, Sarah	1	1			Thos. H. Brenam, att.
86	McFaden, David H.	1	1			
96	Millhouse, David	1	1			Robt.E. Booth Admr.
146	Millapangh, Wm. Dec'd.	1/3				Claiborne West, Cur.
148	Moore, Wm. W.	1/3				
91	Morriss, Elisha		1			
161	McGaffey, John	1	1			
171	Odum, David	1/3				
5	Pleasant, John	1	1			
20	Patilla, George A.		1			
44	Peace, Henry	1	1			
139	Palmer, Silas	1	1			
142	Pevito, Michael, Sr.	1/3				
173	Pulsifer, Joseph P.	1/3				
43	Price, Rease	1	1			
56	Peace, Hiram	1	1			Thos.D. Yocum, Admr.
59	Richie, Wm. Dec'd.	1	1			Hannah Simmons, Admx.
60	Richie, Archibald, Dec'd.	1	1			Hannah Simmons, Admx.
61	Richie, Ewell, Dec'd.			369		Hannah Simmons, Admx.
69	Rome, Thomas M.	1	1			
94	Read, John C.	1	1			
98	Riggs, Pleasant B.	1	1			
114	Roberts, Joseph	1	1			Should be Rubarth
133	Richey, Hiram	1	1			
10	Stephenson, Wm.		1			
48	Scott, David	1/3				
53	Simmons, James		1			
57	Smith, James B.	1/3				
61	Stephenson, Gilbert	1	1			
79	St. Clair, Duncan	1	1			
80	Stephenson, James	1	1			
81	Stephenson, George	1/3				
82	Stephenson, John	1	1			
131	Steward, John, Dec'd.		1			Bradley Garner, Admr.

No.	Name	Lgs.	Lbr.	Acres	Date	Remarks
132	Sills, Wilson W.	1/3				
140	Smith, William D.		1			
156	Stephenson, John, Dec'd.	1	1			Lydia Stephenson, Admx.
165	Smith, William H.	1	1			
9	Tevis, George W.	1	1			
13	Tevis, Nancy	1/2	1			
65	Turner, John	1/3				
66	Turner, Mariah	1	1			John Turner, Admr.
83	Tevis, Andrew J.	1/3				
122	Thomas, Amos	1/3				
138	Townsend, Jacob			369		
175	Turner, Joseph	1	1			
14	Williams, Absalom	1	1			
29	Williams, Charles		1			
43	West, Claiborne		1			
49	Winn, James	1	1			
54	Williams, H.R.	3/4	1			
55	Williams, Oliver H.	1/3				
89	Winfrey, Abraham	1	1			
102	Walea, James	1	1			
112	Williams, Hezekiah, Jr.			369		
120	Williams, Hexekiah, Sr.		1			
160	Wilkerson, George	1/3				
41	Yocum, Christopher A.	1/3				
136	Young, Joseph		1			
158	Yocum, Thomas D.					2,335,413 square varas.

SECOND CLASS

No.	Name	Lgs.	Lbr.	Acres	Date	Remarks
11	Bunker, Thos. C.			640	Jy.5,1838	
12	Barwick, Thos.			1280	Jy.5,1838	
7	Craig, James Alexander			640	Sept.4,1838	
65	Gallier, Frances			1280	Nov.7,1839	
2	Halissy, James			640	Mar.29,1838	
1	Hutchinson, Joseph			640	Mar.8,1838	
13	Jones, Burrel			640	Jy. 6,1838	
9	Keath, George			1280	Jy. 5,1838	
15	McAlpin, Malcom J.			640	Oct. 4, 1838	
1	Sundy, Thomas			640	Mar. 29,1838	
8	Simmons, James, Jr.			1280	Jy.5,1838	
2	Sloan, William			640	Mar. 8,1838	

THIRD CLASS

No.	Name	Lgs.	Lbr.	Acres	Date	Remarks
13	Applewhite, Isaac			640	Apr.4,1839	
98	Anderson, James			320	Jan.2,1840	
129	Allen, John Henry			320	Jan.12,1840	
10	Brazier, William			640	Mar.8,1839	
23	Bonner, Nathaniel			640	Apr.4,1839	
45	Brown, James W.			640	Jy.4,1839	
48	Brown, Joseph M.			640	Jy.4,1839	
71	Baker, Tabitha M.			640	Nov.7,1839	
92	Bark, William			640	Dec.5,1839	
97	Brooks, A.M.			320	Dec.5,1839	
102	Boswell, George W.			320	Jan.2,1840	
103	Booth, Lawrence H.			640	Jan.2,1840	
108	Barwick, Joseph			320	Jan.2,1840	
123	Bonittett, Louis			320	Jan.2,1840	
127	Burwell, George			320	Jan.6,1840	
20	Clark, James			640	Apr.4,1839	
21	Cable, William			320	Apr.4,1839	
24	Chesson, McGuire			640	Apr.4,1839	
53	Calder, Alexander			640	Sept.5,1839	
73	Chesson, Jerard			640	Dec.5,1839	
76	Clayton, James F.			320	Dec.5,1839	
83	Crockett, Martha			640	Dec.5,1839	
128	Crane, Albert			320	Jan.12,1840	
28	Derry, Daniel			320	Apr.4,1839	
67	Dunford, Mathew G.			320	Nov.7,1839	
118	Diekirson, Joseph			320	Jan.2,1840	
131	Dellinable, Lewis			320	Jan.12,1840	
17	Eves, James			320	Apr.4,1839	
18	Eliot, George H.			320	Apr.4,1839	
31	Eddy, Zimri W.			320	May 2,1839	
40	Ewell, Alexander			640	May 2,1839	
54	Elston, Allen W.			320	Sept.5,1839	
114	Ellis, William B.			640	Jan.2,1840	
49	Fee, Henry			320	Jy.4,1839	
64	Frost, Jason			320	Nov.7,1839	
106	Fox, Jonas			320	Jan.2,1840	
133	Franklin, Harvy			320	Jan.12,1840	
5	Gilbert, William			320	Mar.8,1839	
9	Gallies, James			320	Mar.8,1839	
16	Gilchrist, Julius			640	Apr.4,1839	
26	Gavner, Bradley			320	Apr.4,1839	
27	Goodue, Warren			320	Apr.4,1839	
57	Garner, Westley			320	Sept.5,1839	
89	Guedry, Susteen			320	Dec.5,1839	
44	Grigsby, William			320	June 6,1839	

No.	Name	Lgs.	Lbr.	Acres	Date	Remarks
95	Griffs, Thomas			320	Dec.5,1839	
12	Harris, Rector N.			640	Apr.4,1839	
19	Hart, Benjamin			320	Apr.4,1839	
77	Hickman, William			640	Dec.5,1839	
78	Hickman, Jesse			640	Dec.5,1839	
86	Hardin, William O.			640	Dec.5,1839	
101	Hogan, William			320	Jan.2,1840	
110	Hardy, Richard			640	Jan.2,1840	
111	Hardy, Mason			640	Jan.2,1840	
121	Hardinston, Otto			320	Jan.2,1840	
124	Hiorth, C.G.			320	Jan.2,1840	
125	Hildebrand, Levi			320	Jan.6,1840	
47	Howerton, Heritage			320	Jy. 4,1839	
38	Ingols, James			320	May 2,1839	
81	Keezer, Horace P.			320	Dec.5,1839	
105	Kumley, William			320	Jan.2,1840	
107	Kurcher, John C.			320	Jan.2,1840	
119	Kelly, Robert			320	Jan.2,1840	
120	Keezer, Beza T.			320	Jan.2,1840	
85	Lelig, Lewis H.			320	Dec.5,1839	
87	Lad, Anson F.			320	Dec.5,1839	
136	Lewis, Joel			640	Jan.6,1840	
126	Lennox, Thomas			320	Jan.6,1840	
7	Mitchel, Peter			640	Mar.8,1839	
8	Meliheny, Samuel			320	Mar.8,1839	
29	Millard, Sidney H.			320	May 2,1839	
30	Millard, Nancy			640	May 2,1839	
50	May, John			320	Jy.4,1839	
74	McClusky, Jeremiah			320	Dec.5,1839	
82	Muligan, Michael			320	Dec.5,1839	
93	Mixon, Jeremiah			320	Dec.5,1839	
100	McGaffey, Otis			320	Jan.2,1840	
101	McDongle, George			640	Jan.2,1840	
112	Millard, D.J. Otho			640	Jan.2,1840	
113	McNamee, John H.			320	Jan.2,1840	
134	McGaffey, Neil			640	Jan.12,1840	
135	McGaffey, Wyatt			320	Jan.2,1840	
122	Norris, David			320	Jan.2,1840	
15	Piveto, John B.			640	Apr.4,1839	
31	Pine, Thomas Jefferson			320	May 2,1839	
35	Pattillo, James H.			320	May 2,1839	
52	Poindexter, William S.			320	Sept.5,1839	
55	Pumfrey, Archibald			320	Sept.5,1839	
58	Perry, Calvin			320	Nov.7,1839	
109	Pevito, John			320	Jan.2,1840	
115	Porter, William			640	Jan.2,1840	

No.	Name	Lgs.	Lbr.	Acres	Date	Remarks
99	Richie, William			640	Jan.2,1840	
4	Slade, William			640	Mar.8,1839	
39	Swaim, John D.			640	May 2,1839	
66	Sherman, George			640	Nov.7,1839	
90	Sinclair, Daniel			320	Dec.5,1839	
96	Spencer, William			320	Dec.5,1839	
116	Simmons, Daniel H.			320	Jan.2,1840	
137	Stafford, Alci			320	Jan.12,1840	
138	Stafford, Epaminondas			320	Jan.12,1840	
92	Thomas, Larkin R.			640	Apr.4,1839	
60	Taylor, James G.			320	Nov.7,1839	
61	Tabor, Isaac			320	Nov.7,1839	
62	Tabor, Hudson			320	Nov.7,1839	
63	Tabor, Nathan S.			320	Nov.7,1839	
6	White, John			320	Mar.8,1839	
25	Williams, William			320	Apr.4,1839	
32	Wilson, William S.			320	May 2,1839	
33	Wilson, William			640	May 2,1839	
46	Wilds, John Peer			640	Jy.4,1839	
79	Whitmire, John			640	Dec.5,1839	
80	Whitmire, Henry			320	Dec.5,1839	
81	Wait, John			320	Dec.5,1839	
88	Waldirt, John G.			320	Dec.5,1839	
94	White, Isaac B.			640	Dec.5,1839	
130	Watson, Simeon C.			320	Jan.12,1840	
59	Zarnikow, Louis C.			320	Nov.7,1839	

LIBERTY COUNTY

FIRST CLASS

No.	Name	Lgs.	Lbr.	Acres	Date	Remarks
12	Bryant, Luke, Jr.	1	1			
18	Bryan, Kendalles	1/3				
24	Branch, Edward T.	1/3				
38	Bryan, Charles	1				
39	Bryan, Charles		1			
45	Booth, John S.	1/3				
48	Baker, Cabel	1/3				A.B. Hardin, assignee
105	Burrill, Robert	1	1			
121	Bradley, Thomas	1/3				
123	Barker, William	1	1			
136	Banow, Benjamin	1	1			
138	Banow, Sol					6,320,000 square varas.
139	Banow, Levi	1	1			
142	Banow, Reuben, Sr.	1	1			

No.	Name	Lgs.	Lbr.	Acres	Date	Remarks
144	Bradley, Francis, Dec'd.	1	1			
145	Banow, Vincent, Dec'd.	1	1			
158	Bebee, Elnathan	1/3				
165	Bryan, Joseph, Dec'd.	1/3				
204	Barco, Calvin	1	1			A. Garner, assignee
209	Banow, Reuben, Jr.	1/3				
219	Brown, John	1	1			
225	Burks, John D.		1			
231	Bryan, Pryor	1	1			
244	Barber, Amos	1/3				
245	Banow, Benjamin, Jr.	1/3				
252	Beers, David	1				
254	Banow, Reuben, 2nd	2/3	1			
266	Barber, Samuel	1	1			
267	Barber, John	1/3				
298	Byran, Kindales	2/3	1			
333	Boyce, Reason W	1	1			
336	Branch, Edward T.	2/3	1			
342	Berry, Campbell	1	1			Daniel P. Coit assigne
360	Belt, Samuel T.	1	1			
22	Coleman, William	1/3				
25	Clayton, Jas. M.	1	1			
51	Colt, Joseph, Dec'd.	1/3				
53	Clarke, George	1/3				
68	Curry, Jane	1	1			
95	Coronado, Jose		1			
99	Coit, Daniel P.		1			
156	Cheny, John		1			
157	Cape, Thomas	1/3				
161	Cheny, Aaron	1/3				
162	Choate, David, Sr.		1			
163	Choate, Edward	1/3				
164	Choate, John	1/3				
177	Cleveland, Daniel	1/3				
192	Carroll, M.A., Dec'd.		1			
208	Chavenoe, Michael	1/3				
126	Choate, Moses L.		1			
235	Cheny, Herron, Sr.		1			
257	Clark, Esther	1	1			
260	Coleman, Rebecca	1	1			
284	Castillon, Lawrence	1	1			
315	Choate, David, Jr.	1/3				
317	Coy, Alexander	1/3				
107	Cheny, William	1/3				
8	Devore, Jesse		1			
16	Dalton, Wm. K.	1	1			
79	Dunman, Henry	1/3				
80	Dunman, Joseph T.	1	1			
91	Dever, Thomas	3/4	1			

No.	Name	Lgs.	Lbr.	Acres	Date	Remarks
106	Duncan, Wm. B.	1/3				
110	Dever, P.P. Dec'd.		1			A.B. Hardin, Admr.
113	Dever, John C.	1/3				
131	Dunaho, Daniel		1			
146	Deroe, Cornelius	1/3				
150	Dorsett, Thomas M.	1/3				
151	Dorsett, John	1/3				
152	Duncan, Wm., Dec'd.		1			
153	Duncan, Meredith		1			
183	Dorsett, Charles	1/3				
193	Dunman, Martin	1	1			
217	Dunman, Joseph	1/3				
228	Don, Edward	1/3				
233	Dugat, James L.	1	1			
253	Davis, R.N.	1	1			
274	Dobee, Wm., Dec'd.	3/4	1			
278	Davis, Daniel		1			
279	Davis, Zachariah		1			
280	Davis, Geo. Washington	1/3				
301	Dorsett, Thomas		1			
306	Dugat, Joseph, Dec'd.	1	1			
312	Dunahoe, Moses		1			
321	Doane, Jos.	1/3				
350	Dickson, Wm.	1	1			
371	Dugat, Charles E.	1/3				
72	Elender, Joseph	1/3				
188	Eldridge, James	1/3				
201	Everett, Wm.,Dec'd.		1			
369	Edmonds, Margaret	1	1			
5	Farley, H.W.	1				
30	Freeman, Benjamin, Dec'd.	1/3				
52	Faulk, John	1	1			
	Fresby, William		1			
374	Fisher, Ann	1	1			A.B. Hardin, assignee
6	Farley, H.W.		1			
126	Fields, Isah S.		1			
265	Fitzsimmons, P.		1			
13	Green, Richard, Dec'd.	1	1			
54	Garsee, Lemor	1	1			
61	Gill, Prestly	1	1			
94	Gowen, Nancy, Dec'd.	1	1			
140	Green, Wynder L.	1/3				
148	Green, Amos, Dec'd.		1			
200	Green, Benjamin M.		1			
202	Garner, Arthur		1			
203	Garner, James II			369		
237	Garner, Jacob	1	1			
287	Garcio, Macimo	1/3				
370	Green, Reason		1			

No.	Name	Lgs.	Lbr.	Acres	Date	Remarks
4	Hardin, Franklin			369		
23	Hardin, William		1			
34	Harper, Clayton	1	1			
46	Hardin, B.W.		1			
59	Hardin, A.B.	1/2	1			
74	Holshausen, C.	1/3				
87	Hays, Matilda		1			
89	Humphreys, James	1	1			
100	Hardin, Milton A.	3/4	1			
118	Hamilton, Robert	1/3				
129	Hubert, Mathew		1			
135	Haney, James	1	1			
155	Hardin, Jerusha	1	1			
190	Hardin, Wm. B.	1	1			
191	Holshousen, Ann	1	1			
234	Hodges, George	1/3				
71	Isbell, James H.	1/3				
186	Isbell, James H.	2/3	1			
291	Irvine, Jesse B.	1	1			
122	Irwine, James O.	1/3				
9	Johnson, H.B.		1			
117	Jackson, Edward B.	1/3				A.B. Hardin, assignee.
121	Jackson, Hugh	1/3				
134	Johns, Wm.		1			
128	Johnson, John R.	1/3				
195	Jackson, Edward B.	2/3	1			
224	Jones, Jesse R.		1			
276	Jones, Isaac					601 26-100 acres.
325	Jones, Stephen, Dec'd.	1	1			
27	Key, Thomas W.	1/3				
78	Kirkham, Spencer		1			
141	Knight, James		1			
182	Kokenot, D.L.		1			
223	Kibble, William	1/3				
7	Logan, Wm. M.			369		
31	Lanier, Benjamin		1			
43	Littlefield, H.B.	1/3				
60	Lane, Alfred	1	1			
75	Lewis, Frederick, Dec'd.	1/3				
102	Lanier, Samuel S.	1/3				
125	Long, John D.	1/3				
230	Lynch, Reuben	1/3				
283	Lynch, Nicholas	1/3				
285	Lawrence, Joseph	1	1			
288	Lichtle, E.	1	1			
319	Lewis, Abraham	1/3				
332	Littlefield, H.B.	2/3	1			

No.	Name	Lgs.	Lbr.	Acres	Date	Remarks
88	Labadie, N.D.	1	1			
14	Martin, Josiah C.	1/3				
17	McCoy, James	1	1			
21	Magruder, Mary	1	1			
28	Magruder, N.	1/3				
40	Morehead, Thomas	1	1			
47	Miles, George W.	1/3				
82	Moore, Elenor	1	1			Samuel Rogers, att.
103	Martin, James, Dec'd.		1			J.C. Martin, Admr.
179	Maley, Julia Ann		1			
180	Maley, George	1/3				
185	Masters, C.S.	1/3				
178	Moore, William	1	1			
207	Menard, J.P.		1			
210	Maxwell, P.M.	1/3				
227	Morgan, James		1			
250	Munson, M.B. Dec'd.		1			
251	Menard, M.B.		1			
277	Morris, William					497 42-100 Acres
310	McManus, Rob't. O.W.	2/3	1			
322	Miller, P. Dec'd.		1			
335	Miles, Edward, Dec'd.	1	1			
348	Mathias, S.N.	1/3				
263	Morris, William		1			
32	Newman, Wm.	1/3				
132	Normant, Thomas	1/3				
187	Newman, Felix	1	1			
361	Nethuny, Samuel	1/3				
20	Orr, Thomas	1/3				
42	Odom, Lewis	1/3				
93	Ornie, Peter	1/3				
307	Orr, George, Dec'd.		1			
49	Prewitt, Jesse, Dec'd.	1				
184	Pan, Samuel	1	1			
199	Prewitt, Edmond	1/3				
229	Prewett, Beasly	1	1			
248	Prewett, Jesse, Dec'd.		1			
258	Prentiss, Henry B. Dec'd		1			
359	Prewett, Beasly		1			
383	Pinckney, John C.		1			
11	Rodgers, James	1/3				
19	Robinson, Wm.	1/3				
59	Rodgers, Samuel, Dec'd.	1/3				
98	Rodgers, Robert	1				
130	Rector, F.C.	1	1			

No.	Name	Lgs.	Lbr.	Acres	Date	Remarks
212	Rinehart, Asa	1/3				Heirs of.
214	Robinson, James		1			
221	Rankin, David	1/3				
240	Rankin, James M.		1			
255	Richards, Kendal	1/3				
281	Richardson, David L.	1	1			
282	Richardson, J.C.	1/3				Jas. Rodgers, Admr.
305	Rodgers, Robert, Dec'd.		1			
344	Renfro, David			526		
58	Ruddell, John	1/3				
10	Swenny, John	1/3				
29	Smith, William	1/3				
62	Swail, Amy		1			
65	Smith, Silas	1	1			
85	Stephenson, Elisha	1	1			
104	Smith, Charles	1/3				
109	Strang, Samuel		1			
143	Stubblefield, Thomas	1	1			
169	Smith, Mary	1	1			
170	Stearns, H.	1	1			
175	Self, Taylor B. Dec'd.	1/3				
176	Self, Jacob F. Dec'd.		1			
189	Seales, Abraham	1/3				
196	Smith, Adam	1/3				
206	Smith, Wm. H.	1/3				
234	Smith, Stephen		1			
239	Smith, Wm. M.	1	1			
241	Scott, Rozella	1	1			
246	Shaw, Jones	1	1			
256	Smith, Wm. Dec'd.	1/3				
270	Smith, John	1	1			
275	Spinks, B.M.		1			
295	Saul, John		1			
376	Swinghammer, Fred'r.	1/3				Heirs of.
36	Tribble, James M.	1/3				
55	Tanner, Edward	1				
56	Tanner, Edward		1			
61	Tanner, Moses	1/3				
66	Targanton, B.	1	1			
73	Tanner, James R.	1/3				
108	Taylor, Jane		1			
154	Tier, Mary	1	1			
160	Taylor, George	1	1			
166	Taylor, Edward, Dec'd.	1/3				
167	Taylor, James, Dec'd.	1/3				
168	Taylor, George, Dec'd.	1/3				
197	Titton, Charles	1	1			
215	Taylor, Anson, Dec'd.	1	1			
222	Thompson, Narcissa	1	1			
236	Thompson, William	1	1			

No.	Name	Lgs.	Lbr.	Acres	Date	Remarks
308	Thompson, Cyrus W.	1/4				
356	Tatman, Nathan	1	1			Eliz. Stiany Admx.
358	Thomas, G.S.		1			
373	Thouvenour, A.			1033		
115	Thompson, Cyrus W.			369		
114	Thompson, S.O.			369		
95	Tinnen, Jeremiah		1			
173	Van Nordstrand, A.	1	1			
35	Whittock, Robert	1/3				
37	Whittock, Mary		1			
67	White, William	1/3				
69	Wallis, E.H.R.	1	1			
76	Whitcher, Nathaniel	1/3				
77	White, James T.	1	1			
83	Winfree, A.B.,Jr.	1	1			
86	Williams, William	1/3				
92	Winfree, J.T.	1	1			
101	Whittington, M.	1	1			
116	White, John C.	1/3				
120	Wilcox, Charles	1/3				
129	Walless, William	1	1			
133	Wills, William	1	1			
137	White, John	1/3				
172	Williams, Hezekiah	1/3				James Martin, assignee.
181	Welch, C.P.		1			
194	Williams, T.J. Dec'd.	1	1			
198	West, Jerdan		1			
211	Williams, J.L. Dec'd.	1/3				
213	Wilcox, Charles	2/3	1			
216	Weaver, Andrew	1	1			
218	White, Wm. M.	1/3				
220	Woodberry, Jesse, Dec'd.	1/3				
249	Whiting, Samuel		1			
228	Wilborne, R.W.	1/3				
296	Watts, John		1			
297	White, Mathew L.	1/3				
300	Wiseman, Robert	1/2	1			
315	White, Matthew G.Dec'd.		1			
367	Wilbourne, Lucinda G.	1	1			
262	Woods, James B.		1			Geo.M. Patrick, assignee.
380	Winfree, Benjamin		1			Heirs of.
247	Yates, Milton	1	1			
317	Yeoman, James	1/3				
386	Yocum, Adelia	1	1			Heirs of.

SECOND CLASS

No.	Name	Lgs.	Lbr.	Acres	Date	Remarks
355	Andrew, John	1/3			Sept.5,1839	
354	Bryan, John	1/3			Sept.5,1839	
158	Bowen, Wm. F.			610	Feb.2,1838	
323	Brister, Wm.			1280	Oct.4,1838	
324	Brister, Daniel			1280	Oct.4,1838	
311	Barton, Wm.			640	Jan.3,1839	
25	Bryan, Luke, Sr.			640	Jan.18,1838	
111	Bryan, Luke, Sr.			640	Jan.19,1838	
81	Cassady, John	1/3			Jan.18,1838	
147	Clayton, John W.			1280	Feb.1,1838	
303	Carter, Thomas			1280	Aug. 1838	
378	Cortes, Peter			640	Jan.4,1840	
84	Dease, Wm.	1/3			Jan.18,1838	
293	Drew, Gilbert			640	July 5,1838	
330	Denson, John			640	Nov.1,1838	
331	Drysdale, David			640	Nov.1,1838	
365	Deason, John			1280	Dec.5,1839	
90	Edmundson, J.R.	1/3			Jan.18,1838	
96	Eakes, Hexekiah	1/3			Jan.18,1838	
314	Franklin, Benjamin			1280	Sept.6,1838	
320	Forman, David			1280	Oct.4,1838	
346	Freeman, Joseph			640	June 6,1839	
363	Foster, Albert A.			640	Nov.8,1839	
375	Fisher, Jeremiah			640	Jan.4,1840	
302	Grassel, George	1/3			Aug. 1838	
318	Garner, George S.			640	Sept.6,1838	
238	Hunter, B.M.	1/3			Mar.15,1838	
271	Huffman, M.			1280	Apr.26,1838	
272	Huffman, Joseph			1280	Apr.26,1838	
326	Hardin, Jos.B.			1280	Oct.4,1838	
340	Huffman, John			640	Jan.3,1839	
328	Huffman, Jesse			640	Jan.10,1840	
368	Jewel, Ebenezar			640	Dec.5,1839	
337	Kimbrow, George			640	Jan.3,1839	
352	Kincaid, David			1280	Sept.5,1839	
328	Lewis, Wm.T.			640	Oct.4,1838	
338	Loyd, Elizabeth			1280	Jan.3,1839	
339	Loyd, John A.			640	Jan.3,1839	
304	May, Gorham P.			640	Aug. 1838	
291	McWilliams, Alexander			640	June 1838	
273	Mayes, Samuel			1280	Apr.26,1838	

No.	Name	Lgs.	Lbr.	Acres	Date	Remarks
316	Menard, Medard			640	Sept.6,1838	
329	McKimm, John			640	Nov.1,1838	
379	Moralles, Manuel			640	Jan.4,1840	
387	Noulton, Mina			640	Jan.10,1840	
362	Pace, George L.			640	Nov.8,1839	
97	Roberts, A.S.	1/3			Jan.18,1838	
309	Roberts, Alexander S.	2/3	1		Aug. 1838	
301	Robb, Benjamin			640	Sept.6,1838	
149	Sparks, Harmon	1/3			Feb.1,1838	
343	Swinny, Mary C.			1280	May 2,1839	
357	Swinny, Milton			640	Sept.5,1839	
381	Swinny, Newton			640	Jan.4,1840	
327	Tracey, Moses L.			1280	Oct.4,1838	
292	Taylor, Wm. H.			640	June 1838	
268	Van Predelles, A.G.	1/3			Apr.26,1838	
351	Williamson, R.T.			640	June 6,1839	
353	White, S.B.			640	Sept.5,1839	

THIRD CLASS

No.	Name	Lgs.	Lbr.	Acres	Date	Remarks
39	Armstrong, A.			640	Aug.1,1839	
45	Ainsworth, A.S.			640	Aug.1,1839	
42	Ainsworth, J.P.			640	Aug.1,1839	
82	Andrews, Lewis			320	Nov.8,1839	
98	Arnett, James B.			320	Dec.5,1839	
99	Arnett, Cullen C.			640	Dec.5,1839	
111	Arnett, John C.			640	Dec.5,1839	
116	Anderson, W.B.			640	Dec.5,1839	
160	Abby, James W.			640	Jan.4,1840	
176	Abby, Charles E.			320	Jan.4,1840	
192	Allen, Rowland			640	Jan.9,1840	
6	Barber, Rewbin			320	May 2,1839	
7	Barber, Benjamin			320	May 2,1839	
17	Bryan, John			640	May 2,1839	
22	Brooks, Wilson			320	June 6,1839	
30	Barker, Labon			320	July 4,1839	
40	Bryan, Berwick			320	Aug. 1,1839	
54	Butler, Susanna			640	Sept.5,1839	
65	Butler, Landon H.			320	Sept.5,1839	
66	Butler, Stephen A.			320	Sept.5,1839	
67	Butler, John R.			320	Sept.5,1839	
68	Butler, William			640	Sept.5,1839	
81	Blanchard, Benjamin			640	Nov.8,1839	

No.	Name	Lgs.	Lbr.	Acres	Date	Remarks
97	Bouse, A.J.			640	Dec.5,1839	
112	Barclay, David			640	Dec.5,1839	
113	Barclay, Robert			640	Dec.5,1839	
157	Bichenot, Pierre			320	Jan.4,1840	
180	Brooks, John			320	Jan.4,1840	
19	Couch, George W.			640	May 2,1839	
24	Cowan, John F.			320	June 6,1839	
43	Collins, James P.			640	Aug.1,1839	
51	Culbreith, John			640	Aug.1,1839	
58	Carr, John F.			320	Sept.5,1839	
84	Clayton, Henry			320	Nov.8,1839	
85	Clayton, Ann			320	Dec.5,1839	
105	Clayton, Josephus			320	Dec.5,1839	
122	Choate, John H.			320	Dec.5,1839	
128	Carter, Henry W.			320	Dec.5,1839	
145	Clemants, Emanuel			640	Jan.3,1840	
154	Chassaigne, John			320	Jan.4,1840	
158	Choumunt, Nicholas			320	Jan.4,1840	
167	Craig, Benjamin F.			640	Jan.4,1840	
194	Choate, Jefferson			320	Jan.10,1840	
5	Danzey, Bryant			640	May 2,1839	
18	Danzey, Richard			640	May 2,1839	
26	Doles, W.M.			640	June 6,1839	
34	Drew, Monroe			320	Aug.1,1839	
48	Desmuke, A.W.			320	Aug.1,1839	
57	Dugan, William			640	Sept.5,1839	
121	Dodd, Thomas			320	Dec.5,1839	
127	Dickens, D.			320	Dec.5,1839	
129	Davis, Samuel W.			640	Dec.5,1839	
151	Dickens, James W.			320	Jan.3,1840	
161	Detray, John			320	Jan.4,1840	
86	Edmonds, Batiste			640	Nov.8,1839	
100	Enloe, Benjamin			640	Dec.5,1839	
101	Enloe, David			640	Dec.5,1839	
137	Epperson, Thaxton			320	Jan.2,1840	
177	Elian, Francis			320	Jan.4,1840	
8	Fitzgerald, Tilman			640	May 2,1839	
11	Fitzgerald, John			320	May 2,1839	
12	Fitzgerald, Levy			640	May 2,1839	
13	Fitzgerald, William			320	May 2,1839	
15	Fitzgerald, Theophelus			320	May 2,1839	
33	Fitzgerald, F.M.			320	Aug. 1,1839	
195	Fields, Calvin J.			320	Jan.10,1840	
134	Foster, Francis			320	Dec.5,1839	
2	Griffith, Edward			640	May 2,1839	
90	Green, Ellis			320	Dec.5,1839	
91	Green, Joseph			640	Dec.5,1839	
92	Green, James			320	Dec.5,1839	
94	Green, Aaron			640	Dec.5,1839	

No.	Name	Lgs.	Lbr.	Acres	Date	Remarks
103	Gibbs, Alonzo Q.			320	Dec.5,1839	
107	Gibbs, William			640	Dec.5,1839	
136	Gradhandt, Charles			320	Dec.5,1839	
144	Garner, William H.			320	Jan.3,1840	
193	Green, Allen			320	Jan.9,1840	
14	Hendricks, R.			320	May 2,1839	
20	Hobbs, William			320	June 6,1839	
23	Haron, Jacob			640	June 6,1839	
25	Hardin, Wm. C.			320	June 6,1839	
32	Horton, C.B.M.			320	July 4,1839	
49	Humphreys, John			320	Aug.1,1839	
35	Harrell, John B.			320	Sept.5,1839	
56	Hewitt, William			320	Sept.5,1839	
74	Hodges. James			320	Oct.3,1839	
75	Hickman, William			320	Oct.3,1839	
83	Hay, William			640	Nov.8,1839	
108	Hulet, James M.			320	Dec.5,1839	
110	Hulet, Obediah			640	Dec.5,1839	
119	Hardin, A.B., Jr.			320	Dec.5,1839	
149	Hatten, William			320	Jan.3,1840	
153	Hudson, William G.			640	Jan.4,1840	
159	Hardin, Benjamin			640	Jan.4,1840	
162	Hardin, George W.			320	Jan.4,1840	Heirs of.
168	Hunt, Oliver			320	Jan.4,1840	
169	Hobbs, Edward			640	Jan.4,1840	
170	Hill, James J.			640	Jan.4,1840	
172	Harrison, Mary			640	Jan.4,1840	
181	Hendricks, Albert			320	Jan.4,1840	
186	Harrison, William			320	Jan.4,1840	
187	Holdship, George G.			320	Jan.4,1840	
198	Herouard, Lewis			320	Jan.11,1840	
164	Hardin, Benjamin P.			640	Jan.4,1840	
150	Isbell, James R.			640	Jan.3,1840	
165	Ingraham, James			320	Jan.4,1840	
178	Isbell, Duglas			320	Jan.4,1840	
50	Joiner, Y.S.			320	Aug.1,1839	
52	Joiner, Henry			320	Aug.1,1839	
126	Jones, Joseph B.			640	Dec.5,1839	
163	Jones, A.B.			640	Jan.4,1840	
63	Kincaid, William			640	Sept.5,1839	
135	Kendall, Lenard			320	Dec.5,1839	
31	Lurcy, Asa			640	July 4,1839	
44	Lee, John J.			320	Aug.1,1839	
76	Lowe, Daniel			640	Oct.3,1839	
96	Lynch, John R.			640	Dec.5,1839	
106	Logan, N.W.H.			320	Dec.5,1839	
109	Lering, J.G.			640	Dec.5,1839	
143	Logan, James H.			640	Jan.3,1840	

No.	Name	Lgs.	Lbr.	Acres	Date	Remarks
174	Lester, John			320	Jan.4,1840	
190	Logre, Edmund			320	Jan.4,1840	
3	Mayner, S.A.			320	May 2,1839	
21	Martin, James R.			320	June 6,1839	
27	Mayes, Abner D.			320	July 4,1839	
28	Mayes, John J.			320	July 4,1839	
29	Mayes, Garner			640	July 4,1839	
59	Milbourne, E.			640	Sept.5,1839	
77	Mahoffey, Amos			320	Oct.3,1839	
95	Morris, Burrell			640	Dec.5,1839	
102	McDaniel, Margaret			640	Dec.5,1839	
118	McAnella, John E.			640	Dec.5,1839	
120	Mayes, Joshua J.			320	Dec.5,1839	
125	Mies, Jesse			320	Dec.5,1839	
131	McKinney, Roland			640	Dec.5,1839	
138	Mayes, John D.			320	Jan.2,1840	
182	Marchal, Joseph			320	Jan.4,1840	
183	Millsap, James			320	Jan.4,1840	
60	Normant, William			320	Sept.5,1839	
148	Owen, Anthony F.			640	Jan.3,1840	
4	Patton,Wm. A.			640	May 2,1839	
70	Peace, Willie J.			320	Sept.5,1839	
93	Pullen, George W.			640	Dec.5,1839	
114	Parsons, Jason H.			320	Dec.5,1839	
115	Parsons, Edmund J.			320	Dec.5,1839	
124	Palmer, Wm. H.			320	Dec.5,1839	
38	Reeves, William			320	Aug. 1,1839	
41	Reese, George M.			640	Aug. 1,1839	
71	Richardson, William W.			320	Sept.5,1839	
87	Reenie, John			640	Nov.8,1839	
166	Rupe, David M.			320	Jan.4,1840	
196	Rawlings, Edwin			320	Jan.11,1840	
16	Secill, William D.			320	May 2,1839	
35	Stephens, Levi			320	Aug. 1,1839	
36	Stephens, Julia			640	Aug. 1,1839	
61	Slater, Thomas B			320	Sept.5,1839	
64	Summers, A.C.			640	Sept.5,1839	
140	Smith, Bryan			320	Jan. 2,1840	
142	Smith, Noal			320	Jan. 3,1840	
155	Secrest, Charlotte			640	Jan.4,1840	
175	Stockton, John F.			640	Jan. 4,1840	
184	Swinney, Green			640	Jan. 4,1840	
185	Swinney, Wilson R.			320	Jan.4,1840	
197	Snider, Frederick			320	Jan.11,1840	
1	Thomas, John C.			640	May 2,1840	
47	Thompson, Henry D.			320	Aug. 1,1840	

No.	Name	Lgs.	Lbr.	Acres	Date	Remarks
46	Thompson, James			320	Aug. 1,1840	
80	Thompson, James			320	Nov.8,1840	
117	Tanner, Joseph			320	Dec.5,1840	
132	Thompson, Grigsby S.			320	Dec.5,1840	
133	Thompson, William			320	Dec.5,1840	
53	Townsend, B.			640	Aug. 1,1840	
89	Urquhart, Norman			320	Dec.5,1840	
104	Van Benthuzsen, Garrett			320	Dec.5,1840	
9	Wiseman, G.C.			320	May 2,1840	
10	Wooten, John			640	May 2,1840	
37	Wallis, Elisha W.			320	Aug.1,1840	
62	Ward, J.N.			320	Sept.5,1840	
69	White, Wiley B.			640	Sept.5,1840	
72	Williams, Henderson			320	Sept.5,1840	
73	Williams, John R.			320	Sept.5,1840	
78	Westbrook, Hudson			640	Nov.8,1840	
79	Westbrook, Thomas L.			320	Nov.8,1840	
88	Webb, William			640	Dec.5,1840	
123	Wheat, James			320	Dec.5,1840	
130	Williams, J.N.			640	Dec.5,1840	
139	Wilbourne, Charles			320	Jan. 2,1840	
141	Weaver, John			320	Jan.3,1840	
146	Walker, Noah			640	Jan.3,1840	
147	White, Henry			320	Jan.3,1840	
156	Wergenon, Michel			320	Jan.4,1840	
171	Walker, Mathias			640	Jan.4,1840	
173	White, Isaac W.			640	Jan.4,1840	
191	Williams, James			320	Jan.9,1840	
199	White, Leabore G.			320	Jan.11,1840	
179	Young, William			320	Jan.4,1840	

MATAGORDA COUNTY

FIRST CLASS

No.	Name	Lgs.	Lbr.	Acres	Date	Remarks
	Alford, John L.	1/3				
	Anderson, Thomas	1/3				Heirs of.
	Allen, John	1/3				
113	Austin, Andrew J.	1/3				
123	Alexander, George	1/3				Heirs of.
144	Albriecht, Jacob	1/3				
162	Aitkin, John	1	1			Heirs of.
201	Alloway, Samuel	1/3				
353	Allen, Samuel	1/3				Heirs of.
409	Anibal, Bartlett	1/3				
	Baker, D. Davis D.	3/4	1			
	Beaumont, Robert	1/3				Heirs of.

No.	Name	Lgs.	Lbr.	Acres	Date	Remarks
	Brigham, Samuel B.	1/3				
	Bower, Charles A.	1/3				
	Bowling, Burwell B.	1/3				
137	Bullock, Hosea M.	1/3				
168	Belknap, Thomas	1/3				
181	Boom, Garret E.	1/3				
2-0	Burnett, Pumphrey		1			Heirs of.
203	Burknap, Leonard	1/3				Heirs of.
213	Bostick, Caleb R.	1/2	1			
253	Bays, Henry L.	1	1			
281	Blake, Thomas M.	1/3				Heirs of.
289	Bass, Archibald W.	1/3				John P. Cockrill, assignee.
293	Betts, Jacob	1/2	1			Heirs of.
301	Beale, Benjamin	1/3				Heirs of.
333	Bright, George	1/3				Heirs of.
361	Bond, Burr S.	1/3				Heirs of.
380	Brown, Douglass	1/3				Horton & Clements, assignee.
389	Burk, William	1/3				
82	Butler, David	1/3				Heirs of.
18	Bowman, John J.	1/2	1			
175	Banks, Henry P.	1/3				
235	Barns, Turner	1	1			
237	Barnes, William	1/3				
259	Bell, George	1/3				
302	Benson, Wm. B.	1/3				
401	Burnes, Moses	1/3				
150	Bullard, Charles K.	1/3				
	Cook, James	1/2	1			
	Cady, D.C.	1/3				
	Cayce, G.W.	1/3				
	Curtin, Hinton		1			
	Crooks, Henry	1/3				
	Collinsworth, Geo. M.	1	1			
	Collinsworth, D.C.	1/3				Heirs of.
	Clements, Joseph	1/3				
98	Cayce, Henry P.	1/3				
105	Clements, Abner Lee	1/3				
117	Cannon, Thomas	1/3				Dulap & McHugh assignees.
142	Campbell, Elizabeth		1			
153	Cooper, Campbell	1/3				D.C. Gilmour, assignee.
154	Cayce, Shadrack	1/3				
173	Cook, Mary Ann	1	1			Heirs of.
254	Conner, James			370		
300	Cook, Maria		1			Heirs of.
339	Cholwell, Gustavus	1/3				
384	Clopper, Nicholas	1/3				Heirs of.
398	Curry, John P.	1/3				Heirs of.
399	Cooper, John H.	1/3				

No.	Name	Lgs.	Lbr.	Acres	Date	Remarks
403	Craig, Henry R.	1/3				Thom. Fowler, assignee.
7	Cook, Octavius A.	1				Heirs of.
155	Cayce, Thomas		1			
164	Coperland, George	1/3				
174	Cook, Octavius A.	1/3				
198	Cooke, Hamilton L.	1	1			
261	Cazeneau, Wm. L.	1/3				
335	Cavanah, Charles	1	1			
364	Carson, Sam. B.	1/3				
49	Clements, Joseph	2/3	1			
53	Condon, Benj. D.	1/3				
152	Clements, Abner L.	2/3	1			
	Dinsmore, Silas		1			
	DeMoss, Lewis	1	1			
	Decrow, Elijah	1/3				
	Digges, George P.	1	1			Cloptor & Mosby, assignees.
	Dasher, Thomas J.	1/3				Heirs of.
	Duncan, James	1	1			
	Decrow, Howard	1	1			
	Duke, Thomas M.		1			
	Duffield, J.E.	1/3				Heirs of.
	Dennis, Thomas M.	1/3				
102	Dale, Charles	1	1			
106	Downs, John	1/3				
121	Duncan, John	1	1			
131	Dibble, Henry	1/3				
148	Dooley, Spires	1	1			
190	DeMorse, Charles	1/3				
271	DeMoss, William	1	1			
285	Davis, Fields	1	1			Heirs of.
298	Dibble, Edward C.	1/3				Heirs of.
290	Downer, E.D.			370		Heirs of.
367	Duffield, Peter	1/3				Heirs of.
188	Davis, Hatwell T.	1/3				Albert Silsby, assignee.
216	Detrich, Francis	3/4	1			
284	Davis, Jackson	1/3				Heirs of.
347	Dalstorne, John	1/3				Heirs of.
377	Decrow, Thomas	3/4	1			
379	DeMoss, John	1/3				
399	DeMoss, Peter		1			S.Dinsmore & J.E.Dalton,as'gs
430	DeMorse, Charles	2/3	1			
33	Davis, Perry	1/3				
150	Etherton, Daniel	1	1			Hulda Etherton, widow
296	Edwards, Charles		1			
376	Eddy, Peleg	1/3				Heirs of.
383	Ewert, James J.	1/3				Heirs of.

No.	Name	Lgs.	Lbr.	Acres	Date	Remarks
107	Evans, George E.	1/3				
139	Elam, Daniel	1	1			Jos. O'Neil, assignee.
274	Eberly, Jacob		1			
420	Eldridge, Joshua	1/3				
	Flenry, A.B.	1	1			
	Frye, Arnham	1/3				Abram Shepperd,assignee.
	Fowler, Thomas	1/3				Heirs of.
	Farwell, Joseph	1/3				
280	Finney, Andrew L.	1/3				Heirs of.
305	Field, Joseph E.	1	1			
359	Frazier, James	1/3				Heirs of.
242	Fream, William	1	1			
	Gordon, Robert, Dec'd.	1/3				Henry Crooks, Admr.
	Gardner, George W.	1/3				
	Goodwin, Lewis	1	1			Allen Farquhar, assignee.
	Gervais, Sinclair D.		1			
	Gamble, Arthur	1/3				
	Gove, H.N.			370		
101	Green, Elizabeth	1	1			Heirs of.
110	Gilliland, Patrick	1/3				Heirs of.
125	Greene, Robert M.	1/3				Andrew M. Vanslyke,assignee.
141	Graves, Ransom O.	1/3				Heirs of.
166	Garcia, Francisco	1/3				Albert Silsby, assignee.
167	Gilliland, Ellen	1	1			
178	George, Nicholas	1	1			
250	George, David	1/3				
304	Garcia, Thomas	1/3				
327	Griffith, Noah		1			Asa Yeamans, assignee
238	Griffith, Henry		1			Asa Yeamans, assignee.
360	Grabbail, Vincent	1/3				Heirs of.
143	Goodrick, John	1	1			Heirs of.
243	George, John	1/3				
244	George, Holman	1/3				
247	George, Jefferson	1/3				
351	Geraghty, John	1/3				
408	Galbraith, Jane C.	1/3				
37	Goodman, Christopher C.	1/3				Rynd Lawder, assignee.
	Half, J.C.	1	1			
	Howard, Charles	1	1			
	Hardiman, Thomas J.	1	1			
	Hardiman, Thomas M.	1/3				
	Haley, William	1/3				

No.	Name	Lgs.	Lbr.	Acres	Date	Remarks
	Harding, Samuel F.	1	1			
	Hall, John, Dec'd.	1/3				R.R. Royall, assignee.
	Hanson, Thomas	1/3				
	Holmes, John	1/3				
	Hughson, James		1			
	Hand, John J.	1/3				Heirs of.
	Henderson, John F.C.	1	1			
	Hall, Joseph	1	1			Heirs of.
109	Hurst, George	1/3				
128	Hardiman, Bailey	1	1			Heirs of.
129	Hardiman, Wm. P.	1/3				
138	Hughs, Benj. T.	1/3				Heirs of.
143	Hall, Elisha		1			Heirs of.
152	House, James M., Dec'd.	1	1			Sally House, Widow
191	Hurst, Lewis	1	1			Heirs of.
208	Hannum, James	1/3				Heirs of.
233	Haddon, William	1/3				
234	Haddon, Henry H.	1/3				
245	Haddon, Jackson	1/3				Heirs of.
286	Heaton, Ransom	1/3				
315	Hodge, George	1	1			Heirs of.
331	Hunter, Eli		1			Heirs of.
341	Henderson, Charles	1	1			Heirs of.
358	Howard, Levi	1/3				
368	Harper, John	1/3				
388	Hofty, Edmond	1/3				Heirs of.
17	Hardiman, Owen B.	1/3				
127	Hunter, Wiley W.					No quantity specified.
134	Hughes, Thomas J.	1/3				
159	Horton, Albert C.	1	1			
182	Hicks, Milton	1/3				
291	Hubbard, John B.	1/3				J. Tilly & Thos. Decrow, as'gs.
316	Harris, James	1	1			
347	Harmon, Thomas	1/3				
263	Iles, Perry B.		1			
31	Jones, Francis	1/3				R.R. Royall, assignee.
160	Jack, Spencer II			370		Heirs of Andrew Mitchell,as'gs.
104	Jordon, Joseph	1/3				R.R. Royall, assignee.
122	Jackson, Peter	1	1			Heirs of.
170	Jones, Francis	2/3	1			Heirs of.
338	Johnston, George J.	1/3				Elijah Merryman's heirs.
132	Jones, Augustus, II	1/3				

No.	Name	Lgs.	Lbr.	Acres	Date	Remarks
211	Jamison, Thomas		1			
215	Johnson, L. II W.	1/3				
412	Jones, David More	1/3				
	Kendrick, Harvey	1	1			
	Kinsey, Peter	1	1			Heirs of.
	King, Charles F.	1/3				
180	Kemp, Caleb	1	1			Heirs of.
205	Kemp, Jonathan	1	1			
264	Keller, Francis		1			Heirs of.
312	King, Thomas	1/3				
157	Kincheloe, Lewis			370		
238	Kincheloe, Daniel	1/3				
239	Kincheloe, Augustus	1/3				
256	Keller, James	1/3				
330	Keirns, William	1/3				
426	Kraatz, Lewis	1	1			
	Levy, A.M.	1	1			
	Larche, S.A.	1	1			
	Lawder, Rynd	1	1			
112	Lacy, William D.	3/4	1			
145	Linthecum, Wm. E.	1/3				
214	Lewis, James	1/3				Heirs of.
350	Linville, Aaron	1/3				Heirs of.
355	Lidstrand, Ludwick	1/3				
417	Love, Samuel		1			Heirs of.
64	Lopez, Jose Maria	1/3				Heirs of.
224	Lentz, Jacob		1			
251	Ladd, John W.	1/3				
349	Lentz, Jacob G.	1				
357	Living, Thomas H.	1/3				
369	Lewis, Ira R.		1			
	McCoy, Thomas	1/2	1			
	Miller, Travis	1/3				
	Morris, James H.	1/3				
	Morgan, Peter	1/3				
	Mackey, John	1/3				
103	Mackey, Ruth		1			
114	McCartey, James	1/3				
149	Messer, Charles	1/3				
163	Mason, Robert	1	1			Jane Wilkins, Admx.
199	McKinney, Benjamin	1	1			Heirs of.
283	Marshall, John	1/3				
297	McComly, Anthony W.	1/3				Heirs of.
303	McCartey, Daniel	1/3				Heirs of.
352	Moore, Wm.	1/3				Heirs of.
394	Moore, Elisha		1			Heirs of.
407	Matchett, John	1/3				Heirs of.
53	Mitchell, Henry B.	1/3				Heirs of.
206	Martindale, Daniel	1/3				

No.	Name	Lgs.	Lbr.	Acres	Date	Remarks
209	McFarlane, Douglad		1			
212	McManus, R.O.W.	1/3				
225	Moore, James		1			
248	Montgomery, Jas. S.	1	1			
262	Moore, Thomas W.	1	1			
363	McDonald, Abner S.	1/3				
431	Messer, Charles	2/3	1			
258	Moser, Adam	1/3				
76	McLaughlin, Joseph	1/3				
	Norton, James	1/3				
	Neville, Francis S.	1/3				Rufus McLeland, assignee.
146	Nye, Wm. N.	1	1			
354	Noble, Benjamin	1/3				Jos. Oneil, assignee.
375	Ness, David	1/3				Heirs of.
255	Nounnan, Benjamin S.	1/3				
292	Newell, John D.		1			
229	Osborn, John L.	1	1			
230	Osborn, Charles	1/3				
240	Osborn, Thomas	1/3				
413	Osborn, Mary	1	1			
	Page, J. William	3/4	1			
	Plunket, John	1/3				
	Plunket, Elizabeth	1	1			
	Payne, George	1/3				Heirs of.
	Payton, Jonathan C.		1			Heirs of.
308	Parton, John C.		1			Heirs of.
381	Peck, Nicholas	1	1			Heirs of.
410	Parvin, William	1/3				Heirs of.
276	Payton, Alexander G.	1/3				
332	Pace, Albert	1/3				
348	Potter, Michael W.	1	1			
370	Phillips, Isham B.		1			
	Roeder, Mary M.		1			Supposed to be 1 lg., 1 lbr. G.M.Collingsworth, assignee.
	Redman, John	1/3				
	Ringo, William	1/3				
	Royall, Richard R.		1			
	Robinson, Axar	1/3				
	Reding, Robert L.	1/3				
241	Rawls, George	1/3				Heirs of.
314	Rector, Joseph		1			Heirs of.
415	Rivers, Wm. M.	1	1			Heirs of.
223	Ryan, William	1	1			Heirs of.
185	Robertson, Arthur	1/3				
169	Rowland, J.W.	1/3				

No.	Name	Lgs.	Lbr.	Acres	Date	Remarks
268	Rawls, James	1/3				
217	Reed, Essy	1	1			Heirs of.
	Stewart, Robert D.	1	1			Heirs of.
	Smith, Rufus R.	1/3				
	Stewart, Thomas	1	1			
151	Scott, Levi P.	1/3				
193	Smith, Jacob	1/3				
196	Scott, James	1	1			Heirs of.
218	Spencer, Henry	1	1			Heirs of.
220	Smally, Abner	1/3				
226	Sharp, Cyrus R.	1/3				Heirs of.
231	Savery, Asabel		1			
232	Savery, H.P.	1/3				Title in Zavala's colony 1.4 lg.
265	Smally, John G.	1/3				
278	Shropshire, Hicks	1/3				Heirs of.
279	Shropshire, Harrison	1	1			Heirs of.
295	Smith, Francis P.	1/3				
324	Smith, Jacob	1	1			Heirs of.
343	Selkirk, Wm.		1			Heirs of.
344	Smith, Henry S.	1/3				Heirs of.
345	Savage, Emilius		1			
397	Spicer, Joseph A.	1/3				Heirs of.
404	Scott, William	1/3				Heirs of.
405	Scott, Jonathan	1	1			Heirs of.
81	Spencer, William	1/3				Heirs of.
116	Smith, John	1/3				
189	Silsby, Albert			370		
252	Shackleford, Jack	1	1			
288	Simon, John	1/3				
352	Silliman, William S.	1/3				
385	Strode, James	1/3				
135	Thompson, Thomas	1/3				Heirs of.
136	Thompson, Isham	1	1			
140	Thompson, Charles	1/3				Heirs of.
147	Thornton, William S.	1/3				
176	Thompson, Eb	1/3				
202	Threadgill, Joshua	1/3				
337	Treppard, Francis J.	1/3				
115	Tyndal, William	1/3				
219	Tomlin, James	1/3				
246	Tilly, Josiah		1			
260	Tilly, John P.	1/3				
310	Tatum, Thomas S.	1/3				Horton & Clements, assignees
365	Tilotson, James R.	1/3				
365	Thatcher, Thomas	1/3				
	Updike, John H.	1/3				Rufus R. Smith, assignee

No.	Name	Lgs.	Lbr.	Acres	Date	Remarks
317	Utley, Thomas	1/3				
221	Van Darn, Isaac	1/2	1			
290	Vandervier, Cornelus H.		1			
	Williams, Thomas J.	1	1			
	Wright, Gilbert	1/3				
	Wilson, William	1/3				
	Watts, Samuel T.	1/3				
	Wilkins, Jane		1			James Hughson, assignee.
130	Wynne, Robert H.	1	1			
179	Worthington, Andrew	1	1			
184	Wilkinson, John	1	1			
186	Wallace, J.W.E.		1			
197	Williams, Henry		1			
207	Williams, N.B.	1	1			Heirs of.
228	Ward, William	1/3				Heirs of.
306	Witt, Hughs	1/3				Chas.A. Bullard, assignee.
312	Woodward, Alvin	1/3				
313	Wightman, Benjamin		1			Heirs of.
334	Wightman, John	1/3				Heirs of.
374	Wroe, William		1			Heirs of.
386	Wright, Nancy	1	1			Heirs of.
418	Woolridge, Ann S.	1	1			
55	Williams, Thomas, Sr.		1			
79	Watts, William H.	1/3				
126	Williams, Robert H.		1			
165	Williams, Edward	1/3				
201	Williams, Geo. W.	1/3				
355	Wright, Ralph	1	1			
391	White, Peter	1/3				
395	Wilson, Charles	1/3				Munro Edwards, assignee.
422	Wheelwright, George	1				
62	Wootten, Edward	1/3				
192	Yeamans, Horace	1/3				
321	Yeamans, Elias	1/3				Heirs of.
322	Yeamans, Erastus	1/3				Heirs of.
323	Yeamans, Daniel	1/3				
325	Yeamans, Joseph	1	1			
326	Yeamans, Asa		1			

SECOND CLASS

No.	Name	Lgs.	Lbr.	Acres	Date	Remarks
72	Arling, William			640	Apr.16,1838	
112	Ashby, James H.	1/3			Jy.5,1838	
8	Braman, D.E.E.			640	Mar.7,1838	

No.	Name	Lgs.	Lbr.	Acres	Date	Remarks
9	Bryant, Lewis H.			640	Mar.7,1838	
47	Bellinger, Andrew M.			640	Mar.29,1838	
28	Bullard, Charles A.			640	Mar.18,1838	
59	Brown, Allen E.			640	Apr.14,1838	
62	Barlow, Jonathan			640	Apr.14,1838	
78	Belknap, James J.			640	Apr.26,1838	
80	Boyd, William			640	Apr.26,1838	
88	Brown, Thos. H.			640	May 10,1838	
94	Bowmer, Richard			640	May 10,1838	
99	Babcock, Charles J.			640	June 7,1838	
103	Baxter, William P.	1/3			June 7,1838	
110	Barker, John	1/3			Jy.5,1838	
111	Bennett, Benjamin C.			640	Jy.5,1838	
144	Bishop, Joseph			640	Oct.14,1838	
147	Bowman, James H.	1/3			Dec.6,1838	
12	Clark, John			640	Mar.7,1838	
35	Crosby, Cyrus	1/3		640	Mar.29,1838	
43	Caliott, Charles				Mar.29,1838	
50	Clofton, Benj. M.			640	Mar.30,1838	
51	Clofton, Oliver P.			640	Mar.30,1838	
65	Clendenim, Adam	1/3			Apr.16,1838	
68	Cleal, John G.			640	Apr.16,1838	
75	Clements, Alfred			640	Apr.16,1838	
77	Callaghan, James			640	Apr.26,1838	
79	Cobbs, James L.	1/3			Apr.26,1838	
85	Cockrill, John P.			640	May 10,1838	
109	Collinsworth, Joseph F.W.			640	Jy.5,1838	
114	Christy, George			640	Jy.5,1838	
128	Cage, Benjamin			640	Jy.5,1838	
141	Campbell, John			640	Oct.14,1838	
151	Carson, Andrew C.			640	Jan.38,1839	
15	Connor, Daniel G.			640	Apr.30,1839	
148	Cornett, James			640	Dec.30,1839	
185	Crowls, George W.	1/3			Dec.31,1839	
3	Despean, Joseph	1	1		Mar.7,1839	
22	Dunn, Margaret			1280	Mar.15,1839	
27	Doddridge, Eli			640	Mar.18,1838	
30	Dulin, Gerard	1/3			Mar.18,1838	
57	Delap, William L.			640	Mar.30,1838	
60	Dedmore, John C.			640	Apr.14,1838	
69	Depew, Warren S.			640	Apr.16,1838	
83	Denson, Archibald, J.	1/3			May 10,1838	
146	Denson, Archibald J.	2/3			Dec.6,1838	
154	Davis, George	1/3			Jan.3,1839	
47	DuBoseSerra, D.			640	Apr.30,1839	
184	Elkins, David R.	1/3			Dec.31,1839	
116	Forest, Moreau	1	1		Jy.5,1838	
129	Frentress, Lemuel			640	Jy.5,1838	

No.	Name	Lgs.	Lbr.	Acres	Date	Remarks
130	Fanning, John			1280	Aug.2,1838	
131	Fowler, Sam'l O.	1/3			Aug.2,1838	
71	Ferguson, Tolliver			640	Jy.29,1839	
45	Farguhar, Allen			1280	Apr.30,1839	
1	Garrett, John	1	1		Mar.7,1838	Jos.Oneil, assignee.
101	Gosling, Henry			640	June 7,1838	
85	Gorman, James S.	1/3			Oct.20,1839	
19	Hathaway, William L.			1280	Mar.15,1838	
20	Harper, George W.			640	Mar.15,1838	
32	Hare, John			640	Mar.18,1838	
41	Harrington, E.B.	1/3			Mar.20,1838	
49	Hill, Joseph C.	1/3			Mar.30,1838	
56	Harvey, Thomas			640	Mar.30,1838	
61	Hodges, Galen			640	Apr.14,1838	
66	Hardy, Thomas			640	Apr.16,1838	
71	Harris, Wm. A.			640	Apr.16,1838	
113	Haley, Wm. L.			640	Jy.5,1838	
127	Holman, John			640	Jy.5,1838	
150	Hannum, A.B.			640	Jan.3,1839	
156	Huth, Caspar			640	Jan.3,1839	
61	Hotchkiss, William	1/3			June 24,1839	
105	Haley, Robert			640	Nov.24,1838	
111	Hillard, William			640	Dec.20,1839	
113	Hicks, Edward G.			640	Oct.14,1838	
11	Journey, Henry			640	Mar.7,1838	
46	Jenison, William A.	1/3			Mar.7,1838	
67	Johnson, William F.			640	Apr.16,1838	
148	Jack, James	1/3			Dec.6,1838	
35	Jennings, Thomas			640	Apr.30,1838	
136	King, George			640	Sept.6,1838	
140	Kell, Robert			640	Sept.6,1838	
41	Kistler, Philip			640	Apr.20,1838	
5	Lindsey, Benjamin			640	Mar.7,1838	
17	Langford, George No.			640	Mar.15,1838	
36	Landers, David			640	Mar.15,1838	
12	Lathrop, J.S.K.	1/3				
106	Lanningham, Zachariah			640	June 7,1838	
126	Lann, James W.			640	Jy.5,1838	
2	McLellan, Rufus	1	1		Mar.7,1838	
16	McGovern, Edward			640	Mar.15,1838	
31	Miller, William	1/3			Mar.18,1838	
37	Martin, John			640	Mar.29,1838	
45	McGinnis, Joseph	1/3			Mar.29,1838	
48	McKinstry, William C.			1280	Mar.30,1838	
52	Mosby, William O.			640	Mar.30,1838	
70	Moody, Samuel A.			640	Mar.30,1838	
100	McDonald, Alexander			640	Jy.5,1838	

No.	Name	Lgs.	Lbr.	Acres	Date	Remarks
117	Merryman, Elijah			1280	Jy.5,1838	
83	Morey, William D.			640	Oct.29,1838	
88	McHugh, Michael			640	Oct.29,1838	
129	McMillan, Archibald			640	Dec.30,1839	
166	Messina, Ann			640	Dec.30,1839	
34	McFarlane, James			640	Mar.18,1838	
33	Noble, John			640	Mar.18,1839	
107	Netherly, J.S.			640	Jy.5,1839	
21	Nites, J.W.J.			640	Ap4.20,1839	
4	O'Connor, Edward	1/3			Mar.7,1838	
73	Osgood, Charles			640	Apr.16,1838	
102	Oiven, Hugh	1/3			June 7,1838	
119	Oliver, William F.			640	Jy.5,1838	
152	O'Neil, Joseph			640	Jan.3,1839	
58	Peek, Benjamin, B.			640	Apr. 14,1838	
84	Perkins, Leonard			640	May 10,1838	
105	Price, Wm. B.			640	Jy.5,1838	
122	Pague, John H.			640	Jy.5,1838	
81	Quigley, Daniel			640	Apr.26,1838	
13	Reavis, James B.			1280	Mar.7,1838	
21	Rodarmel, S.M.			640	Mar.15,1838	
26	Rice, Charles W.			1280	Mar.18,1838	
86	Rezier, John P.			640	May 10,1838	
133	Reid, David R.			640	Aug.2,1838	
31	Royall, William R.			1280	Apr.30,1839	
38	Reding, William R.			640	Apr.30,1839	
10	Seguine, Bornt			1280	Mar.7,1838	
25	Smith, Lowell P.			640	Mar.15,1838	
55	Sale, Edmund N.			640	Mar.30,1838	
63	Snyder, Conrad			640	Apr.14,1838	
74	Strickland, James			640	Apr.16,1838	
87	Sargeant, Thomas			640	May 10,1838	
91	Selkirk, James H.			640	May 10,1838	
92	Steele, William F.			640	May 10,1838	Geo.R. Beck, assignee.
93	Sterling, Isaac			1280	May 10,1838	
104	Smith, John			640	June 7,1838	
121	Serugge, Henry			640	Jy.5,1838	
134	Simpson, Harrison			640	Aug.2,1838	
146	Scharck, Jacob			640	Dec.30,1839	
182	Sheppard, James G.			640	Dec.31,1839	
54	Townsley, Robert			1280	Mar.30,1838	
64	Tims, Alexander			640	Apr.14,1838	
89	Tilk, Thomas			640	May 10,1838	
97	Thomas, Enoch M.			640	May 10,1838	

No.	Name	Lgs.	Lbr.	Acres	Date	Remarks
98	Tivy, Thomas			640	Jy.5,1838	
123	Taylor, Edward M.	1/3			Jy.5,1838	
120	Tunnard, A.W.			640	Jy.5,1838	
76	Vesteland, Charles A.			640	Apr.26,1838	
156	Vallo, Theodore			640	Dec.30,1838	
18	Wharton, James			640	Mar.15,1838	
39	Welsh, Edward	1/3			Mar.18,1838	
40	Wallace, William	1/3			Mar.29,1838	
53	Wadsworth, Albert			640	Mar.30,1838	
90	Webb, William O.			640	May 10,1838	
115	Ward, Geo. W.			640	Jy. 5,1838	
118	Whitaker, Francis A.			640	Jy. 5,1838	
139	Winfree, Charles			1280	Aug.2,1838	
153	Waterman, E.P.			640	Jan.3,1839	Jos. O'Neil, assignee.
142	Young, Henry			640	Oct.14,1838	

THIRD CLASS

No.	Name	Lgs.	Lbr.	Acres	Date	Remarks
1	Abbey, C.H.			640	Mar.27,1839	
48	Atweil, James			320	Apr.30,1839	
79	Anderson, Alexander			640	Oct.29,1839	
116	Axson, A. Foster			320	Dec.30,1839	
141	Aycock, N.M.			320	Dec.30,1839	
142	Aycock, R.M.			320	Dec.30,1839	
178	Abell, James C.			640	Dec.31,1839	
25	Belknap, Morris L.			320	Apr.30,1839	
73	Booth, George J.			320	Jy.31,1839	
80	Blythe, Samuel C.			320	Oct.29,1839	
86	Barrett, George			320	Oct.29,1839	
94	Boyer, George			320	Oct.29,1839	
106	Baker, Hoadly			320	Dec.30,1839	
109	Bass, Daniel			640	Dec.30,1839	
118	Bray, Isiah			640	Dec.30,1839	
132	Burns, Michael			640	Dec.30,1839	
134	Burns, John			320	Dec.30,1839	
157	Burke, Nicholas			320	Dec.30,1839	
176	Burkhart, George			640	Dec.30,1839	
12	Coriell, George			320	Mar.27,1839	
17	Clements, Nelson			320	Arp.30,1839	
24	Carroll, Sidney A.			320	Arp.30,1839	
42	Collings, George W.			640	Apr.30,1839	
51	Craig, John B.			640	Apr.30,1839	
52	Connor, Abraham V.			320	Apr.30,1839	
59	Caldwell, Robert			320	June 24,1839	
65	Cayce, John			320	Jy.29,1839	
67	Coltart, James			320	Jy.29,1839	
98	Carter, John W.			640	Oct.29,1839	

No.	Name	Lgs.	Lbr.	Acres	Date	Remarks
112	Collins, John Wm.			640	Dec.30,1839	
119	Chester, William H.			320	Dec.30,1839	
122	Clark, William			320	Dec.30,1839	
128	Cox, Joseph			640	Dec.30,1839	
147	Collinsworth, William C.			640	Dec.30,1839	
148	Cornett, James			640	Dec.30,1839	
159	Clark, Charles			320	Dec.30,1839	
162	Cash, John S.			320	Dec.30,1839	
57	Dyas, Robert			320	June 24,1839	
68	Donaldson, Wellington			320	Jy.29,1839	
102	Dunn, John			320	Nov.24,1839	
125	Denison, James			320	Dec.30,1839	
137	Davenport, John G.			640	Dec.30,1839	The Heirs.
4	Elfbrink, Daniel			320	Mar.27,1839	
69	Ewing, Wm. G.			320	Jy.29,1839	
107	Earle, George			320	Dec.30,1839	
108	Earle, Halford			320	Dec.30,1839	
164	Eagan, Gabriel			320	Dec.30,1839	
9	Felt, Henry			320	Mar.27,1839	
75	Feeny, Martin			640	Aug.26,1839	
92	Finlay, Pierce			320	Oct.29,1839	
135	Flood, Thomas			320	Dec.30,1839	
10	Graves, Philip			320	Mar.27,1839	
13	Grainger, C.J.			640	Mar.27,1839	
56	Graban, Theodore			320	June 24,1839	
120	Grosvenor, Lemuel			320	Dec.30,1839	
130	Grier, Eli			640	Dec.30,1839	
131	Grier, Felix			640	Dec.30,1839	
149	Griffith, Charles W.			320	Dec.30,1839	
2	Hierholtzer, John B.			320	Mar.27,1839	
27	Helmbold, Henry			320	Apr.30,1839	
40	Hatch, Ebenezer H.			320	Apr.30,1839	
58	Hemphill, S. Girard			320	June 24,1839	
89	Hunter, William H.			320	Oct.29,1839	
138	Hendon, Henry M.			320	Dec.30,1839	
145	Hillard, James O.L.			320	Dec.30,1839	
161	Hanson, Claus			320	Dec.30,1839	
168	Haley, John			320	Dec.30,1839	
169	Hood, Jeremiah A.			320	Dec.30,1839	
172	Hunter, Lemuel			320	Dec.31,1839	
175	Hubbard, Samuel			320	Dec.31,1839	
3	Ives, Caleb S.			640	Mar.27,1839	
99	Jaques, Gideon R.			320	Nov.24,1839	
171	Johnson, James			320	Dec.31,1839	
23	Kean, Myles			320	Apr.30,1839	

No.	Name	Lgs.	Lbr.	Acres	Date	Remarks
6	Lowell, J.H.			320	Mar.27,1839	
8	Leufstedt, John			320	Mar.27,1839	
18	Lonsdale, John G.			320	Apr.30,1839	
113	Loverin, Wm. H.			320	Dec.30,1839	
121	Ludington, Robert			320	Dec.30,1839	
151	Long, Samuel			320	Dec.30,1839	
179	Layton, William			320	Dec.31,1839	
26	McGuflin, Sam'l			640	Apr.30,1839	
30	Murray, William			320	Apr.30,1839	
60	Marshall, arunah			320	June 24,1839	
66	Martin, James F.			320	Jy.29,1839	
70	Mosby, De Witt C			320	Jy.29,1839	
87	Murray, John R.			320	Oct.29,1839	
93	McDonald, John			320	Oct.29,1839	
97	Morse, James W.			320	Oct.29,1839	
100	Morden, John M.			640	Nov.24,1839	
115	Maynard, Edwin A.			320	Dec.30,1839	
163	Mussina, Jacob			640	Dec.30,1839	
167	Mussina, Ann			640	Dec.30,1839	
174	McGee, Elijah M.			640	Dec.31,1839	
177	Marshall, William A.			320	Dec.31,1839	
180	Mackey, William			320	Dec.31,1839	
181	Miller, Daniel			320	Dec.31,1839	
186	McNabb, John F.			320	Dec.31,1839	Heirs of.
110	Noble, James			640	Dec.30,1839	
124	Newton, Albert G.			320	Dec.30,1839	
160	Noyes, Ira J.			320	Dec.30,1839	
74	O'Brien, Michael			640	Aug.26,1839	
19	O'Flaherty, John			320	Apr.30,1839	
11	Pierce, A.S.			320	Mar.27,1839	
14	Peck, George R.			320	Mar.27,1839	
39	Prescott, Oren			320	Apr.30,1839	
77	Pirie, James			320	Sept.30,1839	
139	Pearson, P.W.			320	Dec.30,1839	
165	Petty, Phillemon H.			640	Dec.30,1839	
20	Ross, Robert M.			320	Apr.30,1839	
29	Russell, William			320	Apr.30,1839	
50	Rawson, Fisher			640	Apr.30,1839	
78	Reed, Perry			320	Oct.29,1839	
133	Robbins,Frederick Wolcot			320	Dec.30,1839	
144	Rhodes, Joseph			640	Dec.30,1839	
153	Robertson, Samuel C.			320	Dec.30,1839	
16	Stewart, W.W.			640	Apr.30,1839	
36	Spaulding, John M.			320	Apr.30,1839	
126	Solomon, John E.L.			320	Dec.30,1839	
127	Scott, William P.			320	Dec.30,1839	
158	Snow, Sylvanus			320	Dec.30,1839	

No.	Name	Lgs.	Lbr.	Acres	Date	Remarks
170	Stockdale, E.B.			320	Dec.31,1839	
173	Sewell, John Y.			320	Dec.31,1839	
183	Sheppard, Dillon J.			320	Dec.31,1839	
103	Stokes, Frederick			320	Nov.24,1839	
101	Vauslyke, Robert T.			320	Nov.24,1839	
5	Williams, E.			320	Mar.27,1839	
28	Winburn, John O.			320	Apr.20,1839	
32	Waldman, Francis			640	Apr.20,1839	
43	Worland, Charles R.			320	Apr.20,1839	
41	Worland, James H.			320	Apr.20,1839	
46	White, Benjamin			320	Apr.20,1839	
96	Wallach, W.D.			320	Oct.29,1839	
101	Whitfield, Robert			640	Nov.24,1839	
114	Wilkins, John A.			320	Dec.30,1839	
123	Weed, John A.			320	Dec.30,1839	
117	Winans, Isaac J.			320	Dec.30,1839	
187	Williams, John			320	Dec.31,1839	

MILAM COUNTY

FIRST CLASS

No.	Name	Lgs.	Lbr.	Acres	Date	Remarks
48	Addison, Isaac	1	1			
75	Anderson, David,Dec'd.	1/4	1			Harriet Anderson, Admx.
47	Addison, Joseph J.	1/3				
63	Bailey, John	1	1			
65	Boates, Calvin	1	1			
84	Bailey, Jesse, Dec'd.	1/3				John Bailey, Admr.
112	Boren, Joseph	1	1			
3	Boren, Michael	1	1			
50	Brown, John D.	1	1			
53	Barron, John M.			369		
56	Beal, John	1	1			
105	Boren, Nancy		1			
115	Bowen, G.B.	1/3				
139	Brightman, Gideon	1/3				
144	Butler, James S.	1/4				
78	Bowen, Jennet	1	1			
91	Bailey, Elizabeth	1/3				
8	Cullins, Daniel	1	1			
87	Coryell, James Dec'd.			369		Massilon Farley, Admr.
2	Craddock, John R.	1/3				
21	Cullum, Soloman, Dec'd.	1/3				John Teal,Admr.
26	Cooke, A.W.	1/3				

No.	Name	Lgs.	Lbr.	Acres	Date	Remarks
29	Cullins, Aaron	1	1			J.W. Porter, Admr.
31	Childers, Thomas	1/3				Gadsby Childers, Admr.
30	Childers, Franklin	1/3				Gadsby Childers, Admr.
33	Curneal, P.T.	1/3				
44	Chance, Samuel	2/3				
51	Childers, Robert	1/3				
68	Clemons, Wm. H.	1/3				
74	Crouch, Isaac		1			Isabella Crouch Admx.
82	Cockrill, John R.	1/3				
183	Curtis, Charles			369		
113	Chapman, G.W.			369		
120	Childers, James R.	1/3				
125	Chapman, Geo. W.	2/3	1			
127	Childers, Goldsby		1			
143	Curneal, Patrick T.	2/3	1			
99	Castleman, Michael	1/3				
60	Darnell, Ansel			369		
15	Dillard, Thomas	1/3				
28	Dean, W.R.	2/3				
39	Drake, James	1/3				James Dunn, Admr.
79	Davidson, Robert		2			Rebeca Davidson, Admx.
24	Erath, G.B.			369		
62	Emmons, C.B.			369		
38	Folkes, Abigail		1			
80	Frazier, William	1/3				
86	Fitch, Benjamin F. Dec'd.	1/3				Charles Curtis, Admr.
88	Frazier, Stephen	1/3				
10	Forbes, R.P.	1/3				Wm. Neill, Admr.
76	Frazier, Margaret		1			
89	Folkes, John L.	1/3				
130	Farmer, David M.	1/3				Wm. W. Bell, assignee.
11	Gross, Jacob	1/3				
85	Garnett, Wm. Dec'd.			369		Massillon Farley, Admr.
57	Graves, Thomas A.	3/4	1			
40	Green, George	1/3				
69	Harvey, John B.	1	1			Massillon Farley, Admr.
73	Hobson, John	1/3				
128	Hannum, Lucien	1/3				A.B. Fleury, Admr.

No.	Name	Lgs.	Lbr.	Acres	Date	Remarks
17	Isaacs, William	1/3				
4	Jones, F.M.	1	1			
54	Johnson, Alfred	1/3				
1	Jackson, Gabriel	1	1			
49	Jones, Joseph P.		1			
1	Johnson, Samuel	1				Permanently disabled.
6	Moore, Joel	1	1			
67	McLennan, Neill		1			
71	McLennan, John	1/3				
41	McLennan, John K.	1	1			
77	Moore, L.L.	1/3				
5	Morrow, Thomas, Dec'd.	1	1			John Teal, Admr.
13	Monroe, Daniel		1			
33	Moore, A.W.	1	1			
45	Maiden, Isaac			369		
58	McKay, Thomas		2			Sarah McKay, Admx.
98	Moore, William	1	1			
100	McCandless, Samuel F.	1/3				David McCandless, Admr.
102	McCandless, William W.	1/3				David McCandless, Admr.
103	Moore, Lewis			369		
37	Milton, Elel	1/3				
9	Neill, Claiborne, Dec'd.	1/3				Wm. Neill, Admr.
43	Neibling, Frederick		1			
72	Neill, James	1	1			Wm. Neill, Admr
	Neill, William Heirs of	1				District Court.
22	Porter, John W.	1				
31	Prater, Philip	1/3				
61	Pool, John C.	1/3				
97	Porter, John T.	1	1			
109	Purson, J.H.			369		
7	Robinson, Neil K. Dec'd.		1			Christian Robinson, Admr.
42	Robinson, Daniel, Dec'd.	1	1			John K. Mc Pherson, Admr.
70	Robinson, Neill	1/3				
144	Robinson, Ezekiel	1/3				
120	Robinson, Daniel	1/3				
131	Robinet, James M.	1/3				
132	Reed, James		1			
20	Roark, Washington	1/3				John Teal, Admr.
	Robertson, James R.	1	1			Proved before District Court.
91	Scott, Elizabeth	1	1			
93	Scott, James W.		1			
106	Sillivan, A.W.	1/3				
108	Shackelford, M.B.			369		

No.	Name	Lgs.	Lbr.	Acres	Date	Remarks
93	Scott, P.B.	1/3				
135	Shackelford, M.B.	2/3	1			
136	Scott, Robert W.	1/4				
137	Scott, L.B.	1/3				
96	Scott, Robert W.			369		
110	Symons, John	1/3				
98	Thomson, J.N.M.	1/3				
12	Taylor, Josiah	1/3				
18	Teal, Richard S.	1/3				
19	Teal, John	1	1			
147	Thompson, Alexander		1			
104	Trudoe, John	1	1			Thomas A. Graves, Admr.
126	Thompson, Empson	1/4				
27	Wilkinson, Melville	1/3				
14	Wilkinson, John M.	1/3				
32	Wilkinson, James A.	1/3				
46	Weaver, Henry C.	1	1			
52	Welch, Charles	1	1			
55	Webb, Thomas R.	3/4	1			

SECOND CLASS

No.	Name	Lgs.	Lbr.	Acres	Date	Remarks
37	Arnett, Timothy			1280		
8	Blair, L.B.			640		
42	Bell, Wm. W.			1280	Sept.29,1838	
4	Couch, Thomas			640	Mar.17,1838	
7	Caspeir, Jacob	1/3			Mar.17,1838	Wm.H.King, Admr.
15	Carr, B.M.			640		
32	Chairs, Samuel A.			640		Calvin Boles agent for Admr.
36	Connelly, Wm.			1280		
19	Dixon, Claiborn M.			640		
29	Eubanks, John T.			1280		
30	Edwards, H.	1/3				
39	Fox, Peter			640		
44	Gravis, Thos. F.			1280	Sept.29,1838	
10	Hughes, Francis			640		
23	Ham, B.L.			640		
45	Ham, B.L.			640		
24	Haggard, Squn			640		
3	Johnson, Samuel	1/3			Mar.17,1838	
21	Jones, Eli			640		
43	Kinney, John			640	Sept.29,1838	

No.	Name	Lgs.	Lbr.	Acres	Date	Remarks
12	Lee, Geo. M.			640		
14	Murry, Wilson L.			640		
33	Middleton, Beboni			640		
34	Middleton, W.B.			640		
38	Middleton, John			1280		
40	Marlin, James	1	1			
41	McKeen, John B.			640		
2	Parsons, Abel			640		
18	Page, Jefferson			640		
20	Price, Thomas	1/3				
27	Rasco, T.L.			640		
32	Randolph, Josiah			640		
1	Thomson, Wm. D.	1	1		Mar.17,1838	
9	Whitton, Elisha H.			1280		
17	White, Charles			1280		
31	Wortham, E.T.			1280		
35	Williams, Wright			640		
11	Zellcur, Francis			640		

THIRD CLASS

No.	Name	Lgs.	Lbr.	Acres	Date	Remarks
49	Addison, Oscar M.			320	Jan.13,1840	
50	Addison, James II			320	Jan.13.1840	
29	Bill, Wm. W.			320	Aug.29,1839	
28	Boucher, Hirm			640	Dec. 3,1839	
48	Beal, John, Dec'd.			320	Jan.13,1840	James Brown, Admr.
6	Chance, James			640	May 14,1839	
34	Chalk, Whitfield,			320	Jan.11,1840	
41	Childers, Prio			320	Jan.11,1840	
8	Custard, William			320	May 14,1839	
10	Dorsey, L.C. Dec'd.			320	May 14,1839	Jos. Rowland, Admr.
32	Duty, Solomon			640	Jan.11,1840	
20	Eraul, B.			640	Jy.27,1839	
15	Gilmer, Wm. R.			320	Jy.27,1839	
40	Green, James O.			640	Jan.11,1840	
41	Humphreys, George W.			320	Jan.11,1840	
13	Jones, John S.			320	May 20,1839	
24	Jones, Wyley			320	Aug.29,1839	

No.	Name	Lgs.	Lbr.	Acres	Date	Remarks
3	King, Hugh C.A.			320	May 13,1839	
4	King, John E.			320	May 13,1839	
2	Lakey, Henry			320	May, 13,1839	
23	Long, Solomon			640	Aug.29,1839	
17	Moore, Wm. C.			320	Jy.27,1839	
5	McKean			640	May 14,1839	
29	Neill, John H.			320	Oct.7,1839	
47	Noe, James			320	Jan.13,1840	
9	Rowland, Joseph			640	May 14,1839	
7	Slator, Samuel			640	May 14,1839	
16	Standifer, Isaac			640	Jy.27,1839	
35	Smith, Plemon L.			320	Jan.11,1840	
37	Scott, John W.			320	Jan.11,1840	
27	Teal, Thomas W.			320	Oct.3,1839	
30	Thomson, Francis A.			320	Oct.8,1839	
31	Thomson, Thomas C.			320	Oct.8,1839	
38	Thorp, Pleasant			320	Jan.11,1840	
39	Thorp, G.H.			640	Jan.11,1840	
1	Williams, J.A.			320	Apr. 4,1839	
36	Yancy, James			320	Jan.11,1840	

MONTGOMERY COUNTY

FIRST CLASS

No.	Name	Lgs.	Lbr.	Acres	Date	Remarks
21	Arnold, Holly	1	1			
25	Arnold, David		1			
36	Atkins, William		1			
167	Armour, Robert		1			
229	Aranandez, Hosea	1/3				
278	Allen, George		1			
286	Allphin, Martha		1			
297	Allen, Ethan		1			
338	Anderson, Nancy		1			
342	Allen, L.D.	1	1			
347	Anderson, Nancy	1				
374	Adams, John W.		1			
385	Arcola, Francis	1	1			
386	Arcola, John	1/3				
387	Arcola, Daloris		1			
390	Anderson, Wyatt	1/3				
405	Arnold, Benjamin F.	1/3				
430	Arnold, Catherine, Dec'd.	1	1			

No.	Name	Lgs.	Lbr.	Acres	Date	Remarks
28	Anglin, William	2/3				
103	Allen, Garret, Dec'd.	1				Estate of.
104	Allen, Garret, Dec'd.		1			Estate of.
410	Ariola, Massima	1/3				Daniel L. Richardson, Asg'n.
294	Allphin, Ransom		1			
188	Andrews, Samuel	1	1			
7	Bennett, Joseph L.	1				
22	Bryan, Stephen	1/3				
119	Busby, William		1			
149	Bowen, Wm. R.	1				
173	Bennett, Joseph L.		1			
178	Bullock, David M.	1/3				
182	Bowen, Wm. R.	1				
191	Bishop, Wm. H.	1/3				Jashua Robins, assignee.
198	Baker, Walter E.	1/3				
225	Bankhead, Richard Dec'd.	1				
227	Bankhead, Richard		1			
232	Ballad, W.W.	1/3				
246	Baker, John	1				
247	Baker, John		1			
282	Barney, William		1			
326	Bricker, John, Dec'd.	1/3				
403	Buryman, Wm.		1			
404	Burnett, James	1/3				
431	Buckhanan, James		1			Chas.B. Stewart, Admr.
197	Baker, John	1	1			
239	Boatright, Thomas		1			
14	Chatham, Thomas	1	1			
32	Cobby, William			369		
41	Collard, Jonathan S.			369		
45	Collard, Jas. H.			369		
47	Cook, Wm. A.		1			
49	Collard, Job S.		1			
63	Clary, Jesse	1				
82	Cooke, Francis S.	1/3				
83	Cooke, Wm. G.					Quantity not specified.
84	Cooke, Henry M. Dec'd.	1	1			Thos. Cooke, executor.
85	Cooke, Thomas	1/3				
97	Corner, Evan	1	1			C.B.Stewart, assignee.
98	Corner, James	1/3				
99	Corner, John		1			
110	Crouch, Jackson	1/3				
114	Corner, Thomas			369		
117	Collard, Sam'l. M.		1			

No.	Name	Lgs.	Lbr.	Acres	Date	Remarks
140	Cude, Timothy		1			
141	Clark, Wm. C.		1			
150	Collard, Elijah		1			
153	Cartwright, Peter	1	1			
154	Cartwright, Willifred	1	1			
155	Cartwright, Mathew	1/3				
156	Cartwright, Wm. P.	1/3				
158	Clary, David	1	1			
162	Clary, George W.	1/3				
163	Clary, William	1/3				
164	Clary, John	1/3				
216	Crothurs, Mary	1/4				Hugh McGuffin, assignee.
224	Castleman, John K.		1			
234	Coker, John	1/3				
236	Cox, Lewis		1			
249	Crabb, H.M.		1			
269	Castleman, Patience	1				John K. Castleman, Admr.
277	Castleman, Patience		1			John K. Castleman, Admr.
311	Corner, Mary		1			
333	Crane, John		1			
334	Chadduck, Richard H.	1/3				
336	Caruthers, John		1			
339	Copeland, Martin	1	1			
340	Crothus, Mary	3/4	1			
345	Copeland, Lawrence	1	1			
367	Cummins, John H.		1			Francis W. Johnson, Admr.
418	Cresap, Thomas A.	1				
424	Cox, James		1			
26	Cooke, Wm. G.	1/3				
20	Cresap, Thomas A.	1/3				
342	Chandter, Hugh			369		
56	Cute, John	1/3				
413	Crouch, Jackson	2/3	1			
65	Clary, Jesse		1			Harvey Murphy, Admr.
62	Donaho, Isaac			369		
248	Decker, Isaac		1			
270	Darwin, John	1				
271	Darwin, John		1			
321	Duncan, James H.	1/3				
375	Davy, Thomas P.	1/4				
436	Davy, Thomas P.	3/4	1			
36	Dugan, Catherine		1			
129	Davy, Thos. P.	1/4				
130	Davy, Thos. P.			369		
111	Dorsey, John	1/3				
52	Edinburg, Christopher		1			
145	Edwards, James	1	1			

No.	Name	Lgs.	Lbr.	Acres	Date	Remarks
223	Elm, Frederick	1/3				
11	Finch, Matt	1/3				
13	Farris, Hezekiah	1	1			
24	Fishr, Wesley		1			
75	Fisher, William			369		
100	Fanthorp, Henry	1	1			
152	Fulton, Samuel, Dec'd.		1			Hugh McGuffin, Admr.
182	Ford, Daniel	1/3				
302	Fuqua, Ephraim		1			
304	Fuqua, Ephraim	1				
314	Foster, James S. Dec'd.	1	1			
444	Fomle, Thos. P.	1/3				Joshna Robins, Admr.
137	Ford, James		1			
2	Graham, J.M.		1			
12	Gillespie, James	1/3				
28	Galbraith, George			369		
31	Garrett, Dickinson	1/3				
38	Geline, John, Dec'd.	1/3				By Benj.Rigby
40	Gilmore, William	1	1			
72	Goodrich, B.B.		1			
122	Goodrich, J.C.	1/3				B.B.Goodrich, Admr.
124	Gray, Pleasant		1			
139	Gilmore, Thomas	1	1			
172	Goodbread, Philip	1				
174	Grimes, A.C.	1/3				Jesse Grimes agent for.
208	Gallatin, Albert	1	1			
210	Greenwood, Joel		1			
211	Greenwood, Franklin, Jr.		1			
212	Greenwood, H.B. Dec'd.	1	1			
215	Goodbread, Philip		1			
327	Garrett, Dickerson	2/3	1			
388	Grimes, Jesse		1			
410	Graham, Elizabeth Jane	1	1			
415	Goodbread, John, Dec'd.	1/3				Philip Goodbread, Admr.
422	Givens, Adnrew	1/3				
24	Garner, Isaac	2/3	1			
20	Harvey, David	1/3				
42	Henderson, Hugh	1/3				
57	Holcomb, James J.	1/3				
73	Harrison, A.L.	1/3				
78	Hadly, Joshua		1			
123	Henderson, P.H. Dec'd.	1/3				B.B. Goodrich, Admr.
125	Hinson, Joseph	1	1			

No.	Name	Lgs.	Lbr.	Acres	Date	Remarks
142	Hadley, J.K.	1/3				
231	Holland, Taply	1/3				
316	Hunter, James S.	1				
317	Hunter, James S.		1			
349	Holland, Francis	1/3				Martin Vancet, Assignee
350	Holland, Francis, Dec'd.	1	1			Wm. Barney, Admr.
360	Harrison, John	1/3				
368	Hampton, Hugh	1/3				
393	Horseley, Thomas	1	1			
391	Horseley, A.J.	1/3				
412	Hampton, Wm., Dec'd.	1	1			Margaret Hampton, Admx.
39	Hill, Obedience &others	1	1			Thos. Gilmore, in trust for.
29	Jones, Benjamin	1/3				
66	Jones, Allen C.	1	1			
87	Jones, Keeton	1/3				
161	Jones, Lewis	1/3				
165	Jones, James	1/3				
245	James, Thomas	1/3				
292	Johnson, Nathan	1/3				
309	James, Thomas		1			
425	James, Thomas	2/3				
426	James, Thomas		1			
171	Johnson, Benjamin	1/3				
101	Kinnard, Wm. E.	1/3				
107	Kinnard, Michael M.	1/3				
126	Kinnard, A.D. Sr.		1			
126	Kinnard, A.D. Jr.	1/3				
361	Kirby, George	1/3				
362	Kirby, Josiah	1/3				
193	Keys, William	1				
194	Keys, William		1			
50	Lindley, Joseph		1			
88	Lindley, James N.	1/3				
91	Little, John	1				
95	Landrum, John		1			
103	Lindley, William	1/3				
104	Little, Hiram	1	1			
115	Lindley, Samuel	1/3				
118	Little, William	1	1			
141	Lee, James	1	1			
226	Lamb, George A. Dec'd.	1				
228	Lamb, George A. Dec'd.		1			
243	Lynch, Patrick		1			
244	Lynch, Patrick	1				
256	Little, John		1			
285	Loyd, John	3/4	1			

No.	Name	Lgs.	Lbr.	Acres	Date	Remarks
392	Larrison, Daniel		1			
433	Longbotham, R.B.		1			
438	Laurence, John, Dec'd.	1	1			
132	Loyd, Peter			369		
17	Landrum, William		1			
18	Landrum, Letitia		1			
120	Loyd, John	1/3				
252	Larence, Geo. W.					No amount given.
318	Larison, Thomas	1/3				
1	McIntire, William	3/4	1			
8	McIntire, Robert	1/3				
9	Montgomery, John			369		
53	McDonald, William		1			
69	Montgomery, Edley			369		
76	McIntire, Margaret		1			
79	Magee, Ralph		1			
93	McFarland, James P.	1	1			
134	McCoy, William	1/3				
143	Milliman, Ira	1/3				
185	Mercer, George R.		1			
189	McGee, Drury		1			
200	Magee, Archibald	1/3				
206	McDillon, John	1/3				B.B. Goodrich, att'y. in fact for.
209	McGuffin, Hugh		1			
213	Miller, Ruth		1			
255	Martin, John F.	3/4	1			
315	Mitchell, James		1			
323	Montgomery, Wm. Dec'd.		1			
353	McIlvale, Harriet	1				
354	McIlvale, Harriet		1			
414	McGuffin, John F.	2/3	1			
420	McCoy, William	2/3	1			
415	Martin, Phillip		1			
21	Montgomery, John	2/3	1			
27	McIntire, Robert	2/3	1			
106	McGary, Daniel H.	1	1			
343	Morse, Matthew	1/3				Cyrus Dykeman, assignee.
391	Manning, Stephen		1			
27	McGuffin, John F.			369		
96	McGuffin, M.G.	1/3				
402	McDowel, Mill		1			
54	Neal, Lewis	1	1			
355	Nixon, L.D.	1				
356	Nixon, L.D.		1			
242	Orr, John William	1/3				

No.	Name	Lgs.	Lbr.	Acres	Date	Remarks
6	Powel, James		1			
71	Pyle, John	1	1			
94	Pyle, Joseph T. Dec'd.	1/3				By his father Jno. Pyle
102	Powel, Archibald G.		1			
136	Patterson, William	1				
148	Parker, Jsees		1			
230	Peterson, Mary	1				
273	Perry, Laurence W.		1			
279	Peterson, John		1			
280	Plummer, Luther T.M.		1			
293	Pillow, Wm. B.		1			
303	Peterson, Mary		1			
357	Parker, James W.		1			
358	Pierson, John H.	1				
364	Prater, Isaac	1/3				
416	Patterson, William		1			Sam'l R. Browning, assignee.
434	Parker, Silas M. Dec'd.		1			Lucinda Parker, Admx.
435	Parker, Wiley		1			
442	Potter, John	1/3				
446	Pierson, John H.	2/3	1			
187	Peterson, Wm., Dec'd.		1			Mary Peterson, Admx.
274	Pritchard, Joseph			369		
401	Perry, Lawrence W.	1				
265	Powell, A.G.		1			
23	Robinson, Yoraster		1			
26	Rogers, Raleigh		1			
37	Rigby, Benjamin		1			
43	Robinson, Benj. W.		1			
48	Robinson, Geo. W.	1/3				
56	Robins, Cinthia		1			
58	Roberts, William	1/3				
68	Rivers, Antonio		1			Benajah Jones, assignee.
74	Raper, Daniel	1/3				
160	Rossin, Hiram	1	1			
177	Rankin, Thos. B.	1/3				
181	Ramsdal, Geo. L.	1/3				
201	Robbins, Joshua	1				
203	Robbins, Rebecca	1				In trust for heirs.
204	Robbins, Rebecca		1			In trust for heirs.
205	Robinson, William		1			
257	Robinson, F.J. Dec'd.	2/3				John F. Martin, Admr.
319	Robbins, John	1				
320	Robbins, John		1			

No.	Name	Lgs.	Lbr.	Acres	Date	Remarks
321	Robbins, Thos., Dec'd.	1/3				John Robbins, Admr.
322	Robbins, Nat., Dec'd.		1			
331	Reisenhoover, Benson	1	1			
411	Ramfield, Soloman	1	1			Jacob Duckworth, Admr.
22	Robinson, Geo. W.	2/3	1			
348	Robinett, John	1/3				M.D. Sandifer, assignee.
300	Roy, Robert	3/4	1			
341	Rea, Elizabeth		1			
366	Roque, Joseph	1	1			
131	Rankin, Wm. M.		1			
202	Robbins, Joshua		1			Jas. Mitchell, assignee.
3	Shannon, Jacob		1			
10	Shepperd, J.H.	1	1			
34	Springer, John M.	1	1			
35	Springer, A.W.	3/4	1			
69	Stephens, John M.	1				
80	Smith, Wiley B.D.	3/4				
81	Smith, Wiley B.D.		1			
89	Smith, John	1/3				
90	Smith, Richard		1			
92	Stephens, Miles G.		1			
105	Sadler, Robert	1/3				
116	Sadler, John		1			
128	Seaton, George W.	1/3				
146	Shannon, Margaret		1			
151	Spillers, John	1				
220	Stewart, Charles B.	2/3				
233	Sandifer, M.D.		1			
258	Stewart, William	1				
259	Stewart, William		1			
267	Stephens, John, Dec'd.	1/3				
283	Stansell, B.B.	1				
287	Spillers, John		1			
284	Stansell, B.B.		1			
288	Spillers, Warrenton	1/3				
289	Spillers, Wm.	1/3				
299	Spillers, Wm. H.	1				
291	Spillers, Wm. H.		1			
298	Smith, James M.	1				
299	Smith, James M.		1			
305	Sidie, Antonio	1/3				
306	Sidie, John B.		1			
325	Steel, Alphonso	1				
330	Svhriers, James		1			
322	Sidie, Peter, Dec'd.		1			
370	Smith, James, Dec'd.	3/4	1			Louise Beck, Admx.
376	Stewart, Charles B.		1			

No.	Name	Lgs.	Lbr.	Acres	Date	Remarks
408	Shannon, John, Dec'd.		1			
441	Steel, Alphonso	2/3	1			
111	Stone, Thomas, Dec'd.	1	1			
157	Smith, Lemuel	1/3				
186	Strambler, Geo. W.	1/3				
344	Stephens, Thomas		1			
129	Smith, Geo. H.	1/3				
133	Steel, Alphonso und	1/3				
192	Shepperd, Wm. W.		1			
207	Slade, Theodore	1/3				
16	Tongue, John B.	3/4	1			
19	Thomas, John	1	1			
30	Thomas, James	1/3				
33	Thomas, David	1/3				
60	Thompson, John	1/3				
86	Talbot, Margaret		1			
183	Taylor, William S.	1/3				
187	Thomas, J.N., Dec'd.	1/3				John Thomas, Admr.
214	Tinny, Ambrose		1			
218	Tumlinson, Peter	1				
222	Tumlinson, Peter		1			
307	Taylor, Levi, Dec'd.		1			
377	Taylor, Abram R.	1/3				
378	Thompson, James		1			
314	Tumlinson, John J.		1			
343	Townsend, William		1			
46	Thomas, Holland	1	1			
384	Taylor, William S.	2/3	1			
407	Thompson, Alexander	1	1			
432	Taylor, Thomas, Dec'd.		1			C.B. Stewart, Admr.
121	Votan, Elijah	2/3	1			
272	Votan, Isaac		1			
397	Votan, Elijah	1/3				
131	Van Norman, William	1	1			
4	Worsham, Joseph	1/3				
5	Worsham, Jeremiah	1	1			
15	Wilson, Zaccheus	1	1			
51	Webb, Isom G.	1	1			
55	Winters, James Sr.		1			
61	Webb, Thomas H.	1/3				
67	Wallace, Caleb		1			
108	Whitley, Sharp	1				
112	Wilson, James	1/3				
138	Whitaker, Peter, Dec'd.	1	1			Joseph Burnett, Admr.
147	Williams, Richard	1	1			
159	Walker, Wm. H.		1			
166	Whitesides, John J.		1			

No.	Name	Lgs.	Lbr.	Acres	Date	Remarks
168	Walker, Sandy H.	1	1			
169	Walker, Daniel E., Dec'd	1	1			Sandy H. Walker, Admr.
170	Walker, John C.	1	1			
175	Winfield, J.M.& H.	1	1			By Caleb Wallace, guardian.
176	Winfield, Henry	1/3				By Caleb Wallace, guardian.
199	Winn, James		1			
219	White, Brigham	1/3				
250	Whitley, Miles	1				
254	Whitley, Miles		1			
253	Whitley, John	1/3				
254	Whitley, Sharp		1			
250	Ware, William		1			
263	Wallace, James		1			
295	Whitaker, Alexander			369		
296	Winters, Williams		1			
335	Winters, James W.	1	1			
363	Whitaker, Alexander	1				
381	Whittaker, Alexander	2/3	1			
398	Webb, Thomas H.	2/3	1			
417	Weedon, George	1				
75	White, John C.	1/3				
123	Walker, Tandy		1			
266	Winters, John	1	1			
135	Young, Wm. F.	1				
221	Young, Wm. F.		1			
346	Young, Jesse		1			
428	Young, Wm. F.	1				
55	Young, Pleasant	1	1			
166	Young, Jesse	1				
64	Zuber, Wm. P.	1/3				
237	Zuber, Abraham		1			

SECOND CLASS

No.	Name	Lgs.	Lbr.	Acres	Date	Remarks
10	Bradford, Thomas			640	Mar.30,1838	
51	Burr, George M.			640	Jy. 6,1838	
64	Beach, John			640	Jy.30,1838	Deceased
65	Brady, Richard			640	Jy.30,1838	
66	Brown, Francis E.			1280	Aug.2,1838	
78	Brothus, John			640	Aug.2,1838	
84	Bobo, Foster			1280	Aug.2,1838	
106	Brock, Daniel E.			640	Sept.6,1838	
239	Brimbeny, Samuel			1280	Dec.30,1839	
2	Corley, C.B.			640	Mar.3,1838	
6	Coode, William			1280	Mar.29,1838	

No.	Name	Lgs.	Lbr.	Acres	Date	Remarks
8	Cunningham, Patrick			640	Mar.30,1838	
88	Cartright, James M.			640	Aug.2,1838	
94	Cailton, John			640	Aug.13,1838	
108	Cartright, Thomas P.			640	Sept.6,1838	
12	Dikeman, Cyrus			1280	Mar.30,1838	
82	Dean, James			1280	Aug.2,1838	
113	Dean, Alfred			640	Sept.24,1838	
143	Davis, Edward B.			640	Sept.26,1839	
76	Edwards, Evan			1280	Aug.2,1838	
117	Elly, Gustar			640	Oct.4,1838	
419	Francis, William	1/3			Aug.2,1838	
28	Foster, Ezekiel			640	June 7,1838	
46	Files, David S.			1280	Jy. 5,1838	
49	Eutler, John			640	Jy.5,1838	
116	Floyd, Robert			640	Oct.4,1838	
1	Goodrich, E.W.			640	Mar.3,1838	
17	Groom, Sander			640	May 3,1838	
52	Gray, Harvey			640	Jy. 7,1838	
53	Gray, E.M.			1280	Jy. 7,1838	
69	Groms, William			1280	Aug.2,1838	
72	Gilbert, Jonas			1280	Aug.2,1838	
73	Gilbert, Jonas, Jr.			640	Aug.2,1838	
74	Gilbert, Jos. T.			640	Aug.2,1838	
75	Gilbert, Jahn			640	Aug.2,1838	
86	Grimmett, Samuel			640	Aug.2,1838	
118	Gilbert, Robert			640	Nov.1,1838	
3	Hulin, Wm.			640	Mar.15,1838	
5	Harper, Andrew			640	Mar.16,1838	
29	Harper, John			640	June 7,1838	
44	Hobbs, Thomas			640	Jy.5,1838	
54	Henson, Absalom			640	Jy.23,1838	
81	Holcomb, Franklin			640	Aug.2,1838	
100	Heath, Simon P.			1280	Aug.14,1838	
107	Hunter, George E.			1280	Sept.6,1838	
76	Halsel, Thomas J.			640	May 13,1839	
41	Jones, Benaiah			1280	Jy.5,1838	
96	Johnson, Wm.			1280	Aug.13,1838	
50	Kesler, Ferdinand			640	Jy.6,1838	
115	King, Sidney S.			1280	Oct.4,1838	
7	Long, Tobias			1280	Mar.29,1838	
55	Larison, Joseph			640	Jy.23,1838	
70	Leman, James			640	Aug.2,1838	
91	Lundon, David E.			640	Aug.3,1838	
20	Lamb, Thomas			1280	Mar.25,1839	
80	Land, Joseph			1280	May 13,1839	

No.	Name	Lgs.	Lbr.	Acres	Date	Remarks
179	Morrison, Guyn	1	3		Feb.2,1838	
21	Milton, David			1280	June 7,1838	Deceased
22	McRae, Alexander			1280	June 7,1838	
23	McRae, William			640	June 7,1838	
33	McGary, Jonathan A.			1280	June 8,1838	
39	McFarland, Samuel J.			640	Jy.5,1838	
45	Murphy, Harvey			1280	Jy.5,1838	
47	Matthews, James R.			640	Jy.5,1838	
58	Marsh, Robert			1280	Jy.23,1838	
59	Marsh, Wm. R.			640	Jy.23,1838	
95	McCollum, Thos. J.			640	Aug.13,1838	
109	McLeod, Daniel			640	Sept.6,1838	
123	Manning, May			640	Nov.1,1838	
51	Meredith, Stewart			640	Apr.29,1839	
59	Mays, Jacob			640	Apr.29,1839	
64	McLane, Peter G.			640	Apr.30,1839	
348	O'Bannon, J.W.			1280	Jan.6,1840	
25	Peel, Thomas R.			1280	June 7,1838	
38	Pomeroy, Frederick			640	Jy.5,1838	
77	Perkins, Alvin			640	Aug.2,1838	
65	Perry, E.W.			640	Apr.30,1839	
90	Quimby, Daniel			1280	Aug.2,1838	Deceased
30	Roberts, Thomas			640	June 7,1838	
48	Roberts, John			640	Jy.5,1838	
112	Ringgold, James W.			1280	Sept.24,1838	
101	Roberts, THomas			640	May 28,1839	
128	Rigdill, Charles B.			640	Aug.12,1839	
4	Spillers, James W.			640	Mar.15,1838	
9	Sharp, James, Dec'd.			640	Mar.30,1838	Jos. L. Bennett Admr. of
34	Shepperd, Sidney			640	June 9,1838	
36	Spillers, John M.			640	June 21,1838	
40	Steel, Augustus			1280	Jy.5,1838	
60	Stotts, George L.			1280	Jy.23,1838	
68	Suitor, William			640	Aug.2,1838	
71	Stoub, Jacob			640	Aug.2,1838	
80	Smithers, Fielding S.			640	Aug.2,1838	
87	Sisson, James			640	Aug.2,1838	
89	Smith, Jesse R.			640	Aug. 2,1838	
102	Smith, Charles			640	Aug.14,1838	
103	Stewart, David			1280	Sept.6,1838	
105	Smith, Jaines H.			1280	Sept.6,1838	
110	Shook, Nathan			640	Sept.6,1838	
111	Smith, Alexander			640	Sept.6,1838	
114	Samuels, Allen			1280	Oct.4,1838	
121	Sanders, Wm. D.			640	Nov.1,1838	
37	Tousey, Isaac			640	Jy.5,1838	

No.	Name	Lgs.	Lbr.	Acres	Date	Remarks
61	Tullons, Ransom			640	Jy.30,1838	
62	Tullons, James			1280	Jy.30,1838	
63	Tullons, Hampton			1280	Jy.30,1838	
83	Tinsley, James			1280	Aug.2,1838	
67	Vincent, Adam			1280	Aug.2,1838	
26	Wood, William H.			640	June 7,1838	
24	Wood, John			1280	June 7,1838	
27	Wood, John H.			640	June 7,1838	
42	Wood, Thomas J.			640	Jy.5,1838	
79	Worley, Anderson			640	Aug.2,1838	
93	Whitting, Wm.			640	Aug.13,1838	
101	Wood, Joel P.			640	Aug.14,1838	
120	Wooldridge, John W.			640	Nov.1,1838	
141	Woodward, James W.			640	Sept.23,1839	
232	White, Zachariah			1280	Dec.30,1839	

THIRD CLASS

No.	Name	Lgs.	Lbr.	Acres	Date	Remarks
134	Allen, James J.			640	Aug.26,1839	
135	Allen, Rebecca H.			640	Aug.26,1839	
137	Allen, James M.			320	Aug.26,1839	
148	Arnold, Epaphras J.			640	Sept.25,1839	
157	Arnold, Eliphalet L.			320	Sept.25,1839	
176	Ariola, Joseph			320	Oct.28,1839	
219	Alston, Nathaniel K.			640	Dec.14,1839	
230	Alston, Henry			320	Dec.30,1839	
235	Allison, John			640	Dec.30,1839	
280	Allison, Absolom H.			320	Dec.31,1839	
339	Anderson, John			320	Jan.1,1840	
19	Bassett, Wm. E.			320	Mar.25,1839	
29	Benyman, Wesley			320	Mar.27,1839	
32	Brantley, Blake			640	Mar.27,1839	
41	Brantly, Joseph John			320	Mar.27,1839	
57	Barrett, Sidney			320	Apr.29,1839	
58	Barrett, Micajah			320	Apr.29,1839	
83	Birch, John			320	May 13,1839	
93	Brigauce, Harvey			320	May 28,1839	
96	Brown, Adam R.			320	May 28,1839	
115	Beaty, James			640	Jy. 1,1839	
150	Bynum, Nicholson G.			320	Sept.23,1839	
180	Barnett, Josiah			320	Oct.28,1839	
183	Bowen, Wm. H.			640	Oct.28,1839	
194	Booth, Robert M.			320	Nov.11,1839	
204	Bays, Peter			640	Nov.25,1839	
277	Brigance, Franklin			320	Dec.31,1839	
279	Brown, Robert			320	Dec.31,1839	
302	Bell, William W.			320	Dec.31,1839	

No.	Name	Lgs.	Lbr.	Acres	Date	Remarks
313	Bailey, John M.			320	Dec.31,1839	
332	Buckhannan, James E.			320	Jan. 1,1840	
333	Burns, Leonard			320	Jan. 1,1840	
11	Clabough, Charles			640	Mar.25,1839	
53	Clark, David			640	Apr.29,1839	
63	Cable, Frederick S.			640	Apr.30,1839	
69	Cooper, Richard			320	Apr.30,1839	
112	Cude, James W.			320	Jan.24,1839	
132	Cawthon, E.W.			320	Aug.13,1839	
154	Cook, Zion W.			320	Sept.24,1839	
172	Conrow, Charles M.			320	Oct.28,1839	
179	Camp, Thomas P.			640	Oct.28,1839	
181	Cressher, John B.			640	Oct.28,1839	
201	Clay, James M.			320	Nov.25,1839	
220	Chesher, Thomas E.			320	Dec.14,1839	
226	Cartright, Joseph C.			320	Dec.14,1839	
233	Curry, William			320	Dec.30,1839	
264	Cooper, Calvin			320	Dec.30,1839	
275	Christian, George A.			320	Dec.31,1839	
276	Carson, Thomas J.			320	Dec.31,1839	
290	Chapel, Henry			320	Dec.31,1839	
294	Cotton, Iredill			320	Dec.31,1839	
295	Cotton, John			640	Dec.31,1839	
296	Crane, Greenberry			320	Dec.31,1839	
344	Cummins, David M.			640	Jan. 6,1840	
10	Davis, Larkin D.			640	Mar.25,1839	
43	Durand, Elijah			320	Arp.29,1839	
70	Dodd, Richard			320	Apr.30,1839	
107	Davidson, Richard			640	June 24,1839	
108	Darlin, Thomas			320	June 24,1839	
120	Dunham, Joseph L.			320	Jy.29,1839	
202	Daily, Timothy M.			320	Nov.25,1839	
246	Dodson, Raleigh			640	Dec.30,1839	
251	Davis, David K.			640	Dec.30,1839	
274	Davis, John H.			320	Dec.31,1839	
281	Dyer, Benjamin F.			640	Dec.31,1839	
347	Dillingham, John			320	Jan. 6,1840	
33	Day, Larkin			320	Mar.27,1839	
306	Downes, Anderson			320	Dec.31,1839	
42	Evans, Nancy			640	Mar.27,1839	
89	Edwards, Nimrod N.J.J.B.L.			320	May 28,1839	
335	Elam, George W.			320	Jan. 1,1840	
350	Easters, James W.			320	Jan. 6,1840	
14	Franks, Benjamin			320	Mar.25,1839	
49	Folsom, Ebenezer			640	Apr.29,1839	
48	Folsom, Ebenezer L.			320	Apr.29,1839	
109	Foley, James			320	June 24,1839	
142	Ford, Lewis H.			640	Sept.23,1839	
160	Ford, James B.			640	Sept.25,1839	

No.	Name	Lgs.	Lbr.	Acres	Date	Remarks
221	Faith, Alex B.			320	Dec.14,1839	
231	Ford, A.J.			640	Dec.30,1839	
234	Fox, John			640	Dec.30,1839	
250	Ford, Henry			640	Dec.30,1839	
252	Finley, Norwood H.			640	Dec.30,1839	
253	Ford, William			640	Dec.30,1839	
259	Ford, Craner			320	Dec.30,1839	
284	Fogleman, Michael			320	Dec.31,1839	
325	Fowler, John M.			640	Jan. 1,1840	
326	Floyd, Wm. F.			640	Jan. 1,1840	Deceased.
351	Ford, Thomas J.			320	Jan. 6,1840	
56	Gammon, Silas			640	Apr.29,1839	
114	Guerrant, Daniel B.			320	June 24,1839	
116	Gammon, Smith M.			320	Jy. 1,1839	
151	Gray, George W.			320	Sept.23,1839	
157	Grimes, Jacob			320	Sept.24,1839	
213	Griffith, Leroy A.			320	Nov.26,1839	
228	Gibbs, Thomas			320	Dec.14,1839	
265	Gray, Arch'd.			320	Dec.30,1839	
270	Griffin, Jackson			640	Dec.30,1839	
312	Gerrard, Samuel			320	Dec.31,1839	
349	Gay, Appleton			640	Jan. 6,1840	
3	Hyatt, Jesse			640	Mar.25,1839	
34	Hagan, Jesse W.			640	Mar.27,1839	
60	Hale, Mashack B.			640	Apr.29,1839	
71	Hosteller, John			640	Apr.30,1839	
72	Hosteller, Rodney			320	Apr.30,1839	
73	Heard, Eleazer F.			640	May 13,1839	
81	Hallum, William V.R.			320	May 13,1839	
87	Heard, Hampton			320	May 27,1839	
92	Hill, Samuel			320	May 28,1839	
124	Hall, Thomas J.			320	My. 29,1839	
138	Harris, James M.			640	Aug.26,1839	
140	Hacket, J. Warren			320	Sept.9,1839	
155	Hutchinson, James P.			640	Sept.24,1839	
156	Hutchinson, Robert			640	Sept.24,1839	
159	Hambelton, Wade			320	Sept.25,1839	
174	Horn, William L.			320	Oct.28,1839	
187	Hightower, John O.			320	Nov.11,1839	
189	Heslip, Clinton			320	Nov.11,1839	
195	Herring, Stephen W.			320	Nov.11,1839	
203	Haighler, Thomas L.			320	Nov.25,1839	
225	Hampton, Edward			320	Dec.14,1839	
241	Harbour, Elijah			640	Dec.30,1839	
242	Harbour, Calloway			320	Dec.30,1839	
243	Hall, John J.			320	Dec.30,1839	
244	Hamilton, Joel			320	Dec.30,1839	
260	Harris, Greenbury			320	Dec.30,1839	
285	Hadley, Grantham H.			320	Dec.31,1839	
291	Houston, Abner			640	Dec.31,1839	
293	Houston, Frederick E.			320	Dec.31,1839	

No.	Name	Lgs.	Lbr.	Acres	Date	Remarks
309	Hutchinson, Lewis P.			320	Dec.31,1839	
320	Hall, Williamson, L.			320	Jan. 1,1840	
321	Hall, Hamson W.			320	Jan. 1,1840	
324	Hall, Thomas J.			320	Jan. 1,1840	
304	Irvin, Benjamin F.			640	Dec.31,1839	
305	Irvin, Benjamin F., Jr.			320	Dec.31,1839	
2	Johnson, Jesse			320	Mar.25,1839	
23	Johnson, Mary			640	Mar.25,1839	
25	Johnson, H.G.			640	Mar.26,1839	
51	Jones, George J.			640	Arp.29,1839	
84	Jones, Jackson N.			320	May 13,1839	
85	Jones, James R.			320	May 13,1839	
197	Johnson, Telephus A.			320	Nov.25,1839	
206	Jordan, Matthew F.			320	Nov.25,1839	
208	Jones, Hardy			640	Nov.25,1839	
209	Jones, Benjamin			320	Nov.25,1839	
255	Jones, Elizabeth			640	Dec.30,1839	
288	Jordan, John			640	Dec.31,1839	
50	Kepler, William			640	Apr.29,1839	
113	Kaminski, Ferdinand Napoleon			320	June 24,1839	
133	Kinnard, Marcus L.			320	Aug.26,1839	
175	Keiser, John			320	Oct.28,1839	
52	Lauderdale, Jeremiah			640	Apr.29,1839	
121	Lanehart, Adam C.			320	Jy. 29,1839	
161	Laugham, Charles			640	Spet.25,1839	
162	Langum, Benjamin B.			320	Sept.25,1839	
173	Lloyd, E.R.			320	Oct.28,1839	
177	Lauderdale, Robert			320	Oct.28,1839	
178	Lauderdale, Sarah			640	Oct.28,1839	
207	Long, Joseph H.			320	Nov.25,1839	
211	Lauderdale, William			320	Nov.26,1839	
212	Lauderdale, Simpson J.			320	Nov.26,1839	
308	Langham, James B.			320	Dec.31,1839	
315	Lowe, William			320	Dec.31,1839	
1	McVicar, John			320	Mar.25,1839	
7	Merton, Andrew			640	Mar.25,1839	
9	Mock, Rudolph			640	Mar.25,1839	J.L. Bennett, assignee.
12	Morris, Ross			320	Mar.25,1839	
30	Manning, Levi			640	Mar.27,1839	
31	Martin, William R.			640	Mar.27,1839	
47	Manning, Mark			640	Apr.29,1839	
68	Magee, William			320	Apr.30,1839	
95	McDonald, William			640	May 28,1839	
106	McGary, Warrick W.			640	June 24,1839	
110	McArthur, John			320	June 24,1839	
145	Moffitt, Thomas			640	Sept.9,1839	
146	Moffitt, Archibald A.			302	Sept.9,1839	

No.	Name	Lgs.	Lbr.	Acres	Date	Remarks
147	Moffitt, Paul G.			320	Sept.9,1839	
168	Manning, John			320	Oct. 7,1839	
169	McCown, James			320	Oct.28,1839	
170	McCown, Alexander			320	Oct.28,1839	
188	Mason, Almon H.			320	Nov.11,1839	
196	McCormick, Calvin			640	Nov.11,1839	
218	Mangrum, Joseph			640	Dec.14,1839	
223	Mitchell, James H.			640	Dec.14,1839	
248	McCalla, Andrew J.			320	Dec.30,1839	
257	Murphy, John D.			320	Dec.30,1839	
267	Mabry, James G.			640	Dec.14,1839	
272	Moon, James W.			320	Dec.30,1839	
278	Milton, Ephraim			640	Dec.31,1839	
283	Mayfield, Spencer C.			320	Dec.31,1839	
287	McLaughlin, Henry			320	Dec.31,1839	
298	Malone, Andrew J.			640	Dec.31,1839	
301	McBride, Alexander			640	Dec.31,1839	
314	McMillian, Drury			320	Dec.31,1839	
327	Matthews, Thomas			320	Jan. 1,1840	
328	McWilliams, James G.			320	Jan. 1,1840	
334	McKissick, Y.W.H.			320	Jan. 1,1840	
336	Musick, Isham			320	Jan. 1,1840	
66	Mifler, William			320	Apr.30,1840	
100	Nyman, Joseph			320	May 28,1840	
119	Nicholson, Anderson D.			320	May 29,1840	
247	Neal, Andrew G.			320	Dec.30,1840	
303	Norman, William H.			640	Dec.31,1840	
338	Newton, Benjamin			320	Jan. 1,1840	
67	Overby, J.W.			640	Apr.30,1840	
263	Osleen, Harvy			320	Dec.30,1840	
38	Pattison, John			640	Mar.27,1840	
45	Pattison, Jacob			640	Apr.29,1840	
62	Pierson, Isaac			320	Apr.30,1840	
192	Park, John			320	Nov.11,1840	
222	Pace, Richard E.			640	Dec.14,1840	
224	Pilkinton, Clinch			320	Dec.14,1840	
237	Porter, William L.			640	Dec.30,1840	
238	Porter, James P.			320	Dec.30,1840	
286	Parker, Lucretia			640	Dec.31,1840	
307	Pyle, Samuel E.			320	Dec.31,1840	
310	Posey, John			320	Dec.31,1840	
329	Preston, Samuel S.			320	Jan. 1,1840	
345	Patterson, Jacob, Sr.			640	Jan. 6,1840	
346	Patterson, Anthony			640	Jan. 6,1840	
40	Quin, James O.			320	Mar.27,1839	
18	Roberts, Allen			640	Mar.25,1839	
77	Robinson, Henry			640	May 13,1839	
78	Robinson, Elijah			320	May 13,1839	

No.	Name	Lgs.	Lbr.	Acres	Date	Remarks
79	Robinson, John H.			320	May 13,1839	
125	Redding, Robert B.			320	Aug.12,1839	
127	Roark, Josiah			320	Aug.13,1839	
144	Rogers, Armstead			640	Sept.23,1839	
152	Rumfield, Solomon			320	Sept.24,1839	
214	Rogers, Emery W.			640	Nov.26,1839	
215	Rogers, Carrol			320	Dec.14,1839	
258	Richardson, John D.H.			320	Dec.30,1839	
269	Roberts, John S.			320	Dec.30,1839	
318	Ray, Charles			320	Dec.31,1839	
319	Ray, Edward			320	Dec.31,1839	
322	Rackley, Wilson			320	Jan.1,1840	
4	Skinner, James			640	Mar.25,1839	
5	Stevens, Andrew J.			640	Mar.25,1839	
6	Stloner, Lewis			640	Mar.25,1839	
37	Shannon, Owen			320	Mar.27,1839	
61	Stevens, Thomas C.			640	Apr.29,1839	
88	Spillers, Harvey N.			320	May 28,1839	
91	Stactater, Joseph			320	May 28,1839	
105	Shannon, William			320	June 21,1839	
149	Shores, Henry			640	Sept.23,1839	
163	Savage, William B.			640	Sept.30,1839	
165	Stokes, Samuel			640	Sept.30,1839	Deceased
167	Sherrod, James H.			320	Oct. 7,1839	
171	Smith, Moses B.			320	Oct.28,1839	
190	Smither, Robert			320	Nov.11,1839	
191	Street, John, Jr.			320	Nov.11,1839	
193	Smith, Raleigh W.			320	Nov.11,1839	
199	Sutton, Isaac			640	Nov.25,1839	
215	Stubblefield, John			320	Dec.30,1839	
273	Simmons, Wm. B.			320	Dec.31,1839	
282	Shaw, Sexins W.			320	Dec.31,1839	
289	Smither, John			320	Dec.31,1839	
292	Smith, William S.			640	Dec.31,1839	
297	Smith, John C.			320	Dec.31,1839	
323	Smith, Henry H.			640	Jan. 1,1840	
331	Sullivan, Edward			320	Jan.1,1840	
39	Townsend, Joshua			320	Mar.27,1839	
41	Teas, Charles			640	Apr.29,1839	
205	Tankersly, William			640	Nov.25,1839	
268	Thompson, David			640	Dec.30,1839	
256	Templeton, Archibald W.			320	Dec.30,1839	
46	Utz, Frederick			640	Apr.29,1839	
210	Uzzell, Thomas M.			320	Nov.25,1839	
217	Uzzell, Elisha			640	Dec.14,1839	
94	Vaudevander, Hugh			320	May 28,1839	
249	Visar, William			640	Dec.30,1839	
261	Visar, Andrew F.			320	Dec.30,1839	
262	Visar, Washington L.			320	Dec.30,1839	

No.	Name	Lgs.	Lbr.	Acres	Date	Remarks
8	Wells, John			640	Mar.25,1839	
13	Winters, Oran			640	Mar.25,1839	
15	Williams, William R.			640	Mar.25,1839	
17	Winters, Benjamin F.			320	Mar.25,1839	
35	Warsham, Isreal			320	Mar.27,1839	
74	White, Robert			640	May 13,1839	
82	Williams, John M.			320	May 13,1839	
99	Westcott, Richard D.			640	May 28,1839	
102	Woolham, John C.			320	May 28,1839	
118	Whittenton, William M.			320	Jy.29,1839	
122	Warren, Hiram			320	Jy.29,1839	
130	Wheeler, Francis A.B.			640	Aug.12,1839	
136	Weekley, George M.			320	Aug.25,1839	
153	White, Henry A.			320	Sept.24,1839	
164	Williams, Thomas			640	Sept.30,1839	
198	White, Abel H.			320	Nov.25,1839	
200	Wood, Bennett			320	Nov.25,1839	
216	Williamson, John H.			320	Dec.14,1839	
236	Winn, Lemuel P.			640	Dec.30,1839	
240	Walarap, Claiborne P.			320	Dec.30,1839	
251	Word, Elizabeth			640	Dec.30,1839	
266	Wood, William W.			320	Dec.30,1839	
271	Walton, Jesse N.			320	Dec.30,1839	
299	Wells, Jackson			640	Dec.31,1839	
300	Wells, Crittendon			320	Dec.31,1839	
316	Wood, Robert			320	Dec.31,1839	
347	Wilson, James W.			320	Dec.31,1839	
330	Weaver, Charles			320	Jan. 1,1840	
337	White, John L.			320	Jan. 1,1840	
340	Wood, Henry			640	Jan. 1,1840	
341	Wood, Mary			640	JAn. 1,1840	
184	Yokiesch, Charles			320	Oct.28,1839	
185	Yokiesch, Augustus			320	Oct.28,1839	

NACOGDOCHES COUNTY

No.	Name	Lgs.	Lbr.	Acres	Date	Remarks
24	Ables, Joseph S.	1	1			
25	Ables, Ezekiel	1	1			
71	Ables, John	1	1			
40	Adams, Jefferson	1	1			
76	Aqualara, Jose Fecunda	1/3				
481	Atwood, James B.	1	1			
111	Arocha, Jose M.	1	1			
174	Ables, Harrison	1	1			
204	Anderson, Elijah		1			
231	Allison, Wm. F.		1			
294	Abshire, Edward	1	1			
347	Anthony, Francis J.	1/3				
362	Allen, Nathan N.G.		1			

No.	Name	Lgs.	Lbr.	Acres	Date	Remarks
483	Albirado, Juan Jose					Quantity not specified.
	Auttry, Micajah	1/3				
521	Allison, James	1	1			
599	Acosta, Juan Ysedro			973		
651	Acosta, Jose Mariano		1			
666	Acosta, Juan Jose	1	1			
688	Autry, Micajah;heirs of	1/3				
695	Alford, George G.	1	1			
469	Ables, Mary	1	1			
480	Alpando, Jose Maria	1	1			Alias, Villa-pando
484	Atwood, James B.	1	1			
621	Alvarado, Quofre	1/3				
505	Albarado, Elijie	1	1			
83	Anderson, Wm. H.	1	1			
243	Barton, Isaac W.		1			
240	Boden, Juan Lorenzo		1			
260	Bernard, Geuenine			369		
263	Bradshaw, James	1	1			
273	Baty, John		1			
645	Brewer, Henry M.	1	1			
316	Bacno, Hene(or Becavro)		1			
	Boden, Juan Batisto	1/3				
377	Brewer, Henry		1			
375	Brewer, James	1/3				
395	Brewer, John	1/3				
623	Brewer, William T.	1	1			
384	Buford, Thomas Y.	1	1			
373	Box, John A.		1			
374	Box, William S.		1			
430	Bailey, Jeremiah	1/3				
447	Beaty, Joseph	1	1			
409	Burnes, Samuel			369		
657	Barnes, Moses	1/3				
495	Bell, Ferdinand	1/3				
508	Balouoye,Francisco Jacinto		1			
652	Box, John M.		1			
653	Box, Samuel C.		1			
564	Brewer, Green B.		1			
565	Burress, Thomas		1			
578	Baker, William; heirs of					Quantity not specified.
608	Boss, George A.	1/3				
503	Bettram, Jose Maria	1	1			
619	Blount, Arch'd.Heirs of	1	1			
633	Bilersal, Juan		1			
681	Brown, James	1/3				
	Boulter, James		1			
690	Bean, Peter G.	1	1			
702	Boslyne, James	1	1			By error, written Rasleyn

No.	Name	Lgs.	Lbr.	Acres	Date	Remarks
713	Bowerman, Leonard	1/3				
288	Basques, Miguel	1	1			
515	Bereva, Jose Maria	1	1			
86	Barola, Jose Antonio		1			
299	Baldez, Bartholome	1/3				
302	Baldez, Francisco	1/3				
	Bajas, Jose Maria	1	1			
	Bradley, Eleanor	1	1			
278	Boden, Jose Lorenzo		1			
164	Bromberry, Sáml.heirs of	1	1			By Mary Bromberry. J. Lee,Admr.
195	Blair, John;heirs of	1/3				
318	Brooks,Francis or Thos.D.	1	1			
288	Basquez, Miguel	1	1			
16	Bell, William W.	1/3				
38	Bailey, Howard W.	1/3				
46	Bell, Samuel	1	1			
51	Burleson, Jonathan	1	1			
6	Bruce, Willis H.	1/3				
93	Bailey, Henry	1/3				
92	Bailey, John	1/3				
124	Barr, Isaac	1/3				
315	Boden, Juan Pdero	1	1			
241	Brown, Jeff. Heirs of	1	1			
2	Clute, John R.	1	1			
20	Chirino, Anastasio	1/3				Francis J. Anthony,assignee
31	Cook, David			368		
72	Childress, George C.	1	1			
77	Crain, Joel B.	1	1			
23	Crain, Ambrose	1	1			
80	Cortez, Felipe	1/3				
84	Cox, Williston M.	1/3				
94	Chapman, Henry	1/3				
103	Collins, Stephen	1/3				
295	Cordova, Jose S.	1	1			
122	Chisum, Wm. J.	1	1			
123	Chisum, Gillington	1/3				
126	Chevallier, Charles	1/3				
139	Cook, Joseph T.		1			
144	Click, George	1	1			
145	Click, Andrew J.	1/3				
210	Click, George W.	1/3				
181	Caro, Thomas	1	1			
165	Chirino, Jose	1	1			
169	Cooke, Joseph T.,Jr.	1/3				
175	Cook, Elihu D.	1/3				
239	Casenova, Estevan	1/3				
189	Casenova, Cresantus	1/3				
238	Casenova, Alfonso	1/3				
191	Carter, James	1/3				

No.	Name	Lgs.	Lbr.	Acres	Date	Remarks
303	Chirino, Antonio	1/3				
265	Chirino, Jose Augle	1/3				
202	Chavano, Guillermo	1/3				
541	Caro, Toribo	1/3				
216	Chavano, Antonio		1			
363	Chirino, Lucas	1/3				
274	Cudler, Francesco	1/3				
285	Cortinez, Miguel		1			
326	Cruz, Guillermo		1			
337	Caro, Jose, Jr.		1			
351	Cook, James	1	1			
423	Cortez, Juan Clement heirs of	1	1			
	Cruz, Manwela Juan		1			
426	Cook, C. Henry	1	1			
494	Cazenave, John B.		1			
489	Craine, Wm. H.	1/3				
	Castanes, Justine	1/3				
	Certines, Maria		1			
516	Cazenova, Gerirudes Maria	1	1			
649	Chirino,Candidi Maria					20 labors,233, 500 varas.
	Calderon, Francisco Juan	1/3				
547	Chirino, Antonio,Sr.	1	1			
572	Coy, Sautos Juan	1/3				
574	Chirino, Polonio	1/3				
585	Coy, Santos Benigro	1/3				
643	Castro, David Maria	1	1			
410	Calderon, Santiago	1	1			
658	Carsmel, Maria del	1	1			
657	Chirino,Juan Baptiste					Quantity not specified.
694	Craft, Samuel	1	1			
697	Carren, Elder	1	1			
701	Cratton, James R.	1	1			
710	Chivano, Santiago	1/3				
45	Carpenter, John M.	1	1			2 certificates (See Augustine ce).
457	Coy, Santos los de Brigado	1/3				
159	Clark, M.B. Heirs of	1/3				
577	Cerda, los de Salvador	1	1			
177	Costley, Michael,heirs of	1	1			
218	Cleveland, James	1/3				
251	Coy, Antonio de los	1	1			
200	Coy, Ignacio de los Santas		1			
321	Cervantez, Domingo		1			
	Castro,Maria Gaudaloupe		1			
383	Culla, Ramon Gonzales			369		
	Clark, Daniel	1	1			E.J. Debard, Admr.
1	Douglas, Kelsey H.	1	1			

No.	Name	Lgs.	Lbr.	Acres	Date	Remarks
18	Dankswerth, William	1/3				
185	Davis, William T.		1			
317	Dickerson, Waller	1/3				
223	Dance, Henry	1/3				
258	Debard, Elijah J.		1			
	Davis, Samuel T.	1/3				
300	Davis, Edward	1/3				
320	Dikes, George B.(alias P.		1			
319	Dikes, Levi B.		1			
	Doswell, James	1/3				
451	Dikes, Mark W. or P.	3/4	1			
456	Duncan, G.A.	1	1			
425	Dorsett, John		1			
524	Domingues, Jose Alfonso		1			
610	Darlin, John H.	1	1			
689	Dunavan, Amos; heirs of		1			
698	Daniel, Reasha(or Oratio)	1/3				By Wm. Bromley
722	Durst, Joseph	1				
110	De Waltz, Napoleon					Quantity not specified.
	David, Lewis		1			
663	Dunagan, Seth;heirs of	1	1			
	Dela, Jose Maria	1	1			
140	Durst, James H.	1/3				
714	Davidson, Washington	1/3				John M. Hansford, Admr.
244	Dexter, Samuel;heirs of	1/3				Rusk & Grant Admrs.
106	Day, F.H.K.;heirs of	1/3				
70	Ersa, Santiago		1			
98	Eubank, Elias M.	1	1			
101	Engledon, Creed S.		1			
107	Emanuel, Albert		1			
132	Elliott, William		1			
237	Engledon, John		1			
255	Earp, Benjamin;heirs of	1/3				
256	Earp, James	1	1			
257	Edwards, John H.		1			
	Elgrezadell, Volentine	1/3				
368	Edwards, Haden	1	1			
	Eldr, Iguacio;heirs of	1/2	1.2			
	Engledon, Oscar	1	1			
187	Escalan, Juana	1	1			
629	Esparza, Encarnacion	1	1			
393	Espaza, Jose Maria	1	1			
684	Espaza, Maria Antonio	1	1			
8	Forbes, John		1			
12	Ferguson, John		1			
62	Frisby, Abram	1	1			
203	Fisher, James		1			
236	Fulcher, Joshua		1			
248	Fulcher, William;heirs of	1	1			

No.	Name	Lgs.	Lbr.	Acres	Date	Remarks
259	Ford, James	1	1			
270	Fitzgerald, Edward	1/3				
272	Ferguson, Alston		1			
275	Falcene, Jose		1			
305	Francisco, Juan	1/3				Alias, Feliciana Lopez
424	Fowler, Thomas P;heirs of		1.3			
512	Frissas, H.E.F.;heirs of	1/3				
605	Foster, John	1	1			
634	Falcen, Juan		1			
648	Frisby, William	1	1			
	Flores, Juan		1			
	Flores, Vetal	1	1			
696	Fortune, James	1/3				
706	Flores, Policaspio	1/3				
712	Flores, Jasnos	1/3				
3	Fanning, Michael	1/3				
331	Flores, Antonio	1/3				
391	Falcin, Deonicio	1	1			
34	Fontino, Julian	1	1			
6	George, Stephen C.	1	1			
48	Gibson, Absalom		1			
114	Gough, Henry	1/3				
115	Garcia, Marcus, Jr.	1/3				
152	Gaines, W.B.P.	1/3				
171	Galland, Miguel	1	1			
193	Grayson, Charles	1	1			
194	Gibson, Jesse		1			
199	Gholson, Jacob J.	1	1			
234	George, Mitchell	1/3				
333	Gonzales, Leno	1/3				
293	Grayson, Jackson	1	1			
	Groce, Joshua,heirs of	1	1			
454	Garcia, Francisco	1/3				
345	Garcia, Marcus, Sr.	1	1			
370	Gee, Eason,;heirs of		1			
	George, William	1/3				
450	Garner, John N.	1/3				Isaac G. Parker, Assignee
324	Gay, John Baptiste	1	1			
504	Gonzales, Andres	1	1			
474	Garcia, Juan	1/3				
545	Goss, Thomas		1			
	Garcia, Trineda		1			
565	Gillaland, Eli	1	1			
635	Garcia, Jose	1/3				
639	Garza, Juan de la	1	1			Widow.
638	Gonzales, Lucelia	1	1			
	Guttierras, Jabel	1	1			
640	Garcia, Gregoria		1			Seth Sheldon, assignee.
708	Graham, John H.		1			

No.	Name	Lgs.	Lbr.	Acres	Date	Remarks
717	Gilliland, Samuel	1/3				
718	Gilliland, James	1/3				
594	Gonzales, Philip	1	1			
348	Gonzales, Juan		1			
497	Gabo, Jose	1	1			
519	Garcia, Ramion	1	1			
	Garcia, Jose Maria	1	1			
206	George, William E.	1/3				
717	Gilliland, Samuel	1/3				
173	Gertrudes, Manuel	1	1			
19	Hoya, Francis Vonder	1/3				
21	Henderson, Wm. F.	1/3				
29	Hoyl, John W.	1/3				
47	Harvey, John	1/3				
55	Hotchkiss, Rinaldo	1/3				
17	Hamilton, Vincent	1	1			
91	Howard, Wm. P.	1	1			
130	Harris, Elbridge G.	1	1			
182	Henri, Archibald	1	1			
158	Hallum, John	1	1			
163	Howard, John	1	1			
215	Haskill, Charles;heirs of	1/3				
216	Hawkins, Benj.;heirs of	1	1			
217	Hamilton, Elias E.	1/3				
	Hilton, Henry	1/3				
323	Hotchkiss, Archibald		1			
	Hernder, H.(or Heder) heirs of	1	1			
	Heinra, Manuel De		1			
	Herren, Moses		1			
380	Hertz, Hyman	1/3				
	Hoya, Anton Vonder			369		
	Henrie, Arthur, Jr.	1/3				
456	Hernandez, Lusano	1/3				
511	Hay, John D;heirs of	1/3				
475	Hamilton, Wm.;heirs of	1	1			
493	Henrie, John M.	3/4	1			
525	Hufferman, John	1/3				
544	Harper, Peter	1	1			
542	Hereia, Maria Gertrudes		1			
625	Hix, Isaac	1	1			
704	Hockaday, Willis;heirs of	1/3				
705	Hampton, Lorry S.		1			
709	Holmes, Peter W.	1/3				
311	Hernandes, Francisco	1	1			
69	Hall, James		1			
498	Hoya,Jos. F. Vonder	1/3				
650	Harris, John;heirs of			369		
	Hendereques, Juana	1	1			
228	Irby, John H.	1/3				
79	Johnson, George	1	1			

No.	Name	Lgs.	Lbr.	Acres	Date	Remarks
85	Johnson, John	1/3				
213	Jordan, Alexander	1	1			
212	Jordan, E.	1	1			
319	Johnson, William		1			
358	Jones, Jesse P.(or Isaac)		1			
509	Justemento, Juan Pascarsia	1/3				
	Jose, Sulegee	1	1			
358	Jones, Isaac		1			
707	Jackson, John; heirs of	1/3				
715	Johnson, Adam	1/3				
	Jeffry, Henry	1	1			
22	Knight, Lewis	1	1			
183	Korn, Mary		1			Alias, Horn
587	Kelly, Michael P.	1/3				
721	Keller, Antonio Dan'l; heirs of	1/3				
146	Kelly, Tobias	1/3				
35	Lacy, Daniel	1/3				
41	Leusch, John	1/3				Alias, Leush
68	Lacy, Martin		1			
121	Logan, O.W.	1/3				
396	Latham, Mary	1	1			
162	Lee, Isaac		1			
610	Lewis, Jacob	1/3				
626	Luna, Gertrudes		1			
108	Lavigna, Jose Polonia	1/3				
516	Leono, Donato	1	1			
500	Lasola, B.	1/3				
	Luna, Encarnacion	1/3				
653	Lazarene, Antonio	1/3				
	Luce, Joseph	1/3				
	Leonard, George G. heirs of	1/3				
	Luna, Sylvester	1/3				
528	Lopes, Jose Cornelio	1/3				
289	Lingorie, Jose	1	1			
	Leonard, George;heirs of	1/3				
437	Lambert, Thomas J.	1	1			
563	Lewis, Jacob	2/3	1			
28	Lazarine, Julion	1/3				
251	Lacy, William Y.	1/3				
11	Milhome, Francis		1			
96	Manwaring, William			369		
97	Morin, Jose		1			
155	Murray, John B.	1/3				
330	Mora, Jose Anastacio	1/3				
198	McNuff, Hamilton	1	1			
301	Mora, Jose Lelerona	1	1			
247	Mast, Jacob	1	1			
559	Mora, Jose	1/3				

No.	Name	Lgs.	Lbr.	Acres	Date	Remarks
269	Marshall, John	1	1			
438	Mancha, Jose S.	1	1			
271	Maffit, James	1/3				
281	Martin, Neal		1			
298	Mora, Jose	1/3				
308	Martinez, Francisco		1			
338	Mancha, Francisco	1/3				
339	Mora, Maria Jose	1	1			
313	Moore, James J.	1	1			Alias, S.
378	Medina, Juan Jose		1			
418	Mendosa, Jose Maria	1/3				Spelled Juan Maria Medina
	Martinez, Antonio	1/3				
522	Murdock, David H. heirs of	1/3				
422	Morison, John C.	1/3				
427	McNutty, James	1/3				
444	Mendez, Jose Antonio	1/3				
455	Marr, Achilla	1/3				
416	Minor, Daniel	1/3				
411	McNutty, Sarah		1			
470	Manchaca, Francisco	1/3				
656	Mora, Mariano, Jr. heirs of					Quantity not specified.
488	McNutty, Bennett	1/3				
413	Mora, Maria Manuella	1	1			
286	May, John	1	1			
502	Martinez, Jose Maria		1			
517	Marroy, Walter	1	1			
540	Melton, James C.P.	1/3				
516	Mitcheson, Edward F.; heirs of	1/3				
	Michamp, John Cigene	1	1			
570	Morales, Andres		1			
586	Medino, Pedro		1			
581	Morris, Robert G; heirs of					Quantity not specified.
607	Myers, Henry			369		
656	Mora, Mariano, Sr.	1	1			
	Martinez, Jose Dolorus	1	1			
611	McIlvain, William					Quantity not specified.
617	Mansola, Juan B.			369		Delores Certimus, Assignee.
615	Metcalf, Isaac J.		1			
612	Musick, Marie (Martha)	1	1			
636	Millard, Robert		1			
624	Mordecai, Benjamin H.	1/3				
616	May, George		1			
556	Montes, Jose Maria	1/3				
	Mayhou, Nathan	1/3				
720	McKenzie, Caster T.	1				
723	Miguel; heirs of		1	119		
90	Martinez, Guadaloupe	1	1			Kelsey H. Douglass, assignee.

No.	Name	Lgs.	Lbr.	Acres	Date	Remarks
58	Medro, Batiste	1/3				Kelsey H. Douglass, assignee.
226	Martinez, Juan Maria	1	1			
88	Michelia, J. Vicente	1	1			
292	Martinez, Pablo	1	1			
	Martinez, Juan Jose	1/3				
439	Madrigal, Manuel	1	1			
	Maloine, Thomas B;heirs of	1/3				
599	Martinez, Gayeuido	1/3				
	McMahon, William	1/3				
661	Maxwell, John	1/3				By John A. Winder
151	Morales, Jose Rodregues	1/3				
330	Mata, Juan	1/3				
172	Navarro, Larenzo	1/3				
168	Neato, Jose	1/3				
233	Nettles, William	1/3				
225	Nelson, William	1	1			
227	Noblett, John	1/3				
289	Nabers, Robert W.	1/3				
650	Nelson, John (or Wm. G.)	1/3				
332	Oseina, Benefacia de	1	1			
610	Odle, Sarah	1	1			
17	Peck, Solomon R.	1/3				Melville Crossman, Admr.
82	Parker, Isaac			369		
102	Pineda, Jose Maria	1/3				
104	Perez, Eugenio	1/3				
385	Patton, Chas. Dec'd.) heirs of	1/3				
148	Porter, J.J.;heirs of		1			
179	Powell, Wm. R.	1/3				
397	Procla, Juan Jesus		1			Alias, Procella
371	Pineda, Juan C.			369		
116	Pollitt, George	1/3	1			
415	Patton, Moses L.			369		
416	Procella, Francisco	1	1			
532	Prado, Martin		1			
539	Pina, Francisco de la	1	1			
576	Peacock, John W.;heirs of	1/3				
588	Peros, Francisca		1			
583	Prado, Jose Anselmo		1			
680	Pantalluin, Bernard		1			
603	Pardilla, Jamire	1/3				
604	Pool, Jonathan		1			
606	Pool, Beverly		1			
618	Pollack, James	1/3				
	Padilla, Juan Antonio	1	1			
665	Park, Alexander	1	1			
	Peres, Jose Ysedro	1/3				
644	Paddilla, Dolores	1/3				

No.	Name	Lgs.	Lbr.	Acres	Date	Remarks
129	Pond, Carlile W.	1/3				
	Pina, Christome	1/3				
344	Prado, Juan, Jr.	1/3				
331	Quiro, Pedro	1	1			
3	Raquet, Henry		1			
5	Reaves, Dirmr W.	1/3				
7	Roark, John		1			
59	Reed, John	1	1			
61	Reed, James	1/3				
99	Rector, James	1	1			
119	Roark, William		1			
120	Roark, Russell			369		
111	Reagan, William		1			
356	Reed, William B.		1			John Forbes, Admr.
157	Rusk, David	1/3				
166	Rial, John W.	1/3				
188	Roderigues, Pedro	1	1			
266	Rosa, Lewis	1/3				
325	Ritter, George W	1	1			
214	Rusk, Thomas J.		1			
219	Russell, Eli		1			
232	Rogers, Robert	1	1			
268	Rameriz, Guerra	1	1			
262	Randal, O.W.	1/3				
356	Reed, Wm. B.		1			
354	Reed, Pleasant	1/3				
361	Rivers, John		1			
369	Rudale, John; heirs of		1			
	Rogers, John; heirs of		1			
421	Roberts, John S.		1			
476	Reinhardt, J.D.	1/3				
492	Rocha Levero	1/3				
548	Reyes, de los Antonio	1/3				
561	Reed, Isaac		1			
576	Reyes, Jose Juan de los		1			
573	Rogales, Francisco	1/3				
582	Rodregues, Jose Antonio		1			
598	Richards, Guadalupe		1			
588	Ryan, John F.	1/3				
597	Rentaria, Maria	1	1			Widow of Jose Gonzales
	Rogers, Bethany		1			
702	Roslyne, James	1	1			Should be Boslyne.
472	Romos, Jose Maria	1/3				
376	Ramsdale, John F.	1/3				
372	Ramsdale, Francis	1	1			
661	Rojas, Francisco de	1	1			
287	Roberts, Matthews	1/3				
314	Roark, Washington; heirs of	1/3				

No.	Name	Lgs.	Lbr.	Acres	Date	Remarks
699	Roof, John Eberhard; heirs of	1	1			
14	Sevier, Eldridge G.	1/3				
22	Sparks, Stephen F.	1	1			
30	Sparks, Richard		1			
32	Strode, Harvey M.	1	1			
52	Sims, Charles H.	1	1			
53	Sims, Matthew F.	1/3				
60	Strode, Stephen	1/3				
78	Smith, Robert W.	3/4				
527	Stanford, Thomas	1	1			
80	Smith, James	1	1			
267	Starr, P.O. & James F.	1	1			Heirs of F.J. Starr
113	Sparks, Matthew	1	1			
118	Sanchez, Antonio	1	1			
128	Stenwick, William	1	1			
136	Silman, Stafford	1	1			
135	Silman, Wesley	1/3				
156	Smith, Henry M.	1/3				
170	Snalum, Thomas C.	1/3				
176	Smith, Leander;heirs of	1	1			
178	Skelton, John; heirs of		1			
471	Soto, Francisco	2/3	1			Alias Manshaca.
429	Sanchez, Maria Gertrudo		1			
197	Stokeley, Thomas;heirs of		1	1		J.S. Ables, Admr.
200	Simpson, Isaac		1			Original entry, 1 lg. & lab.
465	Stokeley, John	1/3				
235	Simpson, John S.		1			
252	Sancido, Dacedia		1			
313	Soto, Jose Maria		1			
301	Santos, Rafael de los		1			
	Sanchis, Francisco; heirs		1	1		A. Sterne, Admr.
316	Simpson, William M.	1/3				
352	Sims, Williams	1	1			
381	Sims, Alfred	1/3				
660	Skellon, James A.	1/3				
	Sanches, Mariana;widow of		1			
419	Sparks, Levi N.	1/3				
428	Sparks, James		1			
	Simpson, Robert H.	1	1			Alias, Bartlett H.
466	Stanley, Willdired		1			
473	Sanches, Ignacio, Jr.	1	1			
501	Sanches, Ignacio, Sr.	1	1			
662	Soto, Madam Maria Delores	1	1			
537	Sanches, Jose Ignacio	1	1			
549	Sanchis, Mariano		1			
562	Stockman, Henry		1			
571	Salasar, Mariano	1	1			

No.	Name	Lgs.	Lbr.	Acres	Date	Remarks
	Sanches, Lewis		1			
	Sanches, David	1	1			
	Sanches, Simeon	1	1			
616	Stadler, Robert G.	1/3				
613	Stanley, Elizabeth		1			
613	Snively, Jacob			369		
614	Smith, Wm. S.		1			
698	Sterne, Adolphus		1			
654	Salasar, Antonio	1/3				
	Sanchez, Gertrudes		1			
419	Sparks, Levi N.	2/3	1			
691	Sewell, M.;heirs of	1/3				
692	Sepulvado, Felipe Seguimundo	1/3				
711	Sibley, Henry	1/3				
407	Simpson, George	1	1			
322	Sylvester, Santos	1/3				
392	Sanches, Ramion	1/3				
411	Santos, Cornelio	1	1			
590	Solis, Doloris	1/3				
491	Shelby, Columbus	1/3				
242	Stewart, Robert	1	1			
385	Shepherd, Hugh		1			
	Sambrano, Antonio Tatiene	1/3				
507	Suligna, Joseph	1	1			Wm. W. Wingfield, assignee.
195	Thorn, John S.			369		
127	Timmons, Thomas G.	3/4	1			
147	Toscano, Santiago	1/2				
119	Tanner, Joseph A.	1	1			
196	Thorn, Leo M.	1/3				
595	Towns, David	1	1			
229	Taylor, John A.	1	1			
261	Tarm, Antonio	1/3				
150	Tesia, Prere (or Techa)	1	1			
310	Tores, Miguel		1			
342	Todd, Jackson	1/3				
340	Tabar, Juan		1			
445	Torres, Maria (or Marcus)	1/3				
498	Trevino, Jose Jesus	1/3				
593	Taylor, Charles S.		1			
602	Thorn, Frost		1			
19	Thraber, Henry	1/3				
108	Trimble, John	1/3				
719	Tipps, George W.	1/3				
	Thomas, Josiah	1	1			
	Tibbles, Frederick A.	1/3				
	Trevada, Ventura		1			
390	Trevino, Juan	1	1			
531	Travino, Francisco	1	1			
	Taylor, James	1/3				
100	Thompson, Bartlett F.	1/3				

No.	Name	Lgs.	Lbr.	Acres	Date	Remarks
211	Vardeman, William	1	1			
253	Vansickle, Benjamin A.	1	1			
261	Vansickle, Hiram	1/3				
359	Villa, Juan Jose		1			
418	Vanwinkle, Mary	1	1			
523	Villerial, N.	1	1			
652	Vela, Maria Catelena	1	1			
600	Vega, Maria de la	1	1			Widow of Juan Lazerine.
677	Veatch, John A.		1			
700	Velard, Lewis	1/3				
703	Vansickle, Elias S.	1/3				
	Vargas, Antonio	1/3				
4	Wood, Benjamin F.	1	1			
13	White, Joseph E.	1	1			
15	White, John M.	1/3				
487	Windle, John A.	1	1			
36	Walters, Wade H.	1	1			
37	Walters, Robert	1	1			
39	Walters, Tilman	1	1			
42	Williams, William F.	1/3				
43	Walling, Thomas J.	1	1			
44	Walling, John,Sr	1	1			
49	Walling, Jesse	1	1			
54	Wright, Benjamin F.	1/3				
21	Walters, George T.	1	1			
27	Walters, Moses	1	1			
33	Walters, Andrew C.	1	1			
26	Walters, Charles M.	1	1			
75	Wade, Nathan	1/3				
64	Wolten, John D.	1/3				
63	Whitaker, Madison G.	1/3				
65	Whitaker, Charles H.	1/3				
138	Walden, Thomas W.	1	1			
117	Walker, John	1	1			
125	Walling, Alfred G.	1/3				
555	Wiess, Simon	1	1			
526	Welch, George	1/3				
551	Williams, Hiram;heirs of	1	1			
542	Wilburn, Daniel		1			
550	Wilburn, Joel	1/3				
686	Walling, John C.	1/3				
693	Walters, B.C.	2/3	1			
725	Williams, Robert	1/3				
264	Walker, Thomas	1	1			
	Ward, Andrew J.	1/3				
50	Walling, John, Jr.		1			
355	Walt, Henry A. (Awalt)		1			
724	Williams, Buck;heirs of		1			
137	Windsor, James	1	1			
167	Walters, Boley C.	1	1			
468	Walker, Lewis	1	1			

No.	Name	Lgs.	Lbr.	Acres	Date	Remarks
	Wagner, George	1	1			
208	Watkins, Richard O.	1/3				
205	Watkins, Robert M.	1/3				
207	Whitaker, B.F.		1			
276	Williams, William	1	1			
282	Whitaker, William; heirs of	1	1			
312	Williams, Thomas;heirs of		1			
349	Wilson, David;heirs of	1/3				
365	Walker, Joel		1			
434	Walter, Boley C.,Jr.	1/3				
490	Watkins, Jesse;heirs of	1	1			
125	Walling, Alfred G.	2/3	1			
56	Ybarba, Ramigo	1/3				
67	Ybarbo, Gregoria	1/3				
81	Ybarbo, Maxmillian	1/3				
87	Ybarbo, Miguel		1			
96	Yordt, D.T.F.	1	1			
142	Ybarbo, Candalaria	1/3				
328	Ybarbo, Juan Jose	1	1			
154	Ybarbo, Manuel Mariano	1/3				
190	Ybarbo, Luciano	1/3				
327	Ybarbo, Jose Maria	1/3				
224	Ybarbo, Jose Antonio	1/3				
417	Ybarbo, Francisco	1/3				
245	Ybarbo, Juan Bemyeno	1/3				
250	Ybarbo, Martin		1			
378	Ybarbo, Demascio		1			
514	Ybarbo, Jose Maria; heirs of	1	1			
592	Ybarbo, Anastacio		1			
591	Ybarbo, Antonio	1/3				
620	Ybarbo, Benigno		1			
647	Ybarbo, Alahandro	1	1			
	Ybarbo, Manuel	1	1			
529	Ybarbo, Francisco, Jr.	1	1			
558	Ybarbo, Jose		1			
k43	Ybarbo, Jesus	1/3				
161	Young, Ezekiel C.	1	1			
297	Ybarbo, Juan	1/3				
716	Yancy, John	2/3	1			
388	Zepada, Juan Maria	1	1			

SECOND CLASS

No.	Name	Lgs.	Lbr.	Acres	Date	Remarks
43	Alvis, Abner			640		
84	Alexander, James			1280	Jy.5,1838	
99	Aldridge, John			1280	Jy.6,1838	
201	Allison, John			1280	Sept.5,1838	

No.	Name	Lgs.	Lbr.	Acres	Date	Remarks
57	Allen, George			1280		
2	Bumes, Charles M.			640	Mar.20,1839	
13	Bell, Charles			640		
14	Bell, James			1280		
15	Belt, Binford			1280		
16	Bell, William			640		
26	Buffington, Joseph			640		
55	Baron, Henry P.			1280		
59	Borner, George			1280		
62	Bingham, John G.			1280		
72	Beard, William A.			640		
76	Black, George H.			640	June 11,1838	
115	Brown, John S.			640	Jy. 6,1838	
143	Bettine, Wiley			1280	Aug. 3,1838	
150	Bromley, William			1280	Aug. 3,1838	
168	Bernitt, Louisa			1280	Sept.6,1838	L.B. Bernitt's widow.
176	Bondus, George			640	Oct. 5,1838	
199	Burrow, William			640	Aug. 3,1838	
208	Brown, Elizabeth			1280	Sept.6,1838	
224	Bivins, James			640	Dec. 5,1838	
9	Corbin, Albert G.			640		
21	Castillo, Florencio			640		
54	Childers, Josiah L.			640		
73	Chisum, Pamela			1280		
131	Conner, Benjamin			1280		
155	Carithers, John S.			1280	Aug. 3,1838	
156	Corbitt, Edwin			640		
190	Chambers, John C.			640	June 6,1838	
193	Childers, John C.			640	Aug. 2,1838	
204	Chisum, James			640	Sept.5,1838	
216	Chisum, Elijah, Jr.			640	Nov. 7,1838	
217	Chisum, Sr.			1280	Nov. 7,1838	
19	Davis, Wm. H.			640		
41	Dorsett, Asa			640		
45	Darst, Isaac			1280		
58	Davis, Wm. C.			640		
96	Draper, James S.			1280	Jy. 6,1838	
125	Dicksin, James G.			640		
	Davis, George N.			640		
32	Eakin, James M.			1280		
51	Eakin, Ephraim M.			1280		
114	Edmundson, Pjilip H.			640	Jy. 7,1838	
161	Eubanks, Edmund V.			640	Sept.6,1838	
219	Elders, Thomas			1280	Nov. 7,1838	
35	Eaton, Alfred			1280		
36	Eaton, John			1280		
33	Ferris, Warren A.			640		

No.	Name	Lgs.	Lbr.	Acres	Date	Remarks
56	Finley, Zachariah P.			1280		
85	Ford, Hazel P.			1280	Jy. 5,1838	
121	Ferguson, John			1280	Jy.13,1838	
138	Fowler, John W.			640		
185	Ford, Levi			640	Apr.12,1838	
192	Floyd, F.R.			640	Aug. 2,1838	
75	Gould, Charles M.			640	June 11,1838	
144	Greer, Alexander			1280	Aug. 3,1838	
148	Grriggs, Asberry			1280	Aug. 3,1838	
149	Grubbs, Winferd			1280	Aug. 3,1838	
86	Giles, Samuel B.			640		
8	Hird, John			640		
23	Hall, Green H.			640		
30	Hamilton, George			640		
34	Hamilton, Andrews			640		
61	Harkeil, Solomon			1280		
67	Harrison, Fitzaymer Wm. S.			640		
81	Hyde, George S.			640	Jy. 5,1838	
82	Hix, Francis F.			640	Jy. 5,1838	
93	Holiness, Charles			640	Jy. 6,1838	
100	Harvey, Leander			640	Jy. 6,1838	
102	Hart, William			1280	Jy. 7,1838	
112	Hart, Alexander			640	Jy. 7,1838	
127	Howard, E.			640		
133	Hall, Bartlett M.			1280		
136	Hang, John F.			640		
154	Hamilton, Andin			1280	Aug. 3,1838	
158	Hubert, John R.			1280	Aug. 3,1838	
167	Holmes, Oscar L.			640	Sept.7,1838	
178	Hall, John			640	Apr. 4,1838	
180	Hamilton, Francis			1280	Apr. 4,1838	Jas. Smith Admr.
182	Hunt, Samuel			640	Apr. 5,1838	
210	Hanks, Elijah D.			1280	Oct. 3,1838	
215	Hyde, John H., Jr.			640	Nov. 7,1838	
225	Hamby, Harvey			1280	Dec. 5,1838	
229	Hyde, John H., Sr.			1280	Dec.20,1838	
108	Hall, John H.			640	Jy. 6, 1838	
212	Ingleton, Ambrose			640	Oct. 3,1838	
74	Jorden, Amstead			640		
198	Jewell, George W.			1280	Aug. 3,1838	
205	Jacobs, Henry			640	Sept.5,1838	
218	Jacobs, Wm.			1280	Nov. 7,1838	
223	Jackson, Y.			1280	Dec. 5,1838	
226	Jacobs, James			1280	Dec.19,1838	
227	Jordon, Samuel J.			640	Dec.19,1838	
7	Keeling, William M.			640		
12	Keyrs, Mary			1280		

No.	Name	Lgs.	Lbr.	Acres	Date	Remarks
139	Killingh, Samuel			1280		
164	Kaufman, David S.			640	Oct. 5,1838	
207	Kelly, Russell			640	Sept.6,1838	
20	Lauson, Augustus			640		
39	Lively, Philip			1280		
46	Little, Jackson			640		
48	Luckett, Thomas A.			1280		
52	Lang, James D.			1280		
53	Lang, Mary M.			1280		
63	Langham, Paschal G.			640		
65	Langham, Monroe			640		
88	Langham, Madison H.			640	Jy. 5, 1838	
89	Langham, Ransom			640	Jy. 5, 1838	
94	Langham, James			1280	Jy. 6, 1838	
97	Long, John			1280	Jy. 6, 1838	
105	Linn, James S.			640	Jy. 7, 1838	
123	Little, John D.			1280	Jy.13, 1838	
165	Langham, Joel			1280	Sept.6,1838	
195	Long, W.D.			1280	Aug. 3,1838	
196	Long, Geo. W.			640	Aug. 3,1838	
209	Long, William T.			640	Sept.5,1838	
1	Lowe, Joseph W.			640	Mar.20,1838	
71	Lewis, Wm. G.			640		
5	McJoer, Alexander			1280		
6	Maas, Samuel			640		
10	Martin, James B.			640		
11	Moreland, Sylvester			1280		
40	Muse. K.H.			1280		
42	McIver, T.T.			1280		
47	Martin, Artemon L.			640		
59	Mead, Aquila M.			640		
68	McGray, Thomas			640		
92	Maxwell, Thomas			640	Jy. 6, 1838	
95	Marlar, Robert M.			1280	Jy. 6, 1838	
109	Miller, Benjamin			640	Jy. 7, 1838	
122	Mayfield, J.S.			1280	Jy. 6, 1838	
131	Miller, John M.			1280		
137	Montgomery, Farris			1280		
141	Mitchell, Bluford			1280		
145	Milander, James			1280	Aug. 3,1838	
152	Merideth, Joseph			640	Aug. 3,1838	
153	Moore, Elijah H.			640	Aug. 3,1838	
166	Mathews, Lyman			1280	Sept.6,1838	
171	Martin, George			1280	Oct. 4,1838	
177	McDonald, John S.			640	Apr. 4,1838	
179	McClure, Wm. F.			640	Apr. 4,1838	
183	McKaughan, William			640	Apr. 5,1838	
187	Martin, Henry			640	June 6,1838	
188	McWilliams, James			640	June 6,1838	
206	Moore, James D.			640	Sept.5,1838	
222	Morse, John			640	Nov.28,1838	By C.W. Waters

No.	Name	Lys.	Lbr.	Acres	Date	Remarks
230	Miller, George W.			640	Dec.27,1838	
231	McCune, James			640	Dec.27,1838	
232	Midkiff, Susana			1280	Dec.29,1838	
104	Newell, William			640	Jy. 7, 1838	
132	Neil, John F.			1280		
191	Noble, S.F.			640	Jy. 4, 1838	
116	O'Kelly, David F.			640	Jy. 6, 1838	
157	Odel, Abraham			640	Aug.3, 1838	
18	Parker, Cyrus			640		
22	Pluker, Wilheilm			1280		
60	Price, Edmund			1280		
110	Parmalle, Richard			640	Jy. 6, 1838	
118	Pope, William			1280	Jy. 6, 1838	
162	Pathun, Robert S.			640	Sept.6,1838	
169	Pate, John			1280	Oct. 4,1838	
181	Pinney, R.H.			640	Apr. 4,1838	
189	Patterson, Thos. J.			640	June 6,1838	
194	Pearson, Lorenzo D.			640	Aug. 3,1838	
202	Pickins, F.D.			640	Sept.5,1838	
24	Quin, Amos			640		
37	Reily, James			1280		
78	Russell, Nancy G.			1280	Jy. 5, 1838	
83	Reynolds, Reynold			1280	Jy. 5, 1838	
117	Rumpff, Martin			1280	Jy. 6, 1838	
119	Reamin, Adolphus			640	Jy. 6, 1838	
151	Royal, Peter			640	Aug. 3,1838	
160	Robinson, James W.			640	Sept.6,1838	
163	Ruth, James			640	Sept.6,1838	
175	Reagan, Charles			640	Oct. 5,1838	
211	Rush, Mary			1280	Oct. 3,1838	
233	Randolph, John			640	Sept.6,1838	
25	Sansum, Sam'l. D., Jr.			640		
44	Shrader, Levi S.			640		
50	Sparks, Eli G.			640		
49	Sparks, William			1280		
66	Starke, Theodore			640		
70	Scott, Abram H.			640		
87	Sandford, James M.			1280	Jy. 5, 1838	
91	Smith, Berry			1280	Jy. 5, 1838	
98	Sing, James M.			1280	Jy. 6, 1838	
107	Sparks, Frederick			1280	Jy. 6, 1838	
111	Stovall, Thomas H.			640	Jy. 6, 1838	
113	Snyder, Michael			640	Jy. 7, 1838	
124	Sparks, James H.			1280	Jy. 13,1838	
130	Shropshin, David M.			640		
135	Sims, Wm. F.			640		
159	Schloss, Leamon			1280	Aug. 3,1838	

No.	Name	Lgs.	Lbr.	Acres	Date	Remarks
170	Stephens, William			640	Oct. 5,1838	
173	Sollar, John			1280	Oct. 5,1838	
176	Samsom, Wm. P.			1280	Apr. 4,1838	
197	Saylor, William W.			640	Aug. 3,1838	
203	Simpson, L.W.			1280	Sept.5,1838	
213	Sparks, John			1280	Nov. 7,1838	
214	Sills, Benjamin F.			640	Nov. 7,1838	
38	Thompson, James C.			640		
106	Thayer, John			640	Jy. 7, 1838	
177	Trvdle, John			1280	Oct.5, 1838	
200	Trumbull, William			640	Aug. 3,1838	
142	Venables, Pleasant			1280	Aug. 3,1838	
220	Vanvaught, John			640	Nov. 7,1838	A. Gibson, Admr.
27	Wright, Samuel C.			640		
28	Wright, Hansel			640		
29	Wright, George H.			640		
31	Wright, Thos. S.			640		
64	Witter, John			640		
77	Wilson, John			1280	June 11,1838	
79	Wilson, Wm. K.			640	Jy. 5, 1838	
80	Wilson, Ira L.			1280	Jy. 5, 1838	
90	Woodson, Henry			1280	Jy. 6, 1838	
120	Williams, Isham			1280	Jy. 6, 1838	
126	Weeks, Daniel			640		
128	Wolverton, George			640		
129	Watkins, John			640		
140	Woods, George W.			1280		
146	Warnel, Wm. R.			1280	Aug. 3,1838	
147	Warnel, Wm. W.			640	Aug. 3,1838	
174	Wyatt, Sam'l.			1280	Oct. 5,1838	
172	Winn, William			640	Oct. 4,1838	
184	Wilds, Sam'l. W.			640	Apr.12,1838	
186	War, Mengurther L.			640	May 11,1838	
221	Walsh, Antonio			640	Nov.21,1838	Jacob Mast, Admr.
228	Walling, James			1280	Dec.20,1838	

THIRD CLASS

No.	Name	Lgs.	Lbr.	Acres	Date	Remarks
68	Abels, Andrew			320	June 6,1839	
105	Anderson, J.Y.			320	Aug. 2,1839	
142	Asqua, Daniel			320	Sept.5,1839	
158	Austin, William			320	Sept.5,1839	
182	Arnold, William			640	Sept.5,1839	
238	Ashmore, Leonard A.			320	Nov. 7,1839	
249	Ashmore, John			320	Nov. 7,1839	
253	Anderson, John			320	Nov. 7,1839	
255	Aiken, S.A.			320	Nov. 7,1839	

No.	Name	Lgs.	Lbr.	Acres	Date	Remarks
287	Allison, Robert M.			320	Nov. 7,1839	
301	Able, Ezekiel			320	Nov.28,1839	
335	Aaron, Thomas N.			320	Dec.5, 1839	
358	Arnoll, John			320	Dec. 5,1839	
486	Alfred, Atkinson			640	Dec.19,1839	
499	Alexander, Christopher C.			640	Dec.19,1839	
594	Aldridge, Joel H.			320	Dec.28,1839	
4	Bradshaw, Mary			640	Apr. 4,1839	
24	Bryant, James L.			640	Apr.11,1839	
34	Brewer, Mary			640	Apr. 4,1839	
38	Busslnner, Martin			640	May 11,1839	
46	Bean, Isaac S.			320	June 6,1839	
63	Brimbury, John N.			320	June 6,1839	
69	Brinbary, Isaac			640	June 6,1839	
83	Banks, ? J.			320	Jy. 4, 1839	
86	Butler, Eumes			640	Jy. 4, 1839	
111	Bissett, Mary C.			640	Aug. 3,1839	
151	Browning, A.			640	Sept.5,1839	
160	Burton, William M.			320	Sept.5,1839	
161	Bright, Alfred			320	Sept.5,1839	
163	Brown, Samuel H.			640	Sept.5,1839	
212	Barner, F.C.			320	Oct. 3,1839	
214	Breley, James			320	Oct. 3,1839	
247	Bean, Samuel M.			320	Nov. 7,1839	
252	Brown, Daniel			320	Nov. 7,1839	
262	Brown, Wilson N.			320	Nov. 7,1839	
263	Brown, James			320	Nov. 7,1839	
283	Bruce, William M.			640	Nov. 7,1839	
299	Berryhill, Thomas			640	Nov.21,1839	
302	Bellah, Samuel			320	Nov.28,1839	
303	Bellah, Reuben			640	Dec. 5,1839	
304	Bellah, Charles			640	Dec. 5,1839	
314	Barkley, Harvey			320	Dec. 5,1839	
315	Barkley, Josiah			320	Dec. 5,1839	
316	Barkley, Scriba			320	Dec. 5,1839	
329	Bean, Robert C.			640	Dec. 5,1839	
330	Bean, Franklin H.			320	Dec. 5,1839	
331	Bean, James K.			320	Dec. 5,1839	
331	Barnes, James P.			320	Dec. 5,1839	
334	Bringham, Moses M.			320	Dec. 5,1839	
337	Brown, John H.			320	Dec. 5,1839	
340	Briley, Shadrack			640	Dec. 5,1839	
363	Bell, Asa			640	Dec. 5,1839	
364	Barnes, William R.			640	Dec. 5,1839	
375	Barks, Samuel P.			640	Dec. 5,1839	
387	Barnes, James			640	Dec. 5,1839	
386	Brigham, Milton S.J.			320	Dec. 7,1839	
407	Belding, Diena			640	Dec. 5,1839	
415	Brown, William			640	Dec. 7,1839	
428	Bradshaw, James N.			320	Dec. 7,1839	
429	Bradshaw, John A.			320	Dec. 7,1839	
440	Brown, Green B.			640	Dec.17,1839	

No.	Name	Lgs.	Lbr.	Acres	Date	Remarks
470	Baxter, Joseph W.			640	Dec.19,1839	
472	Ball, Thomas H.			320	Dec.19,1839	
478	Brookshire, Joseph C.			320	Dec.19,1839	
479	Brookshire, Manning			640	Dec.19,1839	
483	Buttons, Eldridge			320	Dec.19,1839	
484	Berrego, Jose Maria			320	Dec.19,1839	
490	Buford, Christopher Y.			320	Dec.19,1839	
492	Buford, Satia			640	Dec.19,1839	
494	Burren, Benjamin J.			320	Dec.20,1839	
503	Bowers, John A.			640	Dec.20,1839	
504	Bills, Robert			320	Dec.20,1839	
516	Buford, William K.			320	Dec.20,1839	
598	Brookman, Thomas P.			320	Dec.20,1839	
518	Brown, Franklin			640	Dec.20,1839	
519	Burriss, John C.			320	Dec.20,1839	
523	Bass, Isaac T.			320	Dec.20,1839	
527	Bains, Samuel			320	Dec.20,1839	
539	Botton, William			640	Dec.27,1839	
551	Ballard, Franklin M.			640	Dec.27,1839	
560	Ball, Robert, Jr.			640	Dec.28,1839	
574	Brown, Taylor			640	Dec.28,1839	
575	Brown, David			640	Dec.28,1839	
570	Bassey, Jonas			640	Dec.28,1839	
588	Blake, Anderson			320	Dec.28,1839	
603	Bell, D.J.			320	Dec.31,1839	
618	Brown, Robert P.			320	Jan. 2,1840	
620	Brown, Sidney P.			320	Jan. 2,1840	
621	Brown, Beutord W.			320	Jan. 2,1840	
638	Brown, William			320	Jan. 3,1840	
643	Boyd, Thomas A.B.			640	Jan. 4,1840	
3	Cummings, Robert			640	Apr. 4,1839	
17	Chisum, John R.			320	Apr. 5,1839	
20	Crutcher, W.H.			320	Apr. 5,1839	
60	Catson, John			320	June 6,1839	
61	Card, James			640	June 6,1839	
73	Curl, William			320	Jy. 4, 1839	
77	Comb, John			320	Jy. 4, 1839	
80	Cole, Reuben A.			320	Jy. 4, 1839	
85	Carnes, William R.			640	Jy. 4, 1839	
90	Childers, Elizabeth			640	Aug.1, 1839	
143	Chasen, Richard			640	Sept.5,1839	
147	Campbell, James K.			320	Sept.5,1839	
148	Clifford, Adam			320	Sept.5,1839	
155	Carroll, Joseph A.			640	Sept.5,1839	
172	Chisum, Claiborne			320	Sept.5,1839	
174	Chisum, Madison			320	Sept.5,1839	
175	Cardell, A.			320	Sept.5,1839	
184	Carter, J.H.			320	Sept.5,1839	
196	Conner, Henry C.			320	Sept.6,1839	
202	Click, Matischi			320	Sept.6,1839	
206	Calwell, Lemuel			320	Oct.3, 1839	
207	Caldwell, Andrew J.			320	Oct.3, 1839	

No.	Name	Lgs.	Lbr.	Acres	Date	Remarks
210	Crane, A.H.			320	Oct.3,1839	
216	Crawford, Colby W.			320	Oct. 3,1839	
230	Conner, John			640	Oct. 8,1839	
242	Crane, Giles B.			640	Nov. 7,1839	
243	Crane, Boden T.			640	Nov. 7,1839	
271	Cook, William S.			320	Nov. 7,1839	
275	Cook, Lemuel A.			640	Nov. 7,1839	
278	Cheatham, Samuel			320	Nov. 7,1839	
232	Caddell, Jeremiah D.			320	Dec. 5,1839	
361	Chapman, Henry			640	Dec. 5,1839	
381	Cato, Alfred			320	Dec. 5,1839	
391	Cocke, William			640	Dec. 7,1839	
421	Cox, Jenkin			320	Dec. 7,1839	
431	Charlton, N.B.			320	Dec.17,1839	
435	Charleten, James			320	Dec.17,1839	
441	Crumn, Edwin			640	Dec.17,1839	
442	Crump, John			640	Dec.17,1839	
451	Crabb, Thomas G.			320	Dec.19,1839	
455	Camfield, John H.			320	Dec.19,1839	
511	Cox, Benjamin F.			320	Dec.20,1839	
522	Cross, Richard F.			320	Dec.20,1839	
540	Capps, William B.			640	Dec.24,1839	
541	Capps, Demory			640	Dec.24,1839	
544	Charlton, Daneson B.			320	Dec.24,1839	
549	Conner, Uriah			320	Dec.24,1839	
550	Conner, Thomas J.			320	Dec.24,1839	
558	Coeb, William			320	Dec.27,1839	
586	Crane, John F.			320	Dec.28,1839	
610	Clary, John S.			320	Dec.31,1838	
611	Clary, Blaford L.			320	Dec.31,1839	
613	Copender, R.J.			320	Dec.31,1839	
630	Chynoweth, Henry			320	Jan. 3,1840	
628	Connell, William O.			320	Jan. 3,1840	
631	Crow, Enoch			640	Jan. 3,1840	
637	Case, Galusha			320	Jan. 3,1840	
641	Cochran, Robert O.			320	Jan. 4,1840	
13	Davis, William			320	Apr. 5,1839	
15	Dewaal, Sogier			320	Apr. 5,1839	
16	Detiste, J.H.			320	Apr. 5,1839	
18	Davidson, Robert B.			320	Apr. 5,1839	
37	Darst, William			320	May 11,1839	
42	Dufore, Lewis			320	May 11,1839	
57	Dowdie, Abram			320	June 6,1839	
87	Douthet, Benjamin W.			640	Aug. 1,1839	
88	Douthet, Evin			640	Aug. 1,1839	
104	Day, Isaiah			320	Aug. 2,1839	
121	Draper, Henderson			320	Aug. 3,1839	
181	Dunkin, Augustus			320	Sept.5,1839	
201	Dorsett, Theodore			320	Sept.6,1839	
229	Dickerson, Lewis			320	Oct. 8,1839	
231	Dickerson, Joseph			320	Oct. 8,1839	
233	Downs, C. L.			320	Nov. 7,1839	

No.	Name	Lgs.	Lbr.	Acres	Date	Remarks
241	Davis, Bradford			640	Nov. 7,1839	
248	Dougherty, George			640	Nov. 7,1839	
264	Dunkley, Green B.			640	Nov. 7,1839	
280	Dewalt, Martin			320	Nov. 7,1839	
317	Douglas, Joseph			320	Dec. 5,1839	
373	Dyer, Gibson G.			320	Dec. 5,1839	
404	Durrett John			320	Dec. 7,1839	
426	Dollawhitt, Yancy G.			320	Dec.19,1839	
485	Dolores, Canslo			320	Dec. 7,1839	
495	Dunn, Edward F.			320	Dec. 20,1839	
502	Delany, William			320	Dec.20,1839	
515	Davis, James			320	Dec.20,1839	
543	Ducksworth, Samuel			320	Dec.24,1839	
58	Edwards, James			640	June 6,1839	
71	Eliott, John N.			640	June 14,1839	
93	Ellison, Zachariah			640	Aug. 1,1839	
101	Eaten, J.C.			320	Aug. 1,1839	
108	Ederington, James F.			320	Aug. 3,1839	
168	English, Charles F.			320	Sept.5,1839	
221	Evans, John			320	Oct. 3,1839	
254	Ellis, Asa M.			640	Nov. 7,1839	
287	Eubank, Robert			320	Nov. 21,1839	
307	Evans, Edward			320	Dec. 5,1839	
328	Evans, Elisha A.			320	Dec.5,1839	
354	Edmunds, Abel B.			320	Dec. 5,1839	
378	Edens, Balis			320	Dec. 5,1839	
388	Everett, James H.			320	Dec. 7,1839	
450	Eastoff, James W.			320	Dec.19,1839	
457	Eubank, Ambros B.			320	Dec.19,1839	
531	Erwin, James			640	Dec.24,1839	
532	Erwin, Alexander K.			640	Dec.24,1839	
533	Erwin, John A.			640	Dec.24,1839	
534	Erwin, James L.			640	Dec.24,1839	
535	Erwin, George W.			320	Dec.24,1839	
423	Everett, Silvanus			640	Dec.7,1839	
55	Franklin, Resin			640	June 7,1839	
245	Fowler, J.A.			640	Nov. 7,1839	
277	Fox, John H.			320	Nov. 7,1839	
368	Flynn, Solomon K.			320	Dec. 5,1839	
389	Franklin, James S.			320	Dec. 7,1839	
398	Fenton, Joseph			640	Dec. 7,1839	
453	Fowler, Reuben O.			320	Dec.19,1839	
634	Fulgham, Arthur			640	Jan. 3,1840	
635	Fulgham, Pierce			640	Jan. 3,1840	
636	Fulgham, Richard			320	Jan. 3,1840	
294	Finley, William N.			320	Nov.21,1839	
349	Fitzhugh, Rowland S.			320	Dec.5,1839	
593	Friend, Jacob			640	Dec.28,1839	
22	Graham, John F.			640	Apr. 5,1839	
39	Gray, Sylvester			320	May 11,1839	
118	Gwinn, Malcom			640	Aug. 3,1839	

No.	Name	Lgs.	Lbr.	Acres	Date	Remarks
122	Goodwin, James R.			320	Aug. 3,1839	
124	Graham, William C.			320	Aug. 3,1839	
125	Graham, Archibald			320	Aug. 3,1839	
128	Gibson, Abner W.			640	Sept.5,1839	
139	Gann, Solomon			640	Sept.5,1839	
165	Gilbert, Gustavus			640	Sept.5,1839	
195	Gorman, Terril			320	Sept.6,1839	
256	Gill, William			640	Nov. 7,1839	
285	Garrett, William E.			320	Nov.21,1839	
309	Gray, Hubbard S.			320	Dec. 5,1839	
318	Gillespie, Josiah			320	Dec. 5,1839	
338	Graham, Daniel			320	Dec. 5,1839	
348	Gilliland, John			320	Dec. 5,1839	
351	Gibson, George N.			320	Dec. 5,1839	
367	Gullitt, James			320	Dec. 5,1839	
393	Garrett, John			320	Dec. 7,1839	
401	Gilbert, Abraham			640	Dec. 7,1839	
412	Goodwin, Joseph			320	Dec. 7,1839	
466	Griffin, James			320	Dec.19,1839	
475	Greenwood, A.			320	Dec.19,1839	
477	Gray, Samuel E.			320	Dec.19,1839	
497	Givins, Edward A.			320	Dec.20,1839	
561	Griffin, William			320	Dec.28,1839	
582	Gilliland, John			320	Dec.28,1839	
596	Garner, Henry			320	Dec.28,1839	
601	Green, Cassey			640	Dec.31,1839	
602	Green, Berry			320	Dec.31,1839	
607	Gage, David			320	Dec.31,1839	
615	Grigsby, J.P.			320	Dec.31,1839	
615	Gonzales, Robert			320	Dec.31,1839	
622	Gibson, William			320	Jan. 2,1840	
623	Garrett, Thomas N.			320	Jan. 2,1840	
28	Huberson, William F.			320	Apr.11,1839	
33	Harrill, B.C.P.			320	Apr.11,1839	
54	Hamilton, Isaiah			320	June 6,1839	
75	Hotchkiss, Charles			640	Jy. 4, 1839	
76	Hubert, Robert L.			640	Jy. 4, 1839	
79	Hart, James			320	Jy. 4, 1839	
97	Hendon, Solomon			640	Aug. 2,1839	
103	Hutton, James			640	Aug. 2,1839	
106	Hamby, James			640	Aug. 2,1839	
131	Harper, John A.			320	Sept.5,1839	
132	Holdeman, John			640	Sept.5,1839	
149	Hoyd, John Vander			320	Sept.5,1839	
164	Hendon, David A.			320	Sept.5,1839	
171	Hill, J.C.			320	Sept.5,1839	
199	Hamilton, John D.			320	Sept.6,1839	
269	Henry, John W.			320	Nov. 7,1839	
288	Humberson, William F.			320	Nov.21,1839	
293	Hunt, Noah E.			640	Nov.21,1839	
305	Hudson, Stannton			320	Dec.5,1839	
311	Hudson, Edward			640	Dec. 5,1839	

No.	Name	Lgs.	Lbr.	Acres	Date	Remarks
322	Hunter, John			320	Dec. 5,1839	
327	Horton, Calvin J.			320	Dec. 5,1839	
345	Hubbard, John			320	Dec. 5,1839	
350	Hardgrave, Preston			320	Dec. 5,1839	
352	Howell, Willis D.			320	Dec. 5,1839	
355	Hare, Thomas O.			320	Dec. 5,1839	
366	Halmark, James M.			640	Dec. 5,1839	
374	Hutchings, Joel			320	Dec. 5,1839	
379	Haltene, Alfred H.			320	Dec. 5,1839	
380	Hearn, Erasmus			320	Dec. 5,1839	
382	Haltone, William			640	Dec. 5,1839	
397	Harris, Silas			320	Dec. 7,1839	
408	Hamby, Samuel			320	Dec. 7,1839	
409	Hamby, John			640	Dec. 7,1839	
413	Harris, David P.			640	Dec. 7,1839	
446	Haverty, James			320	Dec.19,1839	
447	Haynes, James P.			640	Dec.19,1839	
462	Huson, Winfield			320	Dec.19,1839	
487	Hughs, Daniel H.			640	Dec.19,1839	
517	Hall, Richard			640	Dec.20,1839	
528	Heifner, John			320	Dec.23,1839	
536	Howell, William			320	Dec.24,1839	
542	Hinton, James			320	Dec.24,1839	
566	Hanks, Legrand G.			320	Dec.28,1839	
567	Holland, John H.			320	Dec.28,1839	
585	Hogan, John W.			640	Dec.28,1839	
592	Harrison, James M.			320	Dec.28,1839	
595	Howard, James D.			640	Dec.28,1839	
600	Howard, Robert			640	Dec.30,1839	
605	Harvey, Ferdinand C.			320	Dec.31,1839	
612	Henderson, Thomas			320	Dec.31,1839	
619	Hardiman, Blackstone			320	Jan. 2,1840	
324	Ignight, Mariah			640	Dec.5, 1839	
31	Jarrell, Claiborne			640	Apr.11,1839	
102	Johnson, W.C.			320	Aug. 2,1839	
150	Jowers, W.G.W.			320	Sept.5,1839	
190	Jones, William			640	Sept.6,1839	
215	Johnston, R.L.			320	Oct. 3,1839	
236	James, William			320	Nov. 7,1839	
237	James, Benjamin A.			320	Nov. 7,1839	
320	Johnson, Claiborne			640	Dec. 5,1839	
323	Jones, Elizabeth			640	Dec. 5,1839	
376	Jones, Thomas			640	Dec. 5,1839	
403	Jordon, Eady			640	Dec. 7,1839	
419	Jackson, William			320	Dec. 7,1839	
474	Jackson, Hezekiah			640	Dec.19,1839	
476	Johnson, Samuel F.			320	Dec.19,1839	
537	Jones, Jefferson Y.			320	Dec.24,1839	
632	Johnson, James H.			320	Jan. 3,1840	
646	Jones, Leonard			320	Jan. 3,1840	Heirs of

No.	Name	Lgs.	Lbr.	Acres	Date	Remarks
32	Kuykendall, Simon			320	Apr.11,1839	
47	Knox, George W.			640	June 6,1839	
96	Keiner, Hugh			320	Aug. 2,1839	
112	Killough, Isaac, Sr.			640	Aug. 3,1839	Nath'l. Killough, Admr.
113	Killough, Isaac, Jr.			640		Nath'l. Killough, Admr.
114	Killough, Allen			640	Aug. 3,1839	Nath'l. Killough, Admr.
115	Killough, Nathaniel			640	Aug. 3,1839	
140	Kincannon, Jesse			640	Sept.5,1839	
208	Killough, George P.			320	Oct. 3,1839	Allen Killough, Admr.
259	King, John W.			320	Nov. 7,1839	
292	Kerr, James C.			320	Nov.21,1839	
489	King, Isaac W.			320	Dec.19,1839	
417	Kay, James P.			320	Dec. 7,1839	
10	Lennix, Moses			640	Apr. 5,1839	
23	Lusan, John			320	Apr. 5,1839	
35	Lennix, John			320	May 2, 1839	
41	Lennix, Robert			320	May 11,1839	
110	Long, William W.			640	Aug. 3,1839	
133	Leathers, Joel			640	Sept.5,1839	
145	Leonard, Thomas			320	Sept.5,1839	
156	Luckitt, Noland M.			640	Sept.5,1839	
159	Larkins, Thomas			320	Sept.5,1839	
170	Langham, Theophelus			320	Sept.5,1839	
176	Luckett, Thomas D.			320	Sept.5,1839	
178	Lemon, Isaac			320	Sept.5,1839	
183	Lemon, Felix G.			320	Sept.5,1839	
188	Long, R.M.			320	Sept.6,1839	
194	Leach, Joshua			320	Sept.6,1839	
232	Leach, Joshua			320	Nov. 7,1839	Augmentation.
251	Lane, John C.			320	Nov. 7,1839	
296	Lewis, Joseph F.			320	Nov.21,1839	
362	Long, Matthew L.			320	Dec.5, 1839	
418	Levi, Solomon			320	Dec. 7,1839	
420	Lambert, John			320	Dec. 7,1839	
421	Linn, H.J.			320	Dec. 7,1839	
456	Longstreet, William D.			320	Dec.19,1839	
496	Lacy, George B.			320	Dec.20,1839	
514	Lee, John			320	Dec.20,1839	
557	Lindsey, THomas M.			320	Dec.27,1839	
569	Lane, Robert L.			640	Dec.28,1839	
570	Lane, James F.			320	Dec.28,1839	
572	Lane, Embargo C.			320	Dec.28,1839	
589	Lathrop, Hazael			320	Dec.28,1839	
609	Leach, Admiral W.			320	Dec.31,1839	
644	Loffton, Antonio			320	Jan. 4,1840	
645	Loffton, Eugine			320	Jan. 4,1840	
5	McClure, Houston			640	Apr. 5,1839	

No.	Name	60	Lbr.	Acres	Date	Remarks
8	Moore, William M.			640	Apr. 5,1839	
21	Muckleroy, David			640	Apr. 5,1839	
45	McKnight, James			640	June 6,1839	
48	McKnight, Francis C.			320	June 6,1839	
49	McKnight, William D.			320	June 6,1839	
50	McKnight, James			320	June 6,1839	
64	Medford, Isam			640	June 6,1839	
65	Medford, John Anderson			320	June 6,1839	
66	Medford, Levi			320	June 6,1839	
72	Merideth, Daniel			320	June 14,1839	
92	Miller, William			320	Aug. 1,1839	
98	Merideth, Winney			640	Aug. 2,1839	
99	Milligen, George			320	Aug. 2,1839	
100	Milligen, John			320	Aug. 2,1839	
109	Moon, James			320	Aug. 3,1839	
126	Muleon, Philip			320	Aug. 3,1839	
129	Mayberry, William T.			320	Sept. 5,1839	
135	Mathews, William H.			320	Sept. 5,1839	
136	Mathews, Lyman H.			320	Sept.5,1839	
137	Massingale, George			640	Sept.5,1839	
138	Massingale, Isaac			320	Sept.5,1839	
151	McMahan, A.W.			320	Sept.5,1839	
166	McNutt, Samuel A.			320	Sept.5,1839	
185	McKanghan, Hugh			320	Sept.5,1839	
192	McEntire, HEnry M.			320	Sept.6,1839	
193	McEntire, Archibald H.			320	Sept.6,1839	
203	Massingale, Henry			640	Sept.5,1839	
204	Moore, Milton			640	Sept.5,1839	
205	Moore, Milton J.			320	Sept.5,1839	
223	Mitchell, William			320	Oct. 3,1839	
224	Martin, John E.			320	Oct. 3,1839	
225	Mills, Lorenzo M.			320	Oct. 3,1839	
286	McCormick, Robert S.			320	Nov.21,1839	
295	McCobb, J.W.			320	Nov.21,1839	
317	Morrison, John E.			640	Dec. 5,1839	
319	Moody, John M.			640	Dec. 5,1839	
325	McCline, James H.			320	Dec. 5,1839	
344	Miller, Jacob			320	Dec. 5,1839	
369	Mattison, Thomas			640	Dec. 5,1839	
370	Mattison, Lester B.			640	Dec. 5,1839	
371	Mattison, William P.			320	Dec. 5,1839	
372	Maxfield, William			320	Dec. 5,1839	
406	Murray, Henry F.			320	Dec. 7,1839	
427	Morgan, Elizabeth			640	Dec. 7,1839	
430	Merritt, Robert			320	Dec. 7,1839	
437	McClellen, D.			320	Dec.17,1839	
438	Middleton, Joseph S.			640	Dec.17,1839	
444	McDonald John			320	Dec.19,1839	
481	Merideth, Green			320	Dec.19,1839	
491	Manry, Alfred			320	Dec.19,1839	
498	Myers, John			320	Dec.20,1839	
507	Mungum, Durrell			640	Dec.20,1839	
524	Merrill, Joseph			320	Dec.23,1839	
545	Murphy, Malachi B.			320	Dec.24,1839	

No.	Name	Lgs.	Lbr.	Acres	Date	Remarks
553	Morris, David			320	Dec.27,1839	
559	McDaniel, Moses			320	Dec.27,1839	
568	Milton, Anna			640	Dec.28,1839	
581	Millins, Henry			320	Dec.28,1839	
587	McCutchin, Robert G.			320	Dec.28,1839	
598	Moore, William J.			320	Dec.28,1839	
624	Myers, Abraham			320	Jan. 2,1840	
625	Miller, John C.			640	Jan. 2,1840	
626	McKnight, James			320	Jan. 3,1840	
627	Musick, David			320	Jan. 3,1840	
640	Maze, John			320	Jan. 4,1840	
169	Moore, Thomas J.			320	Sept.5,1839	
2	Noble, Edward B.			640	Apr. 4,1839	
9	Nance, Benjamin			320	Apr. 5,1839	
62	Nail, Joseph			640	June 6,1839	
197	Nelson, Albert A.			320	June 6,1839	
360	Noland, Avery			320	Dec. 5,1839	
385	Nail, Mason			320	Dec. 5,1839	
562	Newton, Matthew A.			320	Dec.28,1839	
573	Nowling, Richard			320	Dec.28,1839	
599	Nelson, Wm. H.			640	Dec.30,1839	
629	Newman, Nathaniel			320	Jan. 2,1840	
244	Noble, A.W.			640	Nov. 7,1839	
279	Orange, Eli			320	Nov. 7,1839	
312	Offeld, James			640	Dec. 5,1839	
341	Outlaw, N.S.			320	Dec. 5,1839	
480	Ogleton, Osborn G.			320	Dec.19,1839	
482	Oswalt, William R.			320	Dec.19,1839	
521	Oxshire, William			320	Dec.20,1839	
56	Powers, James			320	June 6,1839	
81	Price, Elisha M.			320	Jy. 4,1839	
82	Price, Charles L.			320	Jy. 4,1839	
89	Poe, Jedethan			640	Aug. 1,1839	
91	Poe, George			320	Aug. 1,1839	
120	Poe, John			640	Aug. 3,1839	
130	Payne, Wm. G.			320	Sept.5,1839	
157	Patello, John S.			320	Sept.5,1839	
220	Pollard, Richard			320	Oct. 3,1839	
258	Price, Wilson			640	Nov. 7,1839	
268	Pate, David			320	Nov. 7,1839	
282	Penyman, James P.			640	Nov. 7,1839	
306	Powers, Rachel			640	Dec. 5,1839	
308	Pennington, Ellen			640	Dec. 5,1839	
353	Price, Aaron			320	Dec. 5,1839	
359	Pearson, Pleasant H.			320	Dec. 5,1839	
391	Print, James M.			320	Dec. 7,1839	
405	Payne, George			320	Dec. 7,1839	
410	Parmer, H.D.			320	Dec. 7,1839	
449	Pack, Jeremiah			640	Dec.19,1839	
451	Phillpott, Joseph P.			320	Dec.19,1839	

No.	Name	Lgs.	Lbr.	Acres	Date	Remarks
463	Price, Peter C.			320	Dec.19,1839	
493	Palmer, Pleasant			320	Dec.19,1839	
546	Pannell, John			320	Dec.24,1839	
563	Page, John M.			320	Dec.28,1839	
566	Patilla, Jose Antonio			320	Dec.28,1839	
584	Parchman, John			320	Dec.28,1839	
119	Roark, John, Jr.			320	Aug. 3,1839	
123	Rollins, Asa			320	Aug. 3,1839	
144	Ridens, John W.			320	Sept.5,1839	
153	Roarne, John			320	Sept.5,1839	
187	Roddan, P.F.			320	Sept.5,1839	
198	Ragust, Condy			320	Sept.6,1839	
200	Roundtree, James L.			640	Sept.6,1839	
218	Reelly, James M.			320	Oct. 3,1839	
222	Rutledge, John			320	Oct. 3,1839	
234	Ramsey, Stephenson			320	Nov. 7,1839	
240	Rogers, Washington			320	Nov. 7,1839	
267	Rector, George			320	Nov. 7,1839	
289	Rupshire, John			640	Nov.21,1839	
443	Richards, Stephen			320	Dec.19,1839	
461	Roberts, John F.			320	Dec.19,1839	
473	Reagan, John H.			320	Dec.19,1839	
488	Redden, Carrol W.			320	Dec.19,1839	
500	Rentro, John			320	Dec.20,1839	
501	Rogers, Henry			320	Dec.20,1839	
505	Roberts, Henry H.			320	Dec.20,1839	
546	Reynolds, Washington			320	Dec.24,1839	
565	Richardson, James W.			320	Dec.28,1839	
576	Rowan, John			640	Dec.28,1839	
577	Rowan, Milton			320	Dec.28,1839	
578	Restal, William B.			320	Dec.28,1839	
591	Rainny, Isaac			640	Dec.28,1839	
606	Roebuck, Rolly			320	Dec.31,1839	
614	Reins, Robert H.			320	Dec.31,1839	
1	Skelton, David			640	Apr. 4,1839	
7	Steward, John			640	Apr. 5,1839	
11	Sipps, Leander E.			320	Dec. 5,1839	
19	Sipps, Peter			640	Apr. 5,1839	
14	Sims, Edwin T.			320	Apr. 5,1839	
36	Sims, Thomas			640	May 2, 1839	
40	Seliman, James			320	May 11,1839	
67	Sims, James			640	June 6,1839	
70	Smith, Mary			640	June 6,1839	
74	Stokely, Isaac J.			320	Jy. 4,1839	
83	Stone, Robert			640	Jy. 4,1839	
95	Sims, Mary			640	Aug. 1,1839	
134	Snow, John C.			320	Sept.5,1839	
141	Stone, Berry			320	Sept.5,1839	
146	Smith, William			320	Sept.5,1839	
162	Smith, Wiley			640	Sept.5,1839	
167	Slay, William W.			320	Sept.5,1839	

No.	Name	Lgs.	Lbr.	Acres	Date	Remarks
173	Stephen, H.B.			640	Sept.5,1839	
189	Seamore, CHarles			320	Sept.6,1839	
241	Smit, John			320	Oct. 3,1839	
219	Shannon, William F.			640	Oct. 3,1839	
246	Shepherd, Jonas			320	Nov. 7,1839	
260	Spear, Gharles			320	Nov. 7,1839	
261	Smith, William			320	Nov. 7,1839	
266	Stockman, Harvey F.			320	Nov. 7,1839	
270	Sullivan, John M.			320	Nov. 7,1839	
274	Sasser, William			320	Nov. 7,1839	
276	Steed, Moses			320	Nov. 7,1839	
291	Sabin, William			320	Nov.21,1839	
321	Spain, W.K.D.			640	Dec. 5,1839	
326	Stacey, Miles			320	Dec. 5,1839	
377	Stone, George W.			640	Dec. 5,1839	
383	Sory, James L.			640	Dec. 5,1839	
381	Sory, John			640	Dec. 5,1839	
390	Smith, Bennit			320	Dec. 7,1839	
392	Standefer, Luke C.			320	Dec. 7,1839	
395	Stevenson, Samuel R.			320	Dec. 7,1839	
400	Simpson, Wm. P.			640	Dec. 7,1839	
402	Stewart, Thomas			640	Dec. 7,1839	
414	Stewart, John V.			320	Dec. 7,1839	
416	Strong, Alexander H.			320	Dec. 7,1839	
431	Swift, Willis			320	Dec.16,1839	
432	Swift, William			320	Dec.16,1839	
439	Sandlen, Kimsey A.			320	Dec.17,1839	
448	Stephens, Augustus			640	Dec.19,1839	
452	Stanbanck, Benj. D.			320	Dec.19,1839	
458	Sparks, William N.			640	Dec.19,1839	
460	Sorrels, Mathew			320	Dec.19,1839	
465	Sibley, William			320	Dec.19,1839	
467	Stewart, Charles			640	Dec.19,1839	
468	Stewart, Daniel			640	Dec.19,1839	
516	Shorter, Bedford			320	Dec.20,1839	
520	Sampson, J.W.			320	Dec.20,1839	
525	Sharp, James H.			320	Dec.23,1839	
526	Sharp, Joseph D.			640	Dec.23,1839	
530	Saunders, Samuel			320	Dec.23,1839	
538	Surrels, Wm. D.			320	Dec.24,1839	
555	Silliman, Wm. P.			320	Dec.27,1839	
556	Silliman, John			320	Dec.27,1839	
580	Smith, James M.			320	Dec.28,1839	
583	Sugg, John			320	Dec.28,1839	
604	Shepherd, Charles W.			320	Dec.31,1839	
608	Stedman, John			320	Dec.31,1839	
177	Sturdevant, Benjamin			320	Sept.5,1839	
469	Sammons, Wm. G.			640	Dec.19,1839	
25	Thomason, Leonard			640	Apr.11,1839	
27	Thomas, William			640	Apr.11,1839	
30	Tomlinson, Benajah			320	Apr.11,1839	
59	Thompson, Wm.			640	June 6,1839	

No.	Name	Lgs.	Lbr.	Acres	Date	Remarks
94	Taylor, Thomas B.			640	Aug. 1,1839	
235	Thompson, John J.			320	Nov. 7,1839	
255	Thomas, William B.			640	Nov. 7,1839	
272	Thomas, William C.			320	Nov. 7,1839	
273	Thomas, John W.			320	Nov. 7,1839	
284	Tate, John			320	Nov.21,1839	
298	Tubbs, Phillip H.			640	Nov.28,1839	
299	Tubbs, Elisha			320	Nov.28,1839	
343	Townsend, Peter G.			320	Dec. 5,1839	
399	Taylor, Manson			320	Dec. 7,1839	
512	Tomlinson, John			640	Dec.20,1839	
617	Triplett, James C.			320	Dec.31,1839	
186	Upton, James M.			640	Sept.5,1839	
504	Umpstead, Wm. M.			640	Dec.28,1839	
425	Vansickle, R.			320	Dec. 7,1839	
554	Vickry, John			320	Dec.27,1839	
12	Worley, Zach. F.			320	Apr. 5,1839	
43	Wingfield, Wm. M.			640	May 11,1839	
44	Wise, William			320	May 11,1839	
51	Wright, Jones			640	June 6,1839	
52	Wiles, Pinson			640	June 6,1839	
53	Whitlock, Roland			320	June 6,1839	
78	Wright, William P.			640	Jy. 4,1839	
107	Wright, W.C.			320	Aug. 2,1839	
116	Williams, Owen C.			640	Aug. 3,1839	
117	Winsor, Maston			320	Aug. 3,1839	
127	Wickham, Johnson A.			320	Sept.5,1839	
152	Walling, Preston M.			320	Sept.5,1839	
179	Wooton, William			640	Sept.5,1839	
180	Wood, David			640	Sept.5,1839	
191	Welch, John			320	Sept.6,1839	
209	Webb, Lyda			640	Oct. 3,1839	
213	Wickware, Alphus			320	Oct. 3,1839	
217	Wadlington, Jesse			640	Oct. 3,1839	
226	Williams, Albut			320	Oct. 3,1839	
227	Williams, John			640	Oct. 3,1839	
228	Williams, John L.			320	Oct. 3,1839	
239	Ward, Benjamin F.			320	Nov. 7,1839	
250	Wilson, Abel			640	Nov. 7,1839	
257	Wadlington, John			320	Nov. 7,1839	
297	Williams, Nehemiah			640	Nov.21,1839	
300	Williams, John D.			320	Nov.28,1839	
313	Wrigley, John			320	Dec. 5,1839	
336	Woodley, William			320	Dec. 5,1839	
339	West, Amasa			320	Dec. 5,1839	
342	Wilson, Robert C.			640	Dec. 5,1839	
346	Wilhoit, James			320	Dec. 5,1839	
356	Winn, Robert E.			640	Dec. 5,1839	
357	White, Barrel			320	Dec. 5,1839	
365	Wilkinson, John			320	Dec. 5,1839	

No.	Name	Lgs.	Lbr.	Acres	Date	Remarks
386	Watkins, Archibald H.			640	Dec. 7,1839	
411	Wright, Carrol			320	Dec. 7,1839	
422	Wade, Wm. W.			320	Dec. 7,1839	
433	Warden, Samuel			320	Dec.16,1839	
436	Williams, William B.			320	Dec.17,1839	
164	Williams, George L.			320	Dec.19,1839	
171	Whitaker, John H.			320	Dec.19,1839	
509	Warren, John C.			320	Dec.20,1839	
510	Wigginbotham, Linsey			320	Dec.20,1839	
513	Wilson, James			320	Dec.20,1839	
529	Wadsworth, John			320	Dec.23,1839	T.S. McIver, Admr.
547	Wiatt, Dempsey			320	Dec.24,1839	
548	Wiatt, Peter			320	Dec.24,1839	
552	Williams, James			320	Dec.27,1839	
571	Wells, John M.			640	Dec.28,1839	
590	Wright, William			320	Dec.28,1839	
633	Williams, Josephus			320	Jan. 3,1840	
639	Willison, Paulina			640	Jan. 3,1840	
642	Williams, Barchias C.			320	Jan. 4,1840	
310	Walker, Alexander M.			640	Dec. 5,1839	
26	Yates, Arden			640	Apr.11,1839	
29	Yates, Stephen			640	Apr.11,1839	
598	York, William			320	Dec.28,1839	
459	Young, James			320	Dec.19,1839	

RED RIVER COUNTY

FIRST CLASS

No.	Name	Lgs.	Lbr.	Acres	Date	Remarks
42	Akin, Collin M.	1	1			
59	Akin, James	1/3				
143	Arrington, Noel	1	1			
185	Askins, Thomas	1	1			
186	Askins, Wesley	1	1			
186	Aud, Ignatius L.	1	1			
248	Aiguire, Ulysses	1	1			
262	Akin, William	1	1			
362	Atkinson, Joseph	1	1			
410	Anderson, James B.;dec'd	1	1			Heirs of.
526	Askey, Abner, dec'd.	1	1			Heirs of.
527	Askey, Fielding	1/3				Heirs of.
636	Arons, John	1	1			
85	Abraham, James	1/3				Conditionally recommended.
584	Alsop, Samuel S.	1/3				Conditionally recommended.
691	Atkinson, James	1/3				
729	Askey, John	1/3				

No.	Name	Lgs.	Lbr.	Acres	Date	Remarks
5	Ballard, Barckley M.	1	1			
16	Barr, Benjamin F.	1	1			
19	Bull, John	1	1			
20	Box, James F.	1	1			
37	Bagby, Geo. H.	1	1			
38	Barnett, Eli	1/3				
45	Byers, John C.					Quantity not specified.
56	Brinlee, Hiram	1	1			
62	Bivin, HEnry	1/3				
102	Bland, Abel	1	1			
103	Bland, Benjamin	1	1			
105	Beard, Andrew S.	1	1			
107	Berkham, Charles	1	1			
115	Buckler, Henry	1/3				
132	Bason, George	1	1			
138	Boon, John R.	1/3				
140	Bird, John	1/3				
141	Bayley, Amos C.C.	1	1			
155	Bruton, Jonas	1/3				
156	Bruton, David D.	1/3				
158	Bland, Preston	1	1			
159	Becknail, John C.	1/3				
160	Bruton, Benjamin	1	1			
162	Becknell, Wm. A.	1/3				
167	Becknell, Wm. Sr.	1	1			
166	Bruton, Elisha	1	1			
197	Bowrin, Minerva	1	1			
2-0	Butts, Augustus J.	1/3				
232	Brooks, Thos. W.	1	1			
286	Brenton, William	1/3				
288	Berkham, James	1	1			
298	Bell, Alexander	1/3				John Emberson, assignee.
313	Benningfield, Hudson P.	1	1			
321	Brewster, Benjamin F.,Jr.	1/3				
331	Brummett, Harrison	1/3				
349	Barkman, John	1	1			
358	Burris, Sam'l. J.	1/3				
367	Brumley, Thomas	1/3				
377	Brown, Wm. R.	1/3				
381	Bates, John C.	1/3				
384	Barkman, Jacob	1/3				
419	Balloe, Robert	1/3				
420	Boten, Isreal	1/3				
421	Borien, William	1	1			
445	Brewster, Benjamin F.	1	1			
449	Babb, David E.W.;dec'd.	1	1			
457	Browning, Wm. L.	1	1			
498	Blundell, Francis	1/3				
499	Blundell, William	1	1			
507	Burkham, Ahijah	1/3				

No.	Name	Lgs.	Lbr.	Acres	Date	Remarks
519	Burkman, John; dec'd.	1/3				Heirs of.
533	Burnham, Samuel; dec'd.	1	1			Heirs of.
537	Boyce, Jesse T.; dec'd.	1/3				Heirs of.
543	Bowman, Joseph	1/3				
553	Blundell, William	1/3				
555	Blundell, Soloman	1/3				
558	Boyce, James R.	1	1			
568	Boon, Needham	1	1			
574	Buckler, Henry	2/3	1			
585	Boyce, Wm. H.	1	1			
617	Ball, John	1/3				
628	Bowerman, Joshua	1/3				
676	Brown, Harriett	1	1			
714	Burke, Samuel	1/3				
722	Becknell, John	2/3	1			
734	Bottoms, Zachariah	1/3				
738	Bazemore, Freeman	1/3				
742	Bartee, William		1			
744	Boon, James W.	1/3				
745	Brewton, David	1/3				
302	Blanton, John	1	1			
80	Brinley, George	1	1			Conditionally recommended.
219	Benge, Martin	1/3				Conditionally recommended.
279	Byers, Wesley	1	1			Conditionally recommended.
468	Byrnside, William	1/3				Conditionally recommended.
538	Bownan, B. heirs of	1	1			Conditionally recommended.
557	Buzzard, Jacob	1	1			Conditionally recommended.
576	Bryant, John A.	1/3				Conditionally recommended.
577	Birmingham, Patrick W.	1	1			Conditionally recommended.
672	Berry, James	1	1			Conditionally recommended.
698	Bowland, Lewis; dec'd.	1	1			Conditionally recommended.
631	Barkley, John H.;dec'd.	1/3				Conditionally recommended.
645	Barker, James	1	1			
17	Chaffin, Toliver B.	1	1			
21	Collum, Jacob H.	1/3				
22	Clark, James	1	1			
29	Cruse, Isaac	1	1			
34	Crowder, James H.	1/3				
50	Collom, Charles	1	1			
51	Collom, Jonathan	1	1			
63	Clapham, George	1	1			

No.	Name	Lgs.	Lbr.	Acres	Date	Remarks
66	Cherry, John V.	1	1			
82	Collom, George	1	1			
88	Clark, David	1/3				
97	Clark, Gilbert	1	1			
111	Cowen, Thomas L.	1	1			
189	Click, Mathias		1	1		
198	Click, Calvin	1/3				
202	Crow, Joshua W.	1	1			
203	Clark, Benjamin	1/3				
259	Clapp, William	1/3				
276	Cox, George W.	1	1			
304	Clark, Jonathan; dec'd.	1/3				
322	Cullum, Lucy Ann	1	1			
323	Chisholm, David M.	1/3				
253	Collier, Commodore	1/3				
355	Collum, Collin M.; dec'd.		1	1		
359	Craneus, Robert	1	1			
400	Cornelius, Daniel; dec'd.		1	1		
403	Clapp, David	1	1			
422	Carson, John J.	1/3				Heirs of.
461	Clark, Benjamin, dec'd.	1	1			
475	Carson, Charles	1	1			
489	Criger, William	1	1			
501	Cornelius, Phillip	1/3				
518	Collum, Wm.; heirs of	1	1			
657	Clark, George	1/3				
681	Crittendea, Nathan G.	1	1			
368	Crutcher, William	1/3				Conditionally recommended.
622	Crabtree, William	1	1			Conditionally recommended.
275	Craddock, John R.	1/3				
372	Cherry, Smith R.	1/3				
699	Crabtree, Haynes	1	1			Conditionally recommended.
4	Dean, Edward M.	1	1			
172	Dyer, John H.	1/3				
224	Dyer, Dickson	1	1			
227	Dean, Asa	1	1			
230	Dean, Jesse	1	1			
236	Duty, Phillip	1	1			
239	Dixon, James F.	1	1			
250	Doss, Benjamin H.	1/3				
264	Davis, Ralph	1/3				
292	Deck, Joseph; dec'd.	1	1			
314	Danthet, Allen G.; dec'd.	1/3				
318	Downey, John B.	1	1			
319	Dew, Joseph J.	1	1			
320	Dyer, George W.	1/3				
394	Dyer, Robert	1	1			
452	Dennison, Lewis C.;dec'd.	1	1			
485	Duncan, Albert D.	1	1			

No.	Name	Lgs.	Lbr.	Acres	Date	Remarks
603	Dayton, Lewis B.	1/3				
610	Davis, William	1/3				
688	Doss, James W.	1/3				
730	Dyer, John H.	2/3	1			
740	Davis, John	1	1			
239	Dixon, James F.	1	1			
436	Dixon, Alexander J.	1/3				
515	Dunman, Sherod	1	1			Heirs of.
637	Dooley, George	1	1			
235	Doss, John E.	1/3				
460	Dicar, Nancy	1	1			
546	Davis, John	1	1			
675	Deck, John; heirs of	1	1			
139	Douthet, Ambrose	1	1			Conditionally recommended.
69	Epperson, Mark	1	1			
266	Edmondson, William	1	1			
269	Emberson, John	1	1			
364	Elliott, William	1	1			
365	Ethridge, Godfrey	1	1			
369	Ethridge, Howard	1/3				
371	Ellis, Richard	1	1			
523	Everett, Jesse B.	1/3				
604	Edmondson, John	1	1			
588	Edwards, Thomas; dec'd.	1	1			Conditionally recommended.
33	Fowler, John H.	1	1			
154	Frazier, Ebenezer	1	1			
168	Fishback, Isaac H.	1	1			
171	Fowler, Bradford C.	1	1			
251	Fort, John A.	1/3				
335	Fulton, Sam'l. M.	1	1			
389	Franch, Samuel W.; dec'd.	1	1			
605	Fittz Patrick, Hugh	1/3				
665	Fitch, Jabes	1/3				
670	Fort, Elias B.	1/3				
707	Ford, Martin; dec'd.	1/3				
477	Finn, Richard H.	1	1			Conditionally recommended.
634	Fore, William H.	1/3				Conditionally recommended.
299	Fizer, John; dec'd.	1/3				
524	Frazier, Moses G.	1	1			
3	Giddens, Richard F.	1	1			
8	Guest, Joseph	1	1			
48	Gooch, Benjamin	1	1			
52	Greenwood, John	1	1			
69	Gahagan, John C.	1/3				
75	Gragg, Jacob	1/3				

No.	Name	Lgs.	Lbr.	Acres	Date	Remarks
99	Gragg, Samuel	1/3				
106	Gragg, John	1	1			
120	Graham, Alexander N.	1/3				
147	Guest, John	1	1			
191	Giddens, Absalom	1/3				
193	Gear, Garland	1	1			
207	Godley, Marshall G.D.	1/3				
222	Godley, Francis	1	1			
243	Gambell, James M.	1/3				
247	Graham, James	1/3				
254	Gahagan, James	1	1			
257	Gragg, William	1	1			
494	Graham, James; heirs of	1	1			
587	Gragg, Samuel	2/3	1			
647	Gambell, Robert	1/3				James Gambell, assignee.
651	Graham, Richard	1/3				
664	Guest, James J.	1/3				
560	Gray, Robert H.	1/3				
635	Glass, Joseph	1/3				
300	Gragg, Milton	1/3				
9	Hill, Abner	1	1			
12	Hill, Joshua B.	1	1			
31	Herring, John S.	1	1			
35	Hill, Thomas	1	1			
72	Hall, Jesse H.	1/3				
93	Hawkins, Thomas P.	1	1			
108	Hopkins, Rich'd. M.	1	1			
109	Hopkins, James E.	1	1			
118	Hughart, Edward	3/4	1			
123	Harty, Dennis	1	1			
125	Harty, John	1/3				
126	Hamilton, James M.	1/3				
150	Hamilton, Robert S.	1	1			
177	Hampton, Adam	1	1			
181	Hancock, Leander W.	1/3				
212	Humphries, John; dec'd.	1	1			
216	Humphries, John	1/3				
223	Harris, Randolph C.	1	1			
225	Hawnshell, Joseph	1	1			
237	Hancock, Sewel	1	1			
238	Hancock, James W.	1/3				
258	Holbrooks, Daniel	1	1			
277	Hefflefinger, James	1	1			
287	Hart, Marideth	1	1			
297	Hopkins, Francis; dec'd.	1	1			
326	Hill, Thomas H.	1/3				
329	Hampton, Andrew	1	1			
370	Hopkins, Jonathan	1	1			
397	Holmes, Bryant	1	1			
443	Hopkins, Wm. H.H.	1	1			
451	Hanks, John; dec'd.	1	1			Heirs of.

No.	Name	Lgs.	Lbr.	Acres	Date	Remarks
484	Hamilton, Robert	1/3				
540	Hays, Mary	1	1			
554	Harvey, Samuel S.	1/3				
556	Hampton, Lavina	1	1			
600	Hobbs, Jonathan T.	1/3				
602	Harper, James	1	1			
609	Hill, Robert	1/3				
626	Holloway, William	1/3				
686	Hibbard, Lewis B.	1/3				
652	Haslett, Joseph H.	1/3				Bennet T. Logan, assignee.
476	Howard, William	1/3				Conditionally recommended.
625	Hamilton, Mary Ann	1	1			Conditionally recommended.
135	Harmon, Henry J.	1/3				
435	Haygood, Osman S.	1/3				
501	Higgs, Simon M.	1/3				
445	Hill, Thomas D.	1/3				
571	Ingram, Wm. C.	1/3				
706	Ingram, Wm. C.	2/3	1			
408	Ingram, Martha	1	1			
14	Jackson, Edward T.	1/3				
25	Jeffers, Benj. Jr.	1/3				
39	Jeffers, Samuel	1	1			
43	Jeffers, James A.	1/3				
116	Jernigen, Curtis	1	1			
129	Jackson, James	1	1			
164	Johnson, Isaac H.	1	1			
214	Johnson, Baldin C.	1	1			
220	Jones, Robert	1/3				
241	Johnson, William	1/3				
244	Johnston, Alexander	1	1			
317	Johnson, Lindley	1	1			
442	Jackson, John	1/3				
455	Johnson, Thomas	1/3				
510	Jackson, Phillip	1	1			
511	Jones, Massack H.	1	1			
365	Jones, David S.	1/3				
644	Johnston, James H.	1/3				
724	Johnston, James H.	2/3	1			
728	Jackson, John	2/3	1			
337	Jones, Joseph; heirs of	1	1			Conditionally recommended.
373	Jones, Henry S.	1/3				Conditionally recommended.
395	Jones, Garrett	1	1			Conditionally recommended.
458	Jarmon, Asa	1	1			Conditionally recommended.
465	Jones, John E.	1/3				Conditionally recommended.

No.	Name	Lgs.	Lbr.	Acres	Date	Remarks
474	Jones, Isaac N.	1	1			Conditionally recommended.
475	Jones, Isaac H.N.	1/3				Conditionally recommended.
132	Keller, Mitchell	1	1			
145	King, William	1	1			
265	King, Thomas	1/3				
308	Keller, John F.; dec'd.	1	1			
354	Kernols, John H.;dec'd.	1/3				
361	King, James H.	1/3				
530	Kitchens, Jesse; dec'd.	1	1			
534	Keneday, Griswell	1	1			Heirs of.
624	Knight, William	1/3				
703	King, Lewis T.; dec'd.	1	1			
582	Keller, Hesekiah	1	1			Conditionally recommended.
661	King, George W.	1	1			Conditionally recommended.
2	Latimer, Albert H.	1	1			
6	Lemmers, Samuel	1/3				
7	Lyday, Isaac	1/3				
32	Lisk, Richard H.	1/3				
46	Latimer, James	1	1			
56	Lewis, Charles	1	1			
94	Lynn, Benjamin F.	1	1			
210	Levens, Joseph	1	1			
226	Longham, Wiley W.	1	1			
255	Leach, Joseph	1	1			
256	Leach, Evander	1/3				
273	Levins, Nicholas	1/3				
274	Land, John	1	1			
280	Lawson, Isaiah D.	1	1			
311	Logan, Bennet T.	1/3				
338	Lankford, Eleanor	1	1			
341	Levins, James; dec'd.	1	1			
352	Latimer, Henry R.	1/3				
424	Lewis, Kendell	1	1			
466	Lacy, Jacob	1/3				
482	Lick, John; dec'd.	1/3				
496	Leats, Precious	1	1			
612	Longardia, Francisco	1/3				
621	Luckey, Arthur; dec'd.	1	1			
653	Leewright, John; heirs of		1	1		
743	Levens, John	1/3				
350	Lane, Henry L.	1/3				Conditionally recommended.
401	Lloyd, Benager	1/3				Conditionally recommended.
402	Lloyd, Hiram	1/3				Conditionally recommended.

No.	Name	Lgs.	Lbr.	Acres	Date	Remarks
347	Lane, David	1	1			Conditionally recommended.
655	Lloyd, David	1	1			Conditionally recommended.
656	Lloyd, Parker	1/3				Conditionally recommended.
684	Lloyd, Levi; heirs of	1	1			Conditionally recommended.
694	Lloyd, David; heirs of	1	1			Conditionally recommended.
695	Lloyd, Ira; dec'd.	1/3				Conditionally recommended.
413	Lick, John; dec'd.	1	1			Heirs of.
559	Lamb, John C.	1	1			Fulton & Cravens, assignee.
642	Lee, Abner; dec'd.	1	1			Heirs of.
11	Moore, Samuel F.	1	1			
15	McKinney, Blackley	1/3				
27	Matthews, Joseph	1	1			
36	McKinney, Hiram C.	1	1			
41	McKinnay, Daniel	1/3				
47	Matthews, Mansel W.	1	1			
49	Matthews, Wm. O.	1	1			
60	McKinney, George Y.	1/3				
61	McClure, Washington S.	1/3				
70	Milam, Jefferson	1	1			
71	McClenden, Allen	1	1			
89	McKinney, Ashley	1	1			
91	McAneer, Alexander	1	1			
98	McKinney, Collin	1	1			
100	McKinney, Younger S.	1/3				
110	Madding, Robert W.	1/3				
117	McAnear, John B.	1	1			
134	McCarly, Geo. W.	1/3				
148	Midkiff, Pleasant D.	1	1			
149	Mitchell, Rewben D.	1/3				
152	McKenzie, Abner H.	1/3				
161	Milton, Andrew G.	1	1			
170	Miller, Peter; dec'd.	1	1			
180	Maxwell, Robert	1	1			
204	Morton, John	1	1			
283	McKinney, Wm. C.	1	1			
285	McCreery, Wilson	1/3				
295	McCowan, John	1/3				
306	Martin, Gabriel; dec'd.	1	1			
333	Mays, Squire	1	1			
339	McKinney, James	1	1			
357	Momin, Lavina	1	1			
376	Moore, Launson	1	1			
383	Matthews, Elbert	1	1			
386	Moore, Alfred	1	1			
388	Mauray, William	1	1			

No.	Name	Lgs.	Lbr.	Acres	Date	Remarks
423	Majors, John P.	1	1			
429	Mabin, Joseph H.	1/3				
436	McKinney, John A.	1/3				
441	Mowrey, Mathias	1	1			
446	McCurley, John	1	1			
462	Morton, John	1	1			
464	McDaniel, Elijah	1/3				
493	Minn, John	1/3				
580	Mayse, William	1	1			
598	Massie, John W.	1/3				
663	Milam, Benjamin R.	1/3				
668	Morris, George	1	1			
693	Merchoff, Joseph	1	1			Heirs of.
716	McKelly, Hugh	1	1			Heirs of.
727	McCowen, William	1	1			
512	McCabe, Matthew	1	1			James J. Ward, assignee.
1	Morris, Daniel	1	1			Conditionally recommended.
40	Morris, Lee	1/3				Conditionally recommended.
58	Morris, Robert	1/3				Conditionally recommended.
245	McDonald, William	1	1			Conditionally recommended.
463	Moss, Asariah	1/3				Conditionally recommended.
470	Moss, William; dec'd.	1	1			Conditionally recommended.
491	McKinney, Daniel; heirs of	1	1			Conditionally recommended.
579	Mott, Morgan R.	1/3				Conditionally recommended.
660	Harris, Seth	1	1			Conditionally recommended.
683	Morris, Curtis; dec'd.	1	1			Conditionally recommended.
170	McDaniel, James	1/3				
596	McCowen, Rebecca	1	1			Jas. S. Ward, (et alias) assignee.
509	McFarlin, William	1	1			Conditionally recommended.
209	Nugent, Allen B.	1/3				
240	Nelson, John D.	1/3				
261	Nall, Martin G.	1	1			
278	Nall, John	1	1			
289	Nugent, John M.	1/3				
327	Nugent, John	1	1			
398	Nall, Robert	1	1			
409	Nall, John H.	1	1			

No.	Name	Lgs.	Lbr.	Acres	Date	Remarks
356	Osborne, Bushrod W.	1/3				
374	Overtop, Richard	1	1			
418	Oastal, John	1	1			
467	Osgood, James	1	1			Conditionally recommended.
673	Oldham, Willis	1/3				Conditionally recommended.
28	Peters, Richard	1/3				
64	Peters, Lemuel; dec'd.	1	1			
178	Park, Geo. S.	1/3				
190	Peters, Stephen	1	1			
192	Pew, John	1	1			
199	Patterson, John	1/3				
211	Paxton, Hansford L.	1/3				
215	Paxton, John	1	1			
218	Paxton, Wm. J.	1/3				
234	Pew, Samuel	1/3				
282	Proctor, Henry S.	1/3				
310	Pendergrass, Sarah	1	1			
404	Perkins, Daniel	1	1			
405	Perkins, Samuel	1/3				
428	Peters, Joshua	1	1			
450	Price, John	1	1			
654	Pitman, Willis	1	1			
715	Park, Wm. A.	1/3				
733	Parker, Seth	1/3				
573	Pearce, James	1	1			
342	Poor, Eliza	1	1			
221	Paxton, Jesse M.C.	1	1			
425	Pennington, Isaac	1/3				
708	Porter, Juliett; dec'd.	1	1			Heirs of.
41	Richie, Jane	1	1			
57	Rice, Levi M.	1	1			
79	Reed, John A.	1	1			
81	Richie, John M.	1/3				
86	Richie, Samuel A.	1	1			
95	Richie, William	1	1			
101	Reams, Howard	1	1			
128	Ragsdall, Robert	1/3				
130	Roland, Sherrod	1	1			
133	Ragsdale, Thomas	1/3				
146	Reed, Joseph	1	1			
157	Reed, Miles	1	1			
187	Reed, Sally	1	1			
205	Richie, James	1	1			
208	Robbins, John	1	1			
284	Reviere, William K.	1	1			
302	Ragsdale, William; dec'd.		1	1		
375	Riley, James	1	1			
392	Riley, John	1/3				
399	Reed, Isaac	1/3				

No.	Name	Lgs.	Lbr.	Acres	Date	Remarks
412	Ross, Le Roy W.	1	1			
416	Rhoads, James	1	1			
439	Russell, Reddin	1	1			
440	Rattan, Larkin	1	1			
454	Ragsdale, Martin	1	1			
521	Rutherford, John A.	1	1			
522	Riley, Thomas; dec'd.	1	1			Heirs of.
569	Rhoads, Richmond	1	1			
607	Rattan, Daniel	1/3				
614	Richardson, Lewis	1/3				
618	Ragsdale, Charles	1/3				
656	Roads, Leander	1/3				
662	Renfro, Jesse B.	1/3				
674	Robertson, Absolom	1/3				
679	Ross, John; heirs of	1/3				
685	Richey, Renwick	1/3				
709	Roberts, John; dec'd.	1	1			
710	Roberts, John	1	1			
726	Ricker, Nath'l M.	1/3				
739	Roberts, Luke	1	1			
578	Richardson, Henry	1	1			Conditionally recommended.
296	Roland, John	1/3				
13	Simmons, Benj.	1	1			
63	Sherwood, Wilkinson	1/3				
124	Smith, John T.	1/3				
153	Slingland, William	1	1			
165	Satterthite, Thomas	1	1			
174	Sadler, James C.	1	1			
173	Sadler, James M.	1	1			
175	Sadler, Hiram	1	1			
176	Sadler, Felix G.	1/3				
184	Stowell, Willard	1	1			
228	Scarborough, Middleton	1	1			
229	Stiles, John	1	1			
231	Scarborough, Felix	1/3				
249	Stonham, William	1	1			
272	Stonham, James	1	1			
379	Shockey, Henry	1	1			
387	Simmons, Elisha	1	1			
390	Shaw, Hugh B.	1	1			
391	Stout, Henry	1	1			
393	Stout, James S.	1/3				
426	Simmons, Clark	1/3				
444	Shaw, Wm, Jr. dec'd.	1/3				
483	Smith, James N.	1	1			
456	Smith, George W.	1	1			
486	Saunders, John	1/3				
503	Stallenge, Jacob	1	1			
541	Strickland, Joseph; decd	1	1			Heirs of.
545	Smith, Hamman; dec'd.	1				Heirs of.
575	Scott, John T.	1/3				

No.	Name	Lgs.	Lbr.	Acres	Date	Remarks
606	Strickland, David;dec'd	1	1			
669	Smith, Canon	1/3				
687	Savage, Joseph	1/3				
720	Stewart, William	1/3				
85	Smiley, F.J.C.	1	1			
438	Shockley, Wm. D.	1/3				
260	Setzer, Martin	1/3				
114	Trammell, Robert	1	1			
206	Tisdel, John	1	1			
315	Talbot, Thomas	1/3				Williamson & Bowerman, assignees.
324	Thompson, Wm. F.; dec'd.	1	1			
344	Tollett, Wesley	1	1			
343	Tollett, Margarett	1	1			
345	Tollett, Elijah W.	1/3				
363	Thompson, Wiley	1/3				
382	Talbot, John A.	1/3				
492	Tinnin, Lawrence W.	1	1			
506	Tyler, Isaac	1	1			
552	Tidwell, Esram; dec'd.	1	1			Heirs of.
659	Tollett, John	1/3				
705	Tidwell, H; dec'd.	1	1			Heirs of.
4	Tipton, Benj. S.	1/3				Rich. M. Hopkins, assignee.
90	Tarrant, Edward H.	1	1			Conditionally recommended.
83	Ury, Eunis	1/3				
96	Vining, Wade H.	1	1			
532	Vanwinkle, David; heirs of	1	1			
23	Wilson, Jason	1	1			
24	Wood, Caleb B.	1	1			
30	Watson, Coleman	1	1			
67	Watts, William	1/3				
68	Weaver, John W.	1	1			
87	West, David	1	1			
92	Ward, James	1	1			
104	Wilson, Thomas R.	1/3				
112	Ware, John	1	1			
119	Wheat, William	1	1			
122	Wilson, Samuel	1/3				
127	Wright, Geo. W.	1	1			
142	Ward, William C.	1	1			
144	Wheat, Josias T.	1/3				
151	Wilson, William	1/3				
163	Wheat, Robert H.	1/3				
169	Ward, Joseph J.	1	1			
183	Wilson, John	1	1			
194	Ward, James J.Sr.	1	1			
195	Watson, John M.	1	1			
201	Waggoner, David	1	1			

No.	Name	Lgs.	Lbr.	Acres	Date	Remarks
252	Wright, Marcus D.	1/3				
263	Williams, Wm. M.	1/3				
268	Wagley, John	1	1			
270	Widman, Edward	1	1			
271	Wright, Travis G.	1/3				
281	Wilson, Isaac	1/3				
307	Wetmore, Geo. C.; decd.	1	1			
316	Williamson, Isaac C.	1/3				
340	Willett, Andrew; dec'd.	1	1			
346	White, Durant H.	1/3				
366	Wetherspoon, Wiley	1	1			
380	Williams, Silvester	1/3				
431	Williams, Henry G.	1	1			Ennis & Amos Ury, Assignees.
432	Williams, James H.	1/3				
437	Wagley, Abram	1	1			
447	Wyatt, Peyton S.	1	1			
488	Walker, Susanna	1	1			
502	Wagley, Joseph	1	1			
514	Wellborn, Kinchen A.	1	1			
520	Williams, Earl Stanley	1/3				Heirs of.
516	Watson, Evan, Sr. Dec'd.	1	1			Heirs of.
529	Walters, Henry (or Hezekiah)					John J. Jewett, Assignee.
548	Worthington, Samuel; dec'd.	1	1			Heirs of.
586	Wright, James G.		1			
592	Ward, Morris	1	1			
619	Wright, Alexander W.	1/3				
620	Wimbley, James	1/3				
643	Williams, Moses	1	1			Heirs of.
646	Wilson, Isaac	2/3	1			
648	Williams, Thomas; dec'd.	1/3				
671	Williamson, Isaac C.	2/3	1			
697	Ward, Jordon P.	1/3				
723	Wright, Travis G.	2/3	1			
583	Wilson, James R.	1/3				Conditionally recommended.
690	Williams, Wm. B.	1	1			Conditionally recommended.
417	Wood, Joseph; dec'd.	1	1			Heirs of.
595	Watkins, Joseph; dec'd.	1	1			Heirs of.
267	Young, Geo. S.	1	1			
360	Young, Elijah	1/3				

SECOND CLASS

No.	Name	Lgs.	Lbr.	Acres	Date	Remarks
91	Andrews, Thos. H.			640	Aug. 2,1838	
162	Abney, Abner			640	Aug. 3,1838	
180	Archer, Alexander			1280	Aug. 3,1838	
182	Archer, William			1280	Aug. 3,1838	

No.	Name	Lgs.	Lbr.	Acres	Date	Remarks
190	Allen, Hugh			1280	Aug.16,1838	
223	Allen, Levi P.			1280	Sept.6,1838	
224	Andes, Michael			640	Sept.6,1838	
258	Alexander, Daniel J.			1280	Oct. 4,1838	
296	Allen, Almoren			640	Oct. 4,1838	
349	Alfred, Roy			1280	Nov. 1,1838	
354	Andrews, Wm. S.			1280	Nov. 1,1838	
391	Allen, Alfred			640	Jan. 3,1839	
371	Allison, William			640	Nov. 1,1838	
137	Braton, Isaac	1/3			Jan. 3,1839	
2	Bloodworth, John D.			640	Mar. 1,1839	
7	Burrel, Elias A.			640	May 8,'1839	
10	Browning, James E.			1280	June 7,1839	
11	Browning, John A.			640	June 7,1839	
12	Browning, Robert H.			640	June 7,1839	
13	Bradley, Lewis H.			1280	June 7,1839	
15	Boothe, Benjamin			1280	June 7,1839	
49	Birdwell, George			1280	Jy. 5,1839	
52	Burris, Mary			1280	Aug. 2,1839	
63	Bacon, Andrew L.			640	Aug. 2,1839	
69	Baker, Thos. C.			640	Aug. 2,1839	
76	Blanton, Benj.			1280	Aug. 2,1839	
78	Blanton, Francis L.			640	Aug. 2,1839	
79	Blanton, Jacob			640	Aug. 2,1839	
80	Blanton, John			640	Aug. 2,1839	
84	Buchanan, Sam'l.			1280	Aug. 2,1839	
87	Brothers, Jesse			640	Aug. 2,1839	
88	Barrett, Janes			1280	Aug. 2,1839	
90	Blanton, Elijah			1280	Aug. 2,1839	
95	Birdwell, Zachariah			1280	Aug. 2,1839	
96	Birdwell, Thomas G.			640	Aug. 2,1839	
105	Breedin, Calvin			640	Aug. 2,1839	
132	Bryant, Lorenzo D.			1280	Aug. 2,1839	
148	Bridge, James G.			1280	Aug. 3,1839	
149	Bridge, Samuel			1280	Aug. 3,1839	
151	Brown, George A.			640	Aug. 3,1839	
170	Brown, James			640	Aug. 3,1839	
188	Bland, John W.			640	Aug. 6,1839	
198	Blankston, James			1280	Aug.16,1839	
199	Bourland, James			1280	Aug.16,1839	
200	Bourland, Benj. F.			640	Aug.16,1839	
203	Brown, Dempsey			1280	Sept.6,1839	
241	Bell, Daniel			1280	Oct. 4,1839	
261	Bruton, Thursa			1280	Oct. 4,1839	
266	Brigham, Wiley			1280	Oct. 4,1839	
291	Burris, Wm. M.			1280	Oct. 4,1839	
297	Bowland, John M.			1280	Oct. 4,1839	
312	Bingham, Henry			1280	Oct. 4,1839	
321	Beard, Elizabeth			1280	Oct. 4,1839	
323	Bevers, William			640	Oct. 4,1839	
328	Ball, Elisha			640	Oct. 4,1839	
330	Boon, Jacob H.			640	Oct. 4,1839	

No.	Name	Lgs.	Lbr.	Acres	Date	Remarks
331	Bowland, Reuben			640	Oct. 4,1839	
333	Barnes, Edward			640	Oct. 4,1839	
353	Brazzel, Allen			1280	Nov. 1,1839	
356	Blythe, Sam'l K.			1280	Nov. 1,1838	Deceased
358	Boothe, Jessee A.			640	Nov. 1,1838	
370	Bland, John W.			640	Nov. 1,1838	
385	Butler, John			640	Dec. 6,1838	
393	Benton, Nath'l. G.			640	Jan. 3,1839	
418	Boyd, Jesse M.			1280	Mar. 7,1839	
419	Bryarly, Roland T.			640	Mar. 7,1839	
422	Blundell, James H.			640	Mar. 7,1839	
423	Bivins, Susannah			1280	Mar. 7,1839	
424	Birdwell, William B.			640	Mar.21,1839	
9	Bassett, John			1280	Apr. 5,1839	
59	Bassham, James			640	Aug.26,1839	
697	Bailey, Aaron			640	Jan. 7,1840	
626	Baker, Alexander			1280	Jan. 2,1840	
5	Crutcher, Thomas			1280	Apr. 1838	
53	Crowder, William			640	Aug. 2,1838	
77	Cox, Joseph			1280	Aug. 2,1838	
81	Cassidy, James B.			1280	Aug. 2,1838	
99	Calloway, Joshua			1280	Aug. 2,1838	
123	Clifton, James			640	Aug. 2,1838	
131	Chandler, Samuel G.			640	Aug. 2,1838	
157	Clawson, Larkin G.			640	Aug. 3,1838	
158	Clawson, Moses			640	Aug. 3,1838	
173	Cole, William			1280	Aug. 3,1838	
186	Conley, John M.			640	Aug. 3,1838	
204	Chisum, Claiborne			1280	Sept.6,1838	
221	Coots, David			1280	Sept.6,1838	
242	Clapp, Otis, Jr.			640	Oct. 4,1838	
253	Crownover, Benjamin			1280	Oct. 4,1838	
269	Crowder, Jane			1280	Oct. 4,1838	
265	Click, Andrew J.			1280	Oct. 4,1838	
277	Casbier, John			1280	Oct. 4,1838	
300	Craig, John B.			640	Oct. 4,1838	
307	Clark, Minerva			1280	Oct. 4,1838	
368	Croom, Nancy			1280	Nov. 1,1838	
379	Clitton, Henry H.			1280	Nov.12,1838	
381	Chute, James			640	Dec. 6,1838	
394	Cooksey, James			1280	Jan. 3,1839	
399	Cron, John D.			640	Jan. 3,1839	
406	Campbell, John			640	Feb. 7,1839	
408	Craddock, Wm. S.			640	Feb. 7,1839	
22	Click, Rufus K.			640	May 27,1839	
633	Campbell, James A.			640	Jan. 2,1840	
750	Curry, James			640	Jan.11,1840	
54	Crouder, Greenham			640	Aug. 2,1838	
3	Day, Harmon C.			1280	Apr. 1838	
8	Davis, John			1280	June 7,1838	
43	Duncan, Joseph A.B.			640	Jy. 5,1838	Heirs of.

No.	Name	Lgs.	Lbr.	Acres	Date	Remarks
44	Duncan, Alexander			640	Jy. 5,1838	
108	Dean, Levi			1280	Aug. 2,1838	
116	Dabbs, Jonathan W.			1280	Aug. 2,1838	
121	Dixon, James W.			1280	Aug. 2,1838	
122	Davidson, Josiah			1280	Aug. 2,1838	
133	Dillard, Matthew			640	Aug. 2,1838	
193	Dunlap, James P.			640	Aug.16,1838	
207	Davis, David			1280	Sept.6,1838	
210	Duke, Wm. G.			1280	Sept.6,1838	
211	Duke, John H.			1280	Sept.6,1838	
230	Dillard, Wm. N.			1280	Sept.6,1838	
393	Denton, John B.			640	Oct. 4,1838	
337	Dennis, James			1280	Nov. 1,1838	
338	Dolton, Samuel M.			640	Nov. 1,1838	
339	Dolton, James			640	Nov. 1,1838	
340	Dennis, John			640	Nov. 1,1838	
341	Dennis, Thomas			1280	Nov. 1,1838	
346	Davis, Harvey B.			640	Nov. 1,1838	
409	Diment, Lurral M.			640	Feb. 7,1839	
420	Davis, John H.			640	Mar. 7,1839	
438	Davis, Josiah			1280	Dec.23,1839	
439	Davis, Joel S.			640	Dec.23,1839	
441	Davis, Benjamin B.			640	Dec.23,1839	
444	Davis, John L.			640	Dec.23,1839	
92	Eastwood, John			1280	Aug. 2,1838	
102	Elliott, James			640	Aug. 2,1838	
104	Elliott, John W.			640	Aug. 3,1838	
94	Ford, James			640	Aug. 2,1838	
202	Fellers, Henry G.			1280	Sept.6,1838	
205	Fulton, Wm. M.			640	Sept.6,1838	
209	Fellers, Abram G.			640	Sept.6,1838	
237	Farris, Joseph			1280	Oct. 4,1838	
276	Forbes, Thomas C.			640	Oct. 4,1838	
278	Fatts, William S.			640	Oct.11,1838	
289	Fields, Joseph			1280	Oct. 4,1838	
352	Frazier, James			640	Nov. 1,1838	
360	Fields, Edward S.			640	Nov. 1,1838	
361	Field, Wm. A.			640	Nov. 1,1838	
365	Fletcher, George			640	Nov. 1,1838	
386	Fields, Joseph N.			640	Dec. 6,1838	
404	Fort, Josiah W.			1280	Feb. 7,1839	
55	Ferry, Justin			640	Aug. 1,1839	
67	Farris, Isham			640	Sept.14,1839	
68	Farris, John			640	Sept.14,1839	
169	Foster, John			1280	Dec. 5,1839	
170	Foster, Ambrose			1280	Dec. 5,1839	
235	Foster, Isaac M.			640	Dec. 5,1839	
236	Foster, James L.			640	Dec. 5,1839	
269	Frampton, William			640	Oct. 4,1838	
14,	Glover, Martin			1280	June 7,1838	

No.	Name	Lgs.	Lbr.	Acres	Date	Remarks
18	Griffey, Mark			640	June 7,1838	
19	Germany, John			1280	June 7,1838	
22	Glover, John			640	June 7,1838	
85	Gay, Hugh			640	Aug. 2,1838	
86	Green, John			640	Aug. 2,1838	
107	Gerdis, Frederick A.			640	Aug. 2,1838	
124	Green, Thomas			640	Aug. 2,1838	
135	Graham, James H.			640	Aug. 2,1838	
141	Gilliam, James			1280	Aug. 3,1838	
166	Giddens, Wiley W.			640	Aug. 3,1838	
175	Gordon, George			640	Aug. 3,1838	
196	Gnernsey, Lyman			640	Aug.16,1838	
231	Graham, Richard C.			1280	Sept.6,1838	
235	Glover, William			1280	Sept.6,1838	
246	Guffey, John			1280	Oct. 4,1838	
280	Graham, Robert			640	Oct.11,1838	
284	Gaylon, William			640	Oct.11,1838	
321	Gray, George			640	Oct.11,1838	
326	Guest, Isaac			1280	Oct.4, 1838	
362	Gayton, William D.			640	Nov. 1,1838	
367	Gillium, Timmeon			1280	Nov. 1,1838	
374	Gillum, Henry			1280	Nov. 1,1838	
381	Gillespie, Thomas			1280	Dec. 6,1838	
770	Griffen, John F.			1280	Jan.11,1840	
306	Glass, Robert			1280	Oct. 4,1838	
316	Gerdes, Esdert			1280	Oct. 4,1838	
4	Hale, Ann H.			1280	Apr. 1838	
57	Hartsaw, Daniel			640	Aug. 2,1838	
93	Hale, Josias C.			1280	Aug. 2,1838	
97	Hamilton, Robert			1280	Aug. 2,1838	
98	Hamilton, James			1280	Aug. 2,1838	
113	Hudson, John			1280	Aug. 2,1838	
114	Hudson, Benj. J.			640	Aug. 2,1838	
120	Hutchins, Henry R.			640	Aug. 2,1838	
129	Hill, Samuel			640	Aug. 2,1838	
130	Humphries, William			1280	Aug. 2,1838	
137	Hudson, Joshua J.			1280	Aug. 3,1838	
142	Hobbs, William			640	Aug. 3,1838	
155	Holbert, Hampton			640	Aug. 3,1838	
184	Hamilton, John			1280	Aug. 3,1838	
191	Hart, Joseph C.			640	Aug.13,1838	
212	Hamilton, Wm. E.			640	Sept.6,1838	
248	Hall, George H.			1280	Oct. 4,1838	
255	Hamilton, Wm. J.			640	Oct. 4,1838	
271	Harris, Joseph			1280	Oct. 4,1838	
274	Hogan, Ann			1280	Oct. 4,1838	Wm. B. Stout, Assignee.
301	Hazelwood, Richard C.			640	Oct. 4,1838	
320	Harmon, John T.			1280	Oct. 4,1838	
342	Harter, Harvey			640	Nov. 1,1838	
344	Harrison, Wm. M.			640	Nov. 1,1838	
348	Harris, Joseph			1280	Nov. 1,1838	
368	Holland, William			640	Nov. 1,1838	

No.	Name	Lgs.	Lbr.	Acres	Date	Remarks
380	Hendricks, William			640	Dec. 6,1838	
392	Hillis, Samuel W.			640	Jan. 3,1839	
410	Hood, Charles			640	Feb. 7,1839	
425	Harris, Daniel			640	Mar.21,1839	Samuel Rodgers, Assignee.
57	Harris, Virgil H.			1280	Aug.26,1839	
221	Hart, Josiah			1280	Dec. 5,1839	
319	Harmon, Jacob			1280	Dec. 5,1839	
37	Jones, William			640	Jy. 5,1838	
38	Jones, Daniel			640	Jy. 5,1838	
39	Jones, Hiram			1280	Jy. 5,1838	
100	Jones, Isaac			1280	Aug. 2,1838	
106	Janssen, John			640	Aug. 2,1838	
111	Johnson, Avis			640	Aug. 2,1838	
174	Jameson, Daivd K.			1280	Aug. 3,1838	
206	Johnson, John			1280	Sept.6,1838	
234	Johns, Clement R.			640	Sept.6,1838	
252	Johnson, William			640	Oct. 4,1838	Date of certif. & witnesses' names not on original record.
309	Johnson, Peter B.			640	Oct. 4,1838	
365	Jones, Marvel R.			640	Dec.18,1839	
766	Johnson, James S.			1280	Jan.11,1840	
23	Keel, Wiley			640	June 8,1838	
45	Kirkpatrick, Hiram			1280	Jy. 5,1838	
61	Key, David P.			640	Aug. 2,1838	
138	Kennedy, George			640	Aug. 3,1838	
179	Kimbel, Albert G.			640	Aug. 3,1838	
288	Kennedy, John J.			1280	Aug. 4,1838	
313	Kimbell, Edward W.			640	Oct. 4,1838	
314	Kimbell, John M.			640	Oct. 4,1838	
315	Kimbell, Joseph; dec'd.			1280	Oct. 4,1838	
318	Kimbell, Thomas M.			640	Oct. 4,1838	
1	Key, John P.			640	Apr. 5,1839	
58	Keykendal, Isaac			1280	Aug.26,1839	
475	Kiching, John F.			640	Dec.25,1839	
638	Kennedy, Wiatte W.			640	Jan. 2,1840	
24	Logwood, Thos. Y.			1280	June 8,1838	
40	Luckey, Hugh			640	Jy. 5,1838	
41	Largent, John			1280	Jy. 5,1838	
75	Lankston, Isaac P.			640	Aug. 2,1838	
140	Leiper, James W.			640	Aug. 3,1838	
177	Latimer, Cynthia			1280	Aug. 3,1838	
192	Lyday, Andrew			1280	Aug.16,1838	
227	Lilly, Noah			1280	Sept.6,1838	
282	Lane, John W.			1280	Oct. 4,1838	
350	Lovejoy, John L.			1280	Nov. 1,1838	
733	Lawless, William			320	Jan.10,1838	Clerk's returns say 640 acres.

No.	Name	Lgs.	Lbr.	Acres	Date	Remarks
29	Millikin, Hugh			1280	Jy. 5,1838	
33	Millikin, George			1280	Jy. 5,1838	
47	Merritt, James			640	Jy. 5,1838	
50	Miller, John			640	Jy. 5,1838	
71	McWhirter, James			1280	Aug. 2,1838	
160	Moores, Wm. H.			1280	Aug. 2,1838	
127	Mitchell, Joseph			640	Aug. 2,1838	
128	Millsap, Hicks			640	Aug. 2,1838	
153	McDonald, John			640	Aug. 3,1838	
159	Meyers, John			1280	Aug. 3,1838	
161	McCarter, Nancy			1280	Aug. 3,1838	
165	McGauhey, Lee Roy G.			640	Aug. 3,1838	
167	Miller, Peter			640	Aug. 3,1838	
168	McClure, John			1280	Aug. 3,1838	
169	McClure, Milton D.			640	Aug. 3,1838	
183	Milligin, John H.			640	Aug. 3,1838	
214	Matlock, Jones M.			640	Sept.6,1838	
228	McGahee, Robert			640	Sept.6,1838	
232	Morris, Mary			1280	Sept.6,1838	
233	Malias, Thos.			640	Sept.6,1838	
238	McGee, Namon			1280	Oct. 4,1838	
247	Moore, Levin V.			1280	Oct. 4,1838	
251	McDonald, H.G.			1280	Oct. 4,1838	
293	Miller, Richard G.			1280	Oct. 4,1838	
305	Moore, Isaac			1280	Oct. 4,1838	
308	McClanahan, Thos.			640	Oct. 4,1838	
310	Merrill, Wiley B.			1280	Oct. 4,1838	
334	Miller, Zachariah			640	Nov. 1,1838	
345	Mix, Joseph R.			640	Nov. 1,1838	
347	Miller, Sam'l. A.			640	Nov. 1,1838	
363	Moore, Whitfield			640	Nov. 1,1838	
383	Mathews, John H.			640	Dec. 6,1838	
388	Mitchell, Ephraim M.			1280	Jan. 3,1839	
416	Mims, Gideon			640	Mar. 7,1839	
32	Mauldin, Presley			1280	May 27,1839	
654	Mason, Henry D.			640	Jan. 2,1840	
744	Mathews, Ervin			640	Jan.11,1840	
134	Neely, Tallas			640	Aug. 2,1838	
254	Neathery, Abner			640	Oct. 4,1838	
369	Needham, Lewis			1280	Nov. 1,1838	
226	Nobles, Thos.,Sr.			1280	Dec. 5,1839	
227	Nobles, William			640	Dec. 5,1839	
51	Overton, Benjamin			640	Jy. 5,1838	Deceased
82	Oliver, Malich			1280	Aug. 2,1838	
398	Orr, Green			1280	Jan. 3,1839	
417	Obrient, Rankin			640	Mar. 7,1839	
197	Overton, Reddick			1280	Dec. 5,1839	
9	Patrick, Wiley			1280	June 7,1838	Deceased.
73	Pickie, Jacob P.G.			1280	Aug. 2,1838	
83	Parlain, Wm.			1280	Aug. 2,1838	

No.	Name	Lgs.	Lbr.	Acres	Date	Remarks
103	Poor, Wm. B.			640	Aug. 2,1838	
112	Price, Robert			640	Aug. 2,1838	
125	Poor, James, Sr.			1280	Aug. 2,1838	
139	Patten, William B.			1280	Aug. 3,1838	
143	Peck, Seyman			640	Aug. 3,1838	
171	Perry, Leonard W.			640	Aug. 3,1838	
172	Perry, Josiah			1280	Aug. 3,1838	Deceased.
213	Pool, Orlando L.			1280	Sept.6,1838	
263	Patterson, James R.			1280	Oct. 4,1838	
292	Peebles, Ephraim			640	Oct. 4,1838	
397	Peters, John S.			640	Jan. 3,1839	
414	Pirtle, Benjamin			1280	Feb. 7,1839	
14	Price, William			1280	May 2, 1839	
124	Peters, Lemuel			640	Nov.14,1839	
60	Raney, Stephen D.			640	Aug. 2,1838	
68	Richards, Jacob			640	Aug. 2,1838	
70	Reed, John S.			1280	Aug. 2,1838	
117	Ragan, Carey			640	Aug. 2,1838	
150	Ritchil, Thos. J.			1280	Aug. 3,1838	
154	Reed, Henry A.			640	Aug. 3,1838	
221	Ryburn, Mathew			1280	Sept.6,1838	
236	Richardson, Rufus M.			1280	Oct. 4,1838	
259	Richards, Wilson Q.			640	Oct. 4,1838	
295	Reed, George			640	Oct. 4,1838	
299	Redford, William			640	Oct. 4,1838	
355	Ratliff, Benjamin			640	Nov. 1,1838	
372	Riggs, William			640	Nov. 1,1838	
377	Reed, John			1280	Nov. 1,1838	
413	Riker, Abraham			640	Feb. 7,1839	
32	Spain, John D.			1280	Jy. 5,1838	
48	Swan, Lyman			640	Jy. 5,1838	
56	Sheek, Adam			1280	Aug. 2,1838	
66	Speer, Moses			640	Aug. 2,1838	
115	Simons, Peter			1280	Aug. 2,1838	
118	Sorrels, Sam'l W.			640	Aug. 2,1838	
126	Stewart, Benj. F.			640	Aug. 2,1838	
144	Smith, Elial M.			640	Aug. 3,1838	
145	Sample, David			640	Aug. 3,1838	
147	Stephenson, Alexander			1280	Aug. 3,1838	
156	Smith, Sampson			1280	Aug. 3,1838	
160	Seidikum, Frederick			640	Aug. 3,1838	
163	Smith, Joseph E.			640	Aug. 3,1838	
164	Smith, Thomas F.			640	Aug. 3,1838	
176	Sims, James W.			1280	Aug. 3,1838	
178	Sims, William			1280	Aug. 3,1838	
185	Sims, Samuel W.			640	Aug. 3,1838	
189	Sherlock, Benj. F.			640	Aug. 6,1838	
220	Street, Sarah			1280	Sept.6,1838	
243	Saunders, Wm. S.			1280	Oct. 4,1838	
250	Smith, John			640	Oct. 4,1838	
262	Sharp, Ellison			1280	Oct. 4,1838	

No.	Name	Lgs.	Lbr.	Acres	Date	Remarks
264	Sharp, Anthony			1280	Oct. 4,1838	
267	Sandlin, John			1280	Oct. 4,1838	
268	Swinford, Seth			1280	Oct. 4,1838	
273	Smith, Sarah			1280	Oct. 4,1838	
286	Stephenson, Joseph A.			1280	Oct. 4,1838	
287	Smith, Robert			640	Oct. 4,1838	
324	Stallcup, William			640	Oct. 4,1838	
327	Shell, James M.			640	Oct. 4,1838	
335	Sage, Gordon F.			640	Nov. 1,1838	
343	Scurlock, William			640	Nov. 1,1838	
359	Simpson, John P.			1280	Nov. 1,1838	
376	Spears, Joseph			1280	Nov. 1,1838	
387	Smith, Tilmon			1280	Dec. 6,1838	
389	Skidmore, Wm.			640	Jan. 3,1839	
390	Shook, Daniel			640	Jan. 3,1839	
396	Seawright, John			1280	Jan. 3,1839	
402	Scott, William			1280	Feb. 7,1839	
411	Scarbough, William			1280	Feb. 7,1839	
415	Sherwood, Absalom			640	Feb. 7,1839	
421	Smith, Sam'l S.			1280	Mar. 7,1839	
2	Shillings, Jacob			640	Mar. 7,1839	
10	Scott, William			640	Mar. 7,1839	
166	Shelton, Jessee			1280	Dec. 5,1839	
512	Spinin, Oliver			640	Dec.28,1839	
734	Saddler, Thos. R.			640	Jan.10,1840	
735	Saddler, John			640	Jan.10,1840	
55	Talbott, Benjamin			640	Aug. 2,1838	
62	Tapp, William			640	Aug. 2,1838	
67	Trusdal, David			640	Aug. 2,1838	
89	Turner, Joshua			1280	Aug. 2,1838	
146	Thomas, David B.			640	Aug. 3,1838	
304	Titus, James			1280	Oct. 4,1838	
187	Titus, Thomas F.			640	Aug. 3,1838	
104	Trimble, Henry			1280	Aug.16,1838	
208	Turner, Sarah			1280	Sept.6,1838	
225	Tailer, Jacob			1280	Sept.6,1838	
240	Tuggle, Jackson			1280	Oct. 4,1838	
249	Thompson, John			1280	Oct. 4,1838	
279	Thomas, John			640	Oct. 4,1838	
281	Thomas, Richard			1280	Oct. 4,1838	
322	Titus, James, Jr.			640	Oct. 4,1838	
332	Tiller, George W.			1280	Oct. 4,1838	
364	Taylor, Addison			640	Nov. 1,1838	
375	Tidmore, Julius			640	Nov. 1,1838	
437	Tudor, Kinsey L.			1280	Dec.23,1839	
110	Urquhart, Allen			1280	Aug. 2,1838	
216	Ury, Amos			640	Sept.6,1838	
272	Vining, Wm. W.			640	Oct. 4,1838	
329	Vining, John J.			640	Oct. 4,1838	
336	Vizur, Peter			1280	Nov. 1,1838	

No.	Name	Lgs.	Lbr.	Acres	Date	Remarks
401	Vizer, Henry F.			640	Feb. 7,1839	
407	Vizer, Andrew J.			640	Feb. 7,1839	
1	Woods, John			1280	Mar. 1,1838	
6	Willis, Elizabeth			1280	May 8,1838	
17	Williams, William D.			640	June 7,1838	
28	Williamson, Matilda			1280	June 8,1838	
30	Walker, Jeremiah			1280	Jy. 5,1838	
31	Walker, Jesse			1280	Jy. 5,1838	
34	Wardlow, David S.			640	Jy. 5, 1838	
36	Watson, Orren D.			640	Jy. 5, 1838	
35	Watson, James			1280	Jy. 5, 1838	
74	Ward, John M.			1280	Aug. 2,1838	
119	Wootten, Wm. W.			640	Aug. 2,1838	
152	Wyatt, James			640	Aug. 3,1838	
181	Wardlow, James			1280	Aug. 3,1838	
201	Williams, Abram A.			1280	Aug.16,1838	
197	Woods, James			640	Aug.16,1838	
215	Ward, Mathias			640	Sept.6,1838	
217	Wheat, Benjamin			1280	Sept.6,1838	
218	Wheat, James			640	Sept.6,1838	
219	Wheat, John			640	Sept.6,1838	
226	Watson, John T.			1280	Sept.6,1838	
229	Walker, James R.S.			1280	Sept.6,1838	
244	Williams, John W.			1280	Oct. 4,1838	
245	Williams, H.L.			1280	Oct. 4,1838	
256	Wheat, William			640	Oct. 4,1838	
257	Witters, Charles K.			640	Oct. 4,1838	
270	Ward, Isaac			640	Oct. 4,1838	Samuel F.Rogers, Assignee.
285	Warnel, Nolly G.			1280	Oct. 4,1838	
326	Williams, Richard N.			640	Oct. 4,1838	
357	Ward, William			1280	Nov. 1,1838	
366	Wallace, Ezekiel P.			1280	Nov. 1,1838	
373	Williams, Warren			640	Nov. 1,1838	
395	Wetherby, William F.			640	Jan. 3,1839	
400	Ward, Rufus M.			640	Feb. 7,1839	
403	Woodall, Wm. P.			640	Feb. 7,1839	
412	Williams, John S.			1280	Feb. 7,1839	
156	Whitford, Sam'l G.			640	Dec. 5,1839	
440	Webb, Nancy			1280	Dec.23,1839	
442	Webb, Joel D.			640	Dec.23,1839	
378	Wideman, Thomas			640	Nov.12,1838	
286	Word, Madison			1280	Dec. 5,1839	
435	Williams, Hiram			1280	Dec.23,1839	
195	Young, William			640	Aug.16,1838	
351	Young, William C.			1280	Nov. 1,1838	
168	Yates, William			640	Dec.5, 1839	

THIRD CLASS

No.	Name	Lgs.	Lbr.	Acres	Date	Remarks
12	Alley, Daniel N.			640	Apr. 5,1839	
23	Alley, James			640	May 27,1839	
44	Anderson, Mathew			320	Jy. 4, 1839	
191	Arrington, Joel			320	Dec. 5,1839	
198	Atkinson, James			640	Dec. 5,1839	
234	Adams, David			320	Dec. 5,1839	
240	Adams, Daniel			320	Dec. 5,1839	
427	Aska, Abner N.			320	Dec.20,1839	
428	Anderson, Russel G.			320	Dec.20,1839	
696	Ashbrooks, Henry			320	Jan. 7,1840	
8	Allen, Richard C.			640	Mar. 7,1839	
7	Baker, James			640	Apr. 5,1839	
15	Bohannan, Jonathan			640	May 2,1839	
28	Bateman, Jonathan			320	May 27,1839	
29	Bateman, James			320	May 27,1839	
30	Bateman, Esaias			320	May 27,1839	
50	Benson, William			640	Jy. 4,1839	
87	Bland, James			320	Nov. 7,1839	
92	Bishop, Elias S.			640	Nov. 7,1839	
103	Barry, Lewis D.			320	Nov. 7,1839	
104	Bailey, John C.			640	Nov. 7,1839	
110	Burris, James M.			640	Nov.13,1839	
116	Barcroft Daniel, Jr.			320	Nov.14,1839	
117	Barcroft, Elisha H.			640	Nov.14,1839	
145	Barcroft, Daniel			640	Dec. 2,1839	
189	Barnett, Elias D.			320	Dec. 5,1839	
190	Bright,Davis			320	Dec. 5,1839	
194	Bright, Henry			640	Dec. 5,1839	
195	Bright, John M.			320	Dec. 5,1839	
201	Burge, James C.			640	Dec. 5,1839	
210	Ballard, Nicholas G.			320	Dec. 5,1839	
225	Baxter, Edward			320	Dec. 5,1839	
265	Brooks, Christopher			640	Dec. 5,1839	
331	Brown, Harrison			320	Dec.12,1839	
341	Bryarly, Thomas F.			640	Dec.14,1839	
342	Bryarly, George M.			320	Dec.14,1839	
348	Brotherton, William W.			320	Dec.14,1839	
408	Barker, William			320	Dec.20,1839	
424	Bishop, Joseph			640	Dec.20,1839	
426	Bannum, Merret			320	Dec.20,1839	
454	Brown, Reuben			640	Dec.23,1839	
463	Bird, Charles I.			320	Dec.24,1839	
492	Binnion, John			320	Dec.28,1839	
493	Binnion, Martin			640	Dec.28,1839	
504	Brock, Moses			640	Dec.28,1839	
509	Brogden, William H			640	Dec.28,1839	
517	Brandon, Heit			640	Dec.28,1839	
520	Bagwell, Milas			320	Dec.28,1839	
521	Bailden, John			320	Dec.28,1839	

No.	Name	Lgs.	Lbr.	Acres	Date	Remarks
532	Brackeen, Wm. G.			640	Dec.28,1839	
533	Brackeen, Wm.			640	Dec.28,1839	
538	Brackeen, W.S.J.			640	Dec.28,1839	
539	Brackeen, Azariah			640	Dec.28,1839	
540	Brackeen, James. M.			640	Dec.28,1839	
541	Brackeen, Samuel			640	Dec.28,1839	
545	Barnet, John			320	Dec.28,1839	
563	Burchum, David			640	Dec.28,1839	
565	Brown John			320	Dec.28,1839	
566	Burchum, Joseph			320	Dec.28,1839	
567	Burchum, David, Jr.			320	Dec.28,1839	
586	Bogart, Russel			640	Jan. 1,1840	
587	Bush, George W.			320	Jan. 1,1840	
588	Bankston, Hamilton			320	Jan. 1,1840	
610	Bean, Jesse E.			640	Jan. 2,1840	
619	Blair, James			640	Jan. 2,1840	
620	Brantley, Josiah			640	Jan. 2,1840	
641	Brown, William			640	Jan. 2,1840	
666	Brandon, Joel D.			640	Jan. 2,1840	
694	Blevins, William			320	Jan. 7,1840	
712	Bradin, Felix G.			320	Jan. 8,1840	
713	Brewer, Hanson			320	Jan. 8,1840	
714	Box, William Y.			320	Jan. 8,1840	
747	Baker, Joseph			640	Jan.11,1840	
757	Brown, William			640	Jan.11,1840	
759	Baker, Henry			320	Jan.11,1840	
772	Bevans, James S.			640	Jan.11,1840	
14	Box, Thomas W.			320	Mar.21,1839	
399	Booth, Stephen S.			320	Dec.20,1839	
43	Caveatte, John			640	Jy. 4,1840	
65	Clifton, William S.			320	Sept.1,1839	
69	Coots, George			640	Sep.14,1839	
70	Coots, Andrew			640	Sep.14,1839	
109	Clement, Egbert N.			320	Nov. 7,1839	
111	Clayton, Daniel			320	Nov.13,1839	
120	Casey, George W.			320	Nov.14,1839	
127	Cullumber, Allen			640	Nov.20,1839	
135	Cline, Peter			640	Nov.23,1839	
149	Crook, John H.			640	Dec. 5,1839	
152	Crook, Lewis J.			320	Dec. 5,1839	
154	Craig, Samuel			320	Dec. 5,1839	
185	Christian, Henry B.			640	Dec. 5,1839	
208	Cason, Larkin			640	Dec. 5,1839	
216	Carson, Seth			640	Dec. 5,1839	
217	Cason, William			320	Dec. 5,1839	
282	Cunningham, Thomas			320	Dec. 5,1839	
302	Clark, Thomas C.			320	Dec. 5,1839	
304	Chapman, George			320	Dec. 5,1839	
309	Clutter, Grant			640	Dec. 5,1839	
366	Cox, Hugh			320	Dec.18,1839	
368	Cuthberth, Willis			320	Dec.18,1839	
377	Curtis, Evin			320	Dec.19,1839	

No.	Name	Lgs.	Lbr.	Acres	Date	Remarks
383	Compton, John			640	Dec.19,1839	
384	Compton, John B.			640	Dec.19,1839	
385	Compton, Jesse			320	Dec.19,1839	
387	Campbell, William; Sr.			640	Dec.20,1839	
388	Campbell, James			640	Dec.20,1839	
389	Campbell, David S.			640	Dec.20,1839	
390	Campbell, William; Jr.			320	Dec.20,1839	
397	Clubbs, Samuel H.			320	Dec.20,1839	
402	Chism, John E.			320	Dec.20,1839	
495	Chism, Elizabeth R.			640	Dec.20,1839	
421	Cornelius, Thomas J.			640	Dec.20,1839	
453	Crook, Richard			640	Dec.28,1839	
489	Click, Wm. Carroll			320	Dec.28,1839	
495	Canavan, John			320	Dec.28.1839	
496	Chappelear, Henry			320	Dec.28,1839	
501	Carter, Hannah W.			640	Dec.28,1839	
508	Clark, John L.			320	Dec.28,1839	
526	Cooper, Nathan			640	Dec.28,1839	
529	Crisp, Mansel R.			320	Dec.28,1839	
571	Chapman, Samuel			640	Dec.28,1839	Deceased
574	Clark, John T.			640	Jan. 1,1840	
576	Cole, Mason			320	Jan. 1,1840	
579	Collins, James W.			320	Jan. 1,1840	
585	Cochran, Lemuel M.			320	Jan. 1,1840	
627	Cherry, Joel			640	Jan. 2,1840	
637	Cox, William B.			640	Jan. 2,1840	
639	Cox, John			320	Jan. 2,1840	
649	Cornelius, Absalom			640	Jan. 2,1840	
650	Cornelius, William P.			320	Jan. 2,1840	
669	Cornelius, Martin D.			320	Jan. 2,1840	
670	Coor, Wiley			640	Jan. 2,1840	
673	Coor, Gaines			320	Jan. 2,1840	
719	Cox, John G.			320	Jan. 8,1840	
748	Comer, Absalom G.			320	Jan.11,1840	
763	Christmas, Richard			640	Jan.11,1840	
15	Crisp, Wm. M.			640	Mar. 7,1839	
3	Dablin, John; Sr.			640	Apr. 5,1839	
5	Dablin, John; Jr.			320	Apr. 5,1839	
13	David, Isaac			320	May 2,1839	
51	Dial, William			320	Jy. 4,1839	
53	Duncan, William B.			640	Aug. 1,1839	
141	Davis, Isham F.			320	Nov.23,1839	
143	Davis, John N.			320	Nov.23,1839	
144	Davis, Nathaniel F.			320	Nov.23,1839	
158	Deister, George			320	Dec. 5,1839	
222	Dodd, Atlas			320	Dec. 5,1839	
260	Doudle, John			320	Dec. 5,1839	
263	Doudle, David			640	Dec. 5,1839	
270	Dobbs, Cyrus			640	Dec. 5,1839	
271	Davis, Jonathan R.			640	Dec. 5,1839	
272	Davis, James			640	Dec. 5,1839	
299	Derriberry, Harvey M.			320	Dec. 5,1839	

No.	Name	Lgs.	Lbr.	Acres	Date	Remarks
386	Draper, Michael			640	Dec.20,1839	
400	Dabby, Ann			640	Dec.20,1839	
430	Driggers, William			640	Dec.20,1839	
490	Davis, Iredell			640	Dec.28,1839	
500	Duty, Jefferson			320	Dec.28,1839	
502	Dukes, Isham			640	Dec.28,1839	
591	Davidson, Hopkins			640	Jan. 2,1840	
677	Doke, David			320	Jan. 2,1840	
679	Davidson, Thomas			320	Jan. 2,1840	
684	Doke, Jane			640	Jan. 2,1840	
685	Davis, William W.			320	Jan. 2,1840	
720	Doss, Thomas C.			320	Jan. 8,1840	
760	Dilliard, George			640	Jan.11,1840	
761	Dalton, Lamarcus			320	Jan.11,1840	
24	Ellett, Ambrose K.			640	May 27,1839	
27	Ellett, William			640	May 27,1839	
56	Ellett, James			640	Aug. 1,1839	
171	Eastham, James			320	Dec. 5,1839	
229	Ellett, Joseph W.			320	Dec. 5,1839	
230	Ellett, John W.			320	Dec. 5,1839	
259	Evans, John			640	Dec. 5,1839	
262	Early, Elbert			640	Dec. 5,1839	
308	Elbert, Benj. Franklin			320	Dec. 5,1839	
391	Edmundson, Turner B.			640	Dec.20,1839	
429	Ellis, William			640	Dec.20,1839	
543	Ester, James II			640	Dec.28,1839	
653	Eskridge, Harvey F.			640	Jan. 2,1840	
659	Evans, Jesse			640	Jan. 2,1840	
661	Evanas, Malkijah			640	Jan. 2,1840	
706	Ewing, Jno. B.S.			640	Jan. 8,1840	
707	Ewing, Charles L.			320	Jan. 8,1840	
708	Ewing, Anthony B.			640	Jan. 8,1840	
712	Evans, Silas			320	Jan. 8,1840	
2	Erwin, Samuel			640	Mar. 7,1839	
20	Figures, Bartholomew			640	May 27,1839	
36	Farris, George			320	May 27,1839	
155	Frazier, Robert E.			320	Dec. 5,1839	
174	Forkner, William H.			640	Dec. 5,1839	
175	Forkner, Greenberry			320	Dec. 5,1839	
176	Forkner, Harvey			320	Dec. 5,1839	
199	Freeze, Gerd			320	Dec. 5,1839	
232	Fowler, William L.			640	Dec. 5,1839	
237	Foster, John T.			320	Dec. 5,1839	
287	Francis, Robert B.			320	Dec. 5,1839	
359	Ferguson, John			320	Dec.14,1839	
425	Finley, William			320	Dec.20,1839	
449	Fields, Isaac N.			320	Dec.23,1839	
479	Faulks, Jacob			640	Dec.28,1839	
487	Flat, William			320	Dec.28,1839	
506	Foster, Thomas E.			320	Dec.28,1839	
519	Featherstone, Edward H.			640	Dec.28,1839	

No.	Name	Lgs.	Lbr.	Acres	Date	Remarks
564	Farmer, Thomas			640	Dec.28,1839	
642	Fleming, Jacob W.			320	Jan. 2,1840	
643	Fleming, John W.			320	Jan. 2,1840	
644	Fleming, Wm. H.			320	Jan. 2,1840	
645	Fleming, James D.			320	Jan. 2,1840	
646	Fleming, Eldridge H.			320	Jan. 2,1840	
686	Frazier, John H.			320	Jan. 2,1840	
717	Farris, Major			640	Jan. 8,1840	
718	Farris, John C.			320	Jan. 8,1840	
777	Fitzgerald, Jesse			640	Jan.12,1840	
86	Griffith, Evan			640	Nov. 7,1839	
106	Grace, Wm. S.			640	Nov. 7,1839	
128	Garrison, Lloyd M.			640	Nov.23,1839	
129	Garrison, James			640	Nov.23,1839	
142	Goolsby, Francis M.			320	Nov.23,1839	
153	Gunter, Charles			640	Dec. 5,1839	
211	Gilitine, Nicholas			640	Dec. 5,1839	
233	Griner, William G.			640	Dec. 5,1839	
314	Gavin, William G.			320	Dec. 5,1839	
328	Giddeons, Isaac			640	Dec.12,1839	
329	Giddeons, Lewis H.			640	Dec.12,1839	
336	Giddeons, Joseph F.			320	Dec.12,1839	
357	Gresham, George W.			320	Dec.14,1839	
362	Guest, Martin			640	Dec.18,1839	
370	Gutry, Lihu			320	Dec.18,1839	
378	Greenhaw, Bazzel S.			640	Dec.19,1839	
379	Gerdes, Gerhard			320	Dec.19,1839	
398	Greenwood, Elijah			640	Dec.20,1839	
409	George, Presley S.			320	Dec.20,1839	
461	George, Jesse H.			320	Dec.24,1839	
462	Garrison, Peter S.			640	Dec.24,1839	
469	Gilim, Dudly			320	Dec.25,1839	
470	Gardner, Samuel			320	Dec.25,1839	
471	Gardner, Jonathan			320	Dec.25,1839	
562	Goodman, Archibald			320	Dec.31,1839	
655	Groom, Rezin E.			320	Jan. 2,1840	
667	Gillispie, Isaac S.			320	Jan. 2,1840	
693	Gilbert, William			320	Jan. 7,1840	
700	Glover, Joseph			320	Jan. 8,1840	
732	Griffin, Thomas J.			640	Jan.10,1840	
12	Gray, James N.			320	Mar. 7,1839	
31	Hale, Benjamin			320	Mar.27,1839	
136	Hix, Arthur			640	Nov.23,1839	
137	Hix, John			320	Nov.23,1839	
138	Hix, Thomas			320	Nov.23,1839	
192	Hill, Hugh H.			640	Dec. 5,1839	
202	Haney, Benjamin B.			320	Dec. 5,1839	
219	Heath, Thomas J.			640	Dec. 5,1839	
254	Hart, John			320	Dec. 5,1839	
255	Hart, Thomas			320	Dec. 5,1839	
268	Hugh, Isaac			320	Dec. 5,1839	

No.	Name	Lgs.	Lbr.	Acres	Date	Remarks
269	Hemphill, Samuel			640	Dec. 5,1839	
277	Hughs, William V.			320	Dec. 5,1839	
279	Hughs, Robert; Sr.			640	Dec. 5,1839	
280	Hughs, Robert; Jr.			320	Dec. 5,1839	
289	Hamilton, Thomas			320	Dec. 5,1839	
290	Hamilton, Robert W.			320	Dec. 5,1839	
291	Hamilton, James M.			320	Dec. 5,1839	
310	Hix, Harvey			320	Dec. 5,1839	
313	Hugh, Robert			320	Dec. 5,1839	
315	Harrison, Gideon			640	Dec. 5,1839	
347	Harrel, Richard			320	Dec.14,1839	
358	Hart, Henry A.			320	Dec.14,1839	
361	Hill, Bernard			320	Dec.14,1839	
369	Harwick, Martin			320	Dec,18,1839	
375	Harris, John			320	Dec.19,1839	
376	Harris, James S.			640	Dec.19,1839	
448	Hines, Solomon			640	Dec.23,1839	
460	Harian, Enos			320	Dec.24,1839	
483	Howard, Patience			640	Dec.28,1839	
486	Howard, Nacy			320	Dec.28,1839	
488	Howard, William			320	Dec.28,1839	
498	Hunter, Edward			320	Dec.28,1839	
505	Hamie, William			640	Dec.28,1839	
546	Hunt, Merrick			320	Dec.28,1839	
547	Hushshau, Jacob			640	Dec.28,1839	
549	Harrison, Samuel			640	Dec.31,1839	
550	Harrison, Francis E.			320	Dec.31,1839	
551	Harrison, James			640	Dec.31,1839	
557	Havarter, Jacob			320	Dec.31,1839	
558	Hovarter, Artemus			320	Dec.31,1839	
559	Hovarter, Ruel			320	Dec.31,1839	
572	Holloway, James			320	Dec.31,1839	
556	High, James			640	Dec.31,1839	
589	Hagerton, Joseph			640	Jan. 1,1840	
592	Harmon, Lewis			320	Jan. 2,1840	
593	Harmon, Jacob			320	Jan. 2,1840	
595	Harris, Lewis			320	Jan. 2,1840	
630	Heffner, Alford			640	Jan. 2,1840	
656	Hart, William			320	Jan. 2,1840	
657	Hutson, John; Jr			320	Jan. 2,1840	
658	Hamilton, Robert H.			320	Jan. 2,1840	
660	House, Joseph B.			640	Jan. 2,1840	
726	Henderson, James			640	Jan.10,1840	
727	Henderson, John			320	Jan.10,1840	
774	Hudson, James			320	Jan.11,1840	
515	Ischoepiski, Albert			320	Dec.28,1839	
762	Ingram, Wm.			640	Jan.11,1840	
16	Johnson John			640	May 2,1839	
62	Jones, Andrew J.			320	Sep. 1,1839	
83	Johns, Stephen B.			640	Oct. 3,1839	
90	Jordan, John W.			640	Nov. 7,1839	

No.	Name	Lgs.	Lbr.	Acres	Date	Remarks
91	Jones, James B.			320	Nov. 7,1839	
220	Jones, Merriman H.			640	Dec. 5,1839	
224	Johnson, William S.			320	Dec. 5,1839	
238	Jones, Charles			640	Dec. 5,1839	
239	Jones, Martin G.			320	Dec. 5,1839	
292	Johnson, William C.			320	Dec. 5,1839	
338	Jackson, Samuel F.			320	Dec.14,1839	
356	Jones, Jno. N.B.			320	Dec.14,1839	
360	Jones, Thomas			320	Dec.14,1839	
363	Jones, Jesse			640	Dec.18,1839	
364	Jones, Henry W.			640	Dec.18,1839	
534	Johns, John			640	Dec.28,1839	
549	Jewe't, Aaron C.			640	Dec.28,1839	
663	Jones, James M.			320	Jan. 2,1840	
39	King, Augustus W.			640	May 27,1839	
72	King, John			640	Oct. 3,1839	
118	King, James			320	Nov.14,1839	
180	Kimbell, William H.			320	Dec. 5,1839	
212	Keith, Stephen			640	Dec. 5,1839	
213	Keith, Gabriel			640	Dec. 5,1839	
214	Keith, Nocodemus			640	Dec. 5,1839	
215	Keith, William			640	Dec. 5,1839	
275	Kidd, Leander			640	Dec. 5,1839	
318	Kaufman, Lovel			640	Dec. 9,1839	
346	Kaufman, James			320	Dec.14,1839	
350	Kerfoot, John W.			320	Dec.14,1839	
381	Kinsey, Peter			640	Dec.19,1839	
382	Kinsey, Thomas			640	Dec.19,1839	
401	Key, Walter T.			320	Dec.20,1839	
406	King, David T.			320	Dec.20,1839	
407	King, John C.			320	Dec.20,1839	
446	King, John N.			320	Dec.23,1839	
511	King, Aswin H.			640	Dec.28,1839	
525	Kizer, William			640	Dec.28,1839	
628	Kimbrough, Joseph T.			640	Jan. 2,1840	
629	Kimbrough, Wm. P.			320	Jan. 2,1840	
728	King, James			640	Jan.10,1840	
17	Looney, David			640	May 27,1839	
38	Lawson, Nicholas R.			640	May 27,1839	
96	Lilly, Hugh B.			320	Nov. 7,1839	
115	Lane, Rial			320	Nov.13,1839	
133	Lafferty, Wesley Daniel			640	Nov.23,1839	
344	Lupton, Johnathan W.			320	Dec.14,1839	
345	Lupton, Joseph			320	Dec.14,1839	
478	Logsden, Joseph			640	Dec.28,1839	
481	Logsden, Alban			640	Dec.28,1839	
561	Love, Thomas			640	Dec.31,1839	
475	Legg, John G.			640	Jan. 1,1840	
594	Lewis, Lacy			640	Jan. 2,1840	
617	Lawhon, Hugh M.			640	Jan. 2,1840	

No.	Name	Lgs.	Lbr.	Acres	Date	Remarks
684	Logsden, John			640	Jan. 2,1840	
738	Lindsey, Robert M.			640	Jan.10,1840	
740	Lakin, Samuel			640	Jan.11,1840	
741	Lakin, George W.			320	Jan.11,1840	
742	Lakin, William			320	Jan.11,1840	
743	Lakin, James W.			320	Jan.11,1840	
1	Lilly, Harris B.			320	Mar. 7,1839	
9	Lane William			640	Mar. 7,1839	
731	Lawton, George F.			320	Jan.10,1840	
6	Monkhouse, John			640	Apr. 5,1839	
19	Morton, Rufus			320	May 27,1839	
34	McAneer, Samuel			640	May 27,1839	
40	McClary, Stephen A.			320	May 27,1839	
41	Morrell, Amos			320	May 27,1839	
52	McClish, James			640	Aug. 1,1839	
54	McClish, John P.			320	Aug. 1,1839	
66	Mathews, Daniel			640	Sep.14,1839	
80	Miller, Richard			640	Oct. 3,1839	
94	Morrison, James			320	Nov. 7,1839	
105	Moore, Ephraim D.L.			640	Nov. 7,1839	
119	Montgomery, James M.			320	Nov.14,1839	
157	Merril, William H.			640	Dec. 5,1839	
164	Moore, Joshua			640	Dec. 5,1839	
182	Merrill, Alexander			320	Dec. 5,1839	
184	Moore, William			640	Dec. 5,1839	
188	McAnear, Andrew J.			320	Dec. 5,1839	
256	Mathews, Barton W.			320	Dec. 5,1839	
258	Merrick, Griffith			640	Dec. 5,1839	
273	McAdams, Bethany			640	Dec. 5,1839	
274	McAdams, William			320	Dec. 5,1839	
284	Miller, John			320	Dec. 5,1839	
288	McGennis, Cornelius			320	Dec. 5,1839	
312	Moran, William H.			640	Dec. 5,1839	
325	Morrow, Alexander M.			640	Dec.12,1839	
334	Mathews, James			640	Dec.12,1839	
354	Martin, Ezekiel H.			320	Dec.14,1839	
392	Mabin, George A.			320	Dec.20,1839	
393	Madden, Albert			320	Dec.20,1839	
394	Mabin, Robert W.			320	Dec.20,1839	
395	Mabin, Alexander			640	Dec.20,1839	
396	Mabin, James B.			640	Dec.20,1839	Deceased
404	Mathews, Robert L.			640	Dec.20,1839	
419	Morris, William			640	Dec.20,1839	
420	Martin, Thomas T.			640	Dec.20,1839	
422	Martin, Tilman			320	Dec.20,1839	
433	Maxwell, Henry			320	Dec.20,1839	
447	Maxwell, Jackson B.			320	Dec.23,1839	
459	Mitchell, Eli H.			320	Dec.24,1839	
468	McAdams, Jeptha			320	Dec.25,1839	
472	McAdams, William; Jr.			320	Dec.25,1839	
473	McAdams, William; Sr.			320	Dec.25,1839	
474	McPherson, David			320	Dec.25,1839	
476	McAnly, Robert			640	Dec.25,1839	

No.	Name	Lgs.	Lbr.	Acres	Date	Remarks
491	McCraw, Jacob			320	Dec.28,1839	
499	Murphy, Abraham			640	Dec.28,1839	
514	McDonald, Alexander W.			640	Dec.28,1839	
518	McKinzie, John W.P.			640	Dec.28,1839	
522	McGonnel, John			640	Dec.28,1839	
527	Millen, Hiram M.			640	Dec.28,1839	
530	May, Jackson T.			320	Dec.28,1839	
555	Marier, Hilliard			320	Dec.31,1839	
568	Millign, Rheace P.			320	Dec.31,1839	
578	Marsh, Jesse			320	Jan. 1,1840	
602	McMenamy, John			640	Jan. 1,1840	
603	McMenamy, John H.			640	Jan. 2,1840	
604	McMenamy, Wm. W.			320	Jan. 2,1840	
605	McMenamy, Isaac A.			320	Jan. 2,1840	
622	Montgomery, John			640	Jan. 2,1840	
623	Montgomery, James			320	Jan. 2,1840	
624	Montgomery, Benson			320	Jan. 2,1840	
640	Mitchell, William S.			320	Jan. 2,1840	
651	McCowen, Roger			640	Jan. 2,1840	
652	McCowen, William			640	Jan. 2,1840	
702	Montgomery, William T.			640	Jan. 8,1840	
703	McNight, Andrew A.			320	Jan. 8,1840	
715	Mathews, John W.			320	Jan. 8,1840	
724	Maddox, Nicholas			640	Jan.10,1840	
730	Moore, Samuel			320	Jan.10,1840	
753	McAnally, Thomas			320	Jan.11,1840	
754	McAnally, John			320	Jan.11,1840	
768	Morrison, Andrew			640	Jan.11,1840	
776	Mathews, David R.			640	Jan.12,1840	
6	Mathews, Robert E.			640	Mar. 7,1839	
778	Mace, John			640	Jan.12,1840	
42	Numan, Jonathan F.			640	Jun. 1,1839	
101	Nall, Joseph H.			640	Nov. 7,1839	
102	Nall, William			640	Nov. 7,1839	
228	Noble, Henry			320	Dec. 5,1839	
320	Nicholson, John J.			640	Dec.12,1839	
321	Nicholson, Braxton B.			640	Dec.12,1839	
322	Nicholson, Granville N.			320	Dec.12,1839	
323	Nicholson, John D.			320	Dec.12,1839	
324	Nicholson, David M.			320	Dec.12,1839	
403	Northington, Marshall W.			640	Dec.20,1839	
467	Nidaver, John			640	Dec.24,1839	
598	Nowell, Isaac J.			640	Jan. 2,1840	
599	Nowel, Bernard O.G.			320	Jan. 2,1840	
600	Nowel, Abram T.			320	Jan. 2,1840	
601	Nowel, Richard A.			320	Jan. 2,1840	
615	Nall, James			320	Jan. 2,1840	
725	Nix, Benjamin			640	Jan.10,1840	
764	Nelson, Alexander			320	Jan.11,1840	
749	Nichols, George			320	Jan.11,1840	
746	Norris, Wm. S.			320	Jan. 8,1840	

No.	Name	Lgs.	Lbr.	Acres	Date	Remarks
21	Orton, Samuel B.			640	May 27,1839	
590	Osmon, Temperance			640	Jan. 1,1840	
751	Odell, James B.			320	Jan.11,1840	
37	Phillips, Lewis			320	May 27,1839	
49	Price, Andrew J.			320	Jul. 4,1839	
61	Porter, William N.			640	Aug.29,1839	
71	Pulliam, William H.			320	Sep.18,1839	
113	Patton, Robert			640	Nov.13,1839	
132	Patton, James M.			320	Nov.23,1839	
165	Percival, Elisha			320	Dec. 5,1839	
172	Pistole, Anthony			640	Dec. 5,1839	
200	Pruitt, William			640	Dec. 5,1839	
205	Piland, Mills			640	Dec. 5,1839	
206	Piland, Jesse H.			320	Dec. 5,1839	
207	Piland, Elijah H.			320	Dec. 5,1839	
248	Pace, Jesse K.H.			640	Dec. 5,1839	
330	Parker, Burrel			640	Dec.12,1839	
337	Parsons, Thomas			640	Dec.12,1839	
339	Parsons, John G.			320	Dec.12,1839	
340	Parsons, Elizabeth			640	Dec.12,1839	
355	Powell, Mathew N.			320	Dec.14,1839	
367	Pickett, William			640	Dec.18,1839	
455	Poe, James			320	Dec.23,1839	
528	Peveter, David			640	Dec.28,1839	
552	Pickens, James P.			320	Dec.31,1839	
553	Pickens, Britton			320	Dec.31,1839	
554	Pickens, Mathew G.			640	Dec.31,1839	
570	Price, Thomas			320	Dec.31,1839	
647	Patterson, George W.			640	Jan. 2,1840	
648	Pope, James			640	Jan. 2,1840	
689	Parsons, Thomas; Jr.			320	Jan. 6,1840	
691	Philley, Bartis			320	Jan. 6,1840	
698	Pennington, Elias			640	Jan. 8,1840	
779	Pennington, Jemima			640	Jan.12,1840	
418	Pendergraft, Thomas			320	Dec.20,1839	
423	Perryman, Alexander			640	Dec.20,1839	
63	Ripley, Ambrose			640	Sep. 1,1839	
64	Ripley, Thomas I.			320	Sep. 1,1839	
74	Rusworn, Francis E.			320	Oct. 3,1839	
84	Rogers, John K.			640	Oct.21,1839	
93	Ritchie, John			640	Nov. 7,1839	
95	Ritchie, John S.			320	Nov. 7,1839	
121	Ridgeway, John			320	Nov.14,1839	
130	Roland, John			640	Nov.23,1839	
146	Rollings, Elias			640	Dec. 2,1839	
147	Robinson, Thomas			320	Dec. 2,1839	
252	Ritchie, Henry			320	Dec. 5,1839	
253	Rogers, Samuel			320	Dec. 5,1839	
257	Ritchie, Cyrus			320	Dec. 5,1839	
261	Richardson, Drury			640	Dec. 5,1839	
278	Robb, James			640	Dec. 5,1839	
281	Reid, Joseph H.			320	Dec. 5,1839	

No.	Name	Lgs.	Lbr.	Acres	Date	Remarks
283	Ross, Washington			640	Dec. 5,1839	
293	Richardson, William			320	Dec. 5,1839	
316	Ray, Grevious			640	Dec. 9,1839	
352	Rather, James A.			320	Dec.14,1839	
371	Roach, Lewis			640	Dec.18,1839	
414	Reed, Joseph			640	Dec.20,1839	
416	Reid, John R.			640	Dec.20,1839	
531	Ray, James M.			640	Dec.28,1839	
584	Rhodespin, James			320	Jan. 1,1840	
631	Rice, Zachariah B.			640	Jan. 2,1840	
662	Reeves,Samuel P.			320	Jan. 2,1840	
699	Ross, David L.			320	Jan. 8,1840	
711	Robinson, John			320	Jan. 8,1840	
737	Redding, Joseph			640	Jan.10,1840	
745	Redding, Joseph T.			320	Jan.11,1840	
746	Redding, Richard M.J.			320	Jan.11,1840	
769	Rolls, Madison			320	Jan.11,1840	
5	Ragan, Gilbert			320	May. 7,1839	
11	Strickland, Joseph			320	Apr. 5,1839	
18	Shule, James C.			640	May 27,1839	
45	Simpson, Thomas			320	Jul. 4,1839	
60	Sawyers, George W.			640	Aug.26,1839	
73	Smith, Frederick			320	Oct. 3,1839	
107	Smith, Robert			320	Nov. 7,1839	
108	Smith, Mary			640	Nov. 7,1839	
114	Smith, Jesse A.			320	Nov.13,1839	
123	Shannon, John			640	Nov.14,1839	
148	Story, Jesse W.C.			320	Dec. 2,1839	
151	Stell, George W.			640	Dec. 5,1839	
186	Sharp, Franklin			320	Dec. 5,1839	
193	Stallings, Abram			320	Dec. 5,1839	
196	Shockley, John M.			640	Dec. 5,1839	
218	Smith, John W.			320	Dec. 5,1839	
241	Skidmore, Thomas			640	Dec. 5,1839	
242	Skidmore, Schuyler B.			320	Dec. 5,1839	
243	Skidmore John			320	Dec. 5,1839	
244	Skidmore, David A.			320	Dec. 5,1839	
285	Stell, Jeremiah			320	Dec. 5,1839	
297	Stell, George W.			640	Dec. 5,1839	
300	Sinclair, Daniel			640	Dec. 5,1839	
303	Shannon, Thomas J.			640	Dec. 5,1839	
304	Stout, Wm. II			320	Dec.12,1839	
326	Smith, Risden			320	Dec.12,1839	
349	Shelly, James			320	Dec.14,1839	
373	Story, Samuel			320	Dec.19,1839	
380	Smithers, John			640	Dec.19,1839	
421	Stanford, Harrison			320	Dec.20,1839	
480	Simon, Edward			640	Dec.28,1839	
484	Scanling, Fielding			320	Dec.28,1839	
485	Simon, William			320	Dec.28,1839	
477	Stuard, William			320	Dec.28,1839	
507	Slater, Sanford G.			640	Dec.28.1839	

No.	Name	Lgs.	Lbr.	Acres	Date	Remarks
510	Slayton, Lucy			640	Dec.28,1839	
524	Straley, Joseph L.			320	Dec.28,1839	
535	Steel, Samuel			640	Dec.28,1839	
580	Stephenson, Joseph			320	Jan. 1,1840	
596	Stallings, Henry			320	Jan. 2,1840	
611	Smith Britian			320	Jan. 2,1840	
612	Smith, Edmund G.			320	Jan. 2,1840	
613	Smith, Lewis			320	Jan. 2,1840	
618	Smith, Francis			320	Jan. 2,1840	
621	Stell, James			640	Jan. 2,1840	
635	Sillovant, Adam			320	Jan. 2,1840	
665	Simpson, Samuel B.			640	Jan. 2,1840	
671	Smith, Robert B.			320	Jan. 2,1840	
672	Smith, Wm. P.			320	Jan. 2,1840	
674	Shaw, Thomas			320	Jan. 2,1840	
678	Smith, Samuel C.			640	Jan. 2,1840	
680	Scott, George			320	Jan. 2,1840	
690	Stansberry, Moses			320	Jan. 6,1840	
704	Stacy, John F.			320	Jan. 8,1840	
710	Simmons, Obadiah			320	Jan. 8,1840	
739	Simmons, Elisha C.			320	Jan.11,1840	
752	Shelton, Harvey			320	Jan.11,1840	
3	Smith Caleb			640	Mar. 7,1839	
7	Stewart, Samuel			640	Mar. 7,1839	
668	Simpson, Thomas			640	Jan. 2,1840	
26	Talbott, Joseph			320	May 27,1839	
81	Taylor, Preston			320	Oct. 3,1839	
88	Titus, George			640	Nov. 7,1839	
89	Titus, George M.			320	Nov. 7,1839	
112	Truit, Wingate			320	Nov.13,1839	
122	Tuel, Patmos			640	Nov.14,1839	
179	Titus, James; Sr.			640	Dec. 5,1839	
181	Tailey, Wm. B.			320	Dec. 5,1839	
245	Thompson, Edward			320	Dec. 5,1839	
311	Thompson, John			320	Dec. 5,1839	
327	Turley, James M.			320	Dec.12,1839	
343	Trigg, William			320	Dec.14,1839	
415	Terry, John			640	Dec.20,1839	
456	Tankersly, Richard			640	Dec.20,1839	
603	Townsend, Elijah			320	Dec.28,1839	
577	Tucker, Thomas E.			320	Jan. 1,1840	
607	Thompson, Jonathan			320	Jan. 2,1840	
632	Twitty, William C.			320	Jan. 2,1840	
676	Taylor, Joseph P.			640	Jan. 2,1840	
729	Thomas, Daniel P.			320	Jan.10,1840	
736	Tyson, John			640	Jan.10,1840	
756	Taylor, Daniel			640	Jan.11,1840	
755	Taylor, Thomas			640	Jan.11,1840	
758	Thomas, William			640	Jan.11,1840	
705	Turner, Edward			320	Jan. 8,1840	
246	Vaught, Montgomery			320	Dec. 5,1839	
247	Vaught, Andrew			320	Dec. 5,1839	

No.	Name	Lgs.	Lbr.	Acres	Date	Remarks
250	Villines, Nathaniel			640	Dec. 5,1839	
432	Vials, Whitfield			320	Dec.20,1839	
458	Vining, Leroy			320	Dec.23,1839	
536	Vance, David			320	Dec.28,1839	
537	Vance, Nancy			640	Dec.28,1839	
33	Winter, Wiley B.			320	May 27,1839	
35	Walker, Wm. J.			320	May 27,1839	
46	White, Benjamin			640	Jul. 4,1839	
47	White, John L.			320	Jul. 4,1839	
48	White, James			320	Jul. 4,1839	
78	Ward, John			320	Oct. 3,1839	
125	Wright, John			640	Nov.20,1839	
126	Wolf, Elijah G.			640	Nov.20,1839	
131	Waggoner, Solomon			640	Nov.23,1839	
150	Wynn, William H.			640	Dec. 5,1839	
163	Williams, Sterling E.			640	Dec. 5,1839	
203	Ward, Andrew			640	Dec. 5,1839	
204	Ward, James A.			320	Dec. 5,1839	
231	Wilson, James M.			320	Dec. 5,1839	
264	Warner, John			640	Dec. 5,1839	
276	Wilkins, Berry			320	Dec. 5,1839	
294	Wilkins, Bishop			640	Dec. 5,1839	
305	Wheat, Samuel			320	Dec. 5,1839	
317	Wright, McQuinny			320	Dec. 9,1839	
332	Wise, William D.			640	Dec.12,1839	
333	Wise, Isaac			640	Dec.12,1839	
372	Woolsey, John			320	Dec.18,1839	
374	Warren, Abel			320	Dec.19,1839	
477	Whilley, Hobsen			640	Dec.28,1839	
482	Wells, Peter			640	Dec.28,1839	
457	White, John H.			320	Dec.23,1839	
494	Walker, John			320	Dec.28,1839	
513	Weathered, Robert			320	Dec.28,1839	
523	Wafer, Joel			320	Dec.28,1839	
542	Wortham, James R.G.			640	Dec.28,1839	
544	Winters, Lewis W.			320	Dec.28,1839	
569	Waggoner, Francis G.K.			320	Dec.31,1839	
573	Woodrow, Simon K.			640	Dec.31,1839	
582	Wilson, James			320	Jan. 1,1840	
583	Wright, Joseph F.			320	Jan. 1,1840	
597	Wilbanks, Gardner			640	Jan. 2,1840	
603	Ward, James A.; Sr			640	Jan. 2,1840	
614	Wellison, Thomas			320	Jan. 2,1840	
615	Wilbanks, Jesse			640	Jan. 2,1840	
636	West, John W.			320	Jan. 2,1840	
675	Wallace, Wm. N.			640	Jan. 2,1840	
682	Watson, John			640	Jan. 2,1840	
701	Walker, Walban			320	Jan. 8,1840	
709	Warton, James			640	Jan. 8,1840	
723	Wilbanks, Hiram			320	Jan.10,1840	
10	Walkup, William			640	Mar. 7,1830	
11	Winter, Lavina			640	Mar. 7,1840	
664	Withers, Stephen T.			320	Jan. 2,1840	

REFUGIO COUNTY

FIRST CLASS

No.	Name	Lgs.	Lbr.	Acres	Date	Remarks
7	Crain, Phebe		1			
8	Fagan, Nicholas		1			
14	Garza, Lucitia de la	1	1			
6	Hart, Elizabeth		1			
10	Hynes, Peter		1			
4	Kehoa, Simon	1/3				James Power,Admr
3	O'Brien, Andrew	1/3				J.W.Bower,Admr.
5	O'Brien, Elizabeth		1			J.W.Bower,Admr.
	Power, John W.	2/3	1			Proved before District Court
9	Riley, Michael		1			
2	Williams, John	1/3				John Fagan,Admr.

SECOND CLASS

No.	Name	Lgs.	Lbr.	Acres	Date	Remarks
6	Cahill, Michael			1280	Oct.12,1839	
22	Miller, Fredric L.			640	Dec.28,1839	

THIRD CLASS

No.	Name	Lgs.	Lbr.	Acres	Date	Remarks
19	Armstrong, John			640	Dec.26,1839	
1	Bryne, William			320	May 26,1839	
10	Cody, Mathew			320	Oct.16,1839	
13	Case, Joel T.			640	Dec. 3,1839	
34	Clark, William			320	Jan. 9,1840	
35	Clark, Henry			320	Jan. 9,1840	
36	Clark, Nancy			640	Jan. 9,1840	
37	Cushman, Carpenter			640	Jan. 9,1840	
39	Collins, Alexander			640	Jan. 9,1840	
40	Compton, George			320	Jan. 9,1840	
15	Drew, Edward			640	Dec. 3,1839	
27	English, Charles			320	Jan. 4,1840	
4	Fox, John			320	Aug.26,1839	
7	Findley, Jeremiah			640	Oct.16,1839	

No.	Name	Lgs.	Lbr.	Acres	Date	Remarks
9	Findley, William			320	Oct.16,1839	
18	Fitzgerald, Edward			640	Dec.26,1839	
33	Freeman, George			320	Jan. 9,1840	
21	Gunderman, Fredric			640	Dec.28,1839	
30	Heikus, Joseph			320	Jan. 7,1840	
16	Keating, Dennis			320	Dec.17,1839	
3	Lawler, Patrick			320	Aug.26,1839	
24	Lowd, John			320	Dec.30,1839	
26	Littig, Joshua W.			320	Jan. 4,1840	
38	Lyons, Francis B.			640	Jan. 9,1840	
11	McDaniel, John			320	Dec. 3,1839	
14	McCray, Archibald			640	Dec. 3,1839	
20	Mann, William			320	Dec.26,1839	
29	Neggeratto, Joseph			320	Jan. 7,1840	
2	O'Brien, Thomas			320	Jun.24,1839	
31	Ortel, William			320	Jan. 7,1840	
17	Power, Richard			640	Dec.26,1839	
8	Ryals, Henry			640	Oct.16,1839	
12	Ransom, Thomas			320	Dec. 3,1839	
25	Ross, John			320	Dec.30,1839	
42	Spooner, Thomas II			320	Jan. 9,1840	
28	Thomburg, William			640	Jan. 7,1840	
32	Truman, Benjamin			640	Jan. 9,1840	
23	Vogle, Fredric			320	Dec.28,1839	
5	Whaland, Michael			320	Aug.26,1839	
41	Woods, Washington			320	Jan. 9,1840	

ROBERTSON COUNTY

FIRST CLASS

No.	Name	Lgs.	Lbr.	Acres	Date	Remarks
146	Anglin, Abraham	3/4	1			
154	Anglin, Elisha		1			
155	Anglin, William	1/3				
175	Anglin, Abraham	1/4				
9	Boggus, Leroy	1/3				
20	Boyne, Griffin	1	1			

No.	Name	Lgs.	Lbr.	Acres	Date	Remarks
70	Bowman	1	1			
86	Boren, Elijah, Dec'd.	1	1			
87	Bond, George	1/3				
103	Bryant, Benjamin	1	1			
111	Burton, Samuel	1	1			
144	Bates, Seth H.		1			
147	Bates, Silas H.	1	1			
42	Boon, James M.	1/3				
49	Chamblee, John	1	1			
48	Carter, Richard		1			
49	Carter, Wiley	3/4	1			
50	Collins, W.; Dec'd.	1/3				M. Reed, Assignee
62	Curry, David	3/4				
63	Curry, Thomas	1	1			
78	Chalmers, John	1				
79	Chalmers, John		1			
107	Campbell, Ruth; Dec'd.		1			Thos, Morrow, Admr.
124	Cox, George W.	3/4	1			
130	Cochran, B.	1				Heirs of.
131	Cochran, B.		1			Heirs of.
140	Copeland, Nicholas	1	1			
141	Copeland, Joseph	1	1			
142	Copeland, John	1/3				
156	Cox, Wm. R.			369		
157	Cox, Samuel H.	1/3				
158	Cox, Ann	1	1			
179	Campbell, David W.	3/4	1			
6	Cooke, A. W.	2/3	1			
18	Campbell, Walter	2/3	1			
39	Copeland, Richard	1/3				
54	Covitt, Andrew; Dec'd.	1	1			
56	Covitt, Richard W.	1/3				
74	Chandler, Eli	1	1			
35	Duncan, Mahala	1	1			
38	Duncan, Charles	1/3				
55	Dawson, Dread	1	1			
61	Dawson, Britten	1/3				
66	Duncan, Greenburry	1/3				
94	Dunn, James, Sr.		1			
105	Dawson, David	1/3				
112	Davlin, Hugh	1	1			
159	Danis, Brinkley		1			
64	Dunham, Dan'l A.	1	1			
117	Eaton, Thomas H.	1/3				
133	Eaton, Alfred P.	1/3				
73	Fullerton, Henry, Sr.		1			
75	Fullerton, Henry, Jr.	1/3				
120	Fullerton, William	1	1			
122	Furguson, Joseph	1	1			

No.	Name	Lys.	Lbr.	Acres	Date	Remarks
123	Furguson, Robert M.	1/3				
163	Fullerton, Henry; Jr.	2/3	1			
92	Farris, Edward	1/3	1			
43	Gravis, John A. F.	1				
44	Gravis, John A. F.		1			
46	Griffin, Moses		1			
52	Galloway, John F.	1	1			
92	Greer, Thomas N. B.	1/3				
151	Greer, Thomas N. B.	2/3	1			
181	Gholson, Samuel		1			
12	Henry, William	1	1			
22	Henry, Hugh		1			
26	Hicks, Alfred	1/3				
27	Hill, John A.	1				
28	Hill, John A.		1			
29	Hill, H. J. A.	1				
30	Hill, H. J. A.		1			
31	Hill, Allen	1				
32	Hill, Allen		1			
33	Hill, James W.	1				
34	Hill, James W.		1			
36	Harl, Leander	1	1			
71	Henry, Robert		1			
69	Hinson, Absolom	1	1			
108	Hudson, James	1				
109	Hudson, James		1			
115	Hudson, John; Dec'd.	1	1			
127	Harlin, Isair		1			
149	Head, James A.		1			
174	Harvey, Thomas	1/3				
15	Harlan, Joseph	1	1			
145	James, James; Dec'd.	1	1			
170	Jones, Wiley; Dec'd.	1	1			Jas. Wilkinson, Admr.
171	Jones, A. J.	1/3				
172	Jones, G. M.	1/3				
15	Jackson, Levi; Dec'd.	1/3				
98	James, Lydia	1				
99	James, Lydia		1			
113	Kimbell, S.A.; Dec'd.	1/4				
114	Kimbell, S.A.; Dec'd.	3/4				
16	Lane, James	1				
17	Lane, James		1			
159	Lockridge, Wm; Dec'd.	1/3				
8	Morrow, Thomas		1			
13	McGrew, Hardin R.	1/3				
10	McGrew, Geo, W.	1/3				
23	McCandless, David	1	1			

No.	Name	Lgs.	Lbr.	Acres	Date	Remarks
24	McGrew, William	3/4	1			
25	McMillan, Andrew	1/4				
41	Matthews, Robert H.	1/3				
45	McGrew, James F.	1				
54	McMillan, Ann	1	1			
60	McMillan, James	1/3				
64	Moss, Wm. L.		1			
65	Millican, A. A.	1	1			
68	Moss, James L.	1	1			
72	McMillan, Edward	1/3				
89	Mumford, David		1			
90	McGrew, J. L.		1			
104	Morgan, H. G.	1/3				
106	McCullough, Jas. A.	1/3				
81	Morrow, Thomas	1				
121	McMillan, Edward	2/3	1			
128	McGrew, George W.	2/3				
129	McDaniel, Jer. K.	1/3				
162	Morgan, A. J.	1	1			
165	Morgan, Wm. J.	1/3				
167	Morgan, George		1			
168	Morgan, Claiborne; Dec'd.	1/3				Geo.Morgan,Admr.
169	Marlin, John		1			
173	Maness, Shadrack		1			
8	Matthews, Joseph	2/3	1			
11	Morgan, Wm. S.	2/3	1			
150	Morgan, Martin; Dec'd.	1/3				
183	McDaniel, Granger	1	1			
150	Neville, Hardin	2/3	1			
96	Owen, Harrison	1				
97	Owen, Harrison		1			
76	Pearce, B. B.	1/3				
88	Proctor, Joseph W.	1/3				
182	Powers, Elijah	1	1			
184	Powers, W. C.	1/3				
86	Parker, John; Dec'd.	1	1			
24	Reed, Wilson	3/4	1			
39	Reed, Michael		1			
74	Reed, Henry		1			
77	Rogers, Stephen		1			
82	Robertson, Geo, W.		1			
125	Rogers, Robert, Jr.		1			
143	Ross, Thomas	1	1			
169	Robinett, Enoch	1/3				
161	Rogers, Robert C.	1	1			
164	Robinett, Thos.; Dec'd.	1	1			E.Robinett,Admr.
75	Reilly, James		1			
18	Slauter, Francis	1	1			
42	Smith, John D.	3/4				
110	Souls, Charles	1/3				

No.	Name	Lgs.	Lbr.	Acres	Date	Remarks
119	Smith, Lee C.	1	1			
152	Smith, Samuel C.;Dec'd.			369		
8	Simons, S. M.; Dec'd.	1/3				
148	Seal, Eli		1			
95	Tinnen, Jerimiah		1			
1	Welch, Joseph	1				
2	Welch, Joseph		1			
3	Welch, Thomas	1/3				
4	Welch, John	1				
5	Welch, John		1			
11	Webb, William	1/3				
14	Wheelock, G. Ripley	3/4				
15	Wheelock, G. Ripley		1			
37	Webb, Azra	1/3				
51	Wheelock, E. L. R.		1			
56	Walker, William	1				
57	Walker, James	1/3				
58	Walker, John	1/3				
83	West, Joseph	1/3				
84	West, John	1				
85	West, John		1			
93	Walker, William		1			
134	Webb, Jesse		1			
138	West, John	1/3				
139	White, Samuel W.		1			
153	West, Joseph	2/3	1			
177	Wheelock, G. W.; Dec'd.		1			
19	Webb, Joseph		1			
55	Wheelock, Geo. W.	1				
85	Welch, John; Dec'd.	1	1			

SECOND CLASS

No.	Name	Lgs.	Lbr.	Acres	Date	Remarks
58	Armstrong, Cavitt			640	Jul. 8,1839	
59	Armstrong, John G.			640	Jul. 8,1839	
157	Anderson, Mathew			640	Dec.14,1839	
9	Barton, David A.			640	May 3,1839	
26	Barton, Thos			640	Jul. 5,1839	
33	Barkley, David			1280	Apr. 4,1839	
44	Barry, John M.			640	Jun. 5,1839	
20	Caraway, Patrick H.			640	Jun. 7,1839	
37	Cattenhead, John E.			1280	Sep. 6,1839	
45	Collins, David W.			640	Sep. 6,1839	
46	Culp, Josiah			640	Sep. 6,1839	
25	Cobb, Stancil			1280	Apr. 4,1839	
26	Cobb, Clark			1280	Apr. 4,1839	
40	Cattenhead, Levi P.			1280	Jun. 6,1839	
16	Dalrymple, Wm. C.			640	May 3,1838	
24	Dunlap, John G.			1280	Jul. 5,1838	
27	Duncan, John			1280	Apr. 4,1839	

No.	Name	Lgs.	Lbr.	Acres	Date	Remarks
24	England, Harvey P.			640	Jul. 5,1839	
27	Fifer, Forest			1280	Jul. 5,1839	
35	Fifer, Bradey			280	Jul. 5,1839	
9	Flint, Wm. F.			640	Mar. 1,1839	
63	Fullerton, John			640	Jul. 8,1839	
160	Flint, Sanford P.			1280	Dec.14,1839	
44	Graham, John			1280	Sep. 6,1838	
41	Grubbs, Friendley			640	Jun. 6,1839	
5	Harden, Allen G.			640	Mar.15,1838	
7	Harrison, James			1280	Apr.19,1838	Wm.C.Watson,Admr
18	Henry, John R.			640	Jun. 7,1838	
31	Hill, W. B.			640	Jul. 7,1838	
60	Harrington, John M.			640	Sep. 6,1839	
78	Holis, David			1280	Aug. 3,1839	
10	Killough, samuel B.			640	May 3,1838	
38	Lewis, Andrew J.			1280	Sep. 6,1838	
55	Louchstone, John			640	Sep. 6.1838	
56	Lawson, John			640	Sep. 6,1838	
90	Lockemy, Hugh			640	Aug. ,1839	
12	McCuistian, Robert			1280	May 3,1838	
13	McMahan, Andrew			640	May 3,1838	
14	Maynard, Oven			640	May 3,1838	H.Owen,Admr.
17	McKnight, Wm			640	May 3,1838	
21	Moreland, John			640	Jun. 7,1838	
29	Menefee, Laban			1280	Jul. 5,1838	
30	McDaniel, Elisha			1280	Jul. 5,1838	
34	Menifee, Thos. S.			640	Jul. 5,1838	
39	Mitchel, M. M.			1280	Sep. 6,1838	
51	Moore, Wm. D.			1280	Sep. 6,1838	
67	Melton, E.			640	Aug. 1,1839	
103	Marlin, Sam'l W.			640	Dec.14,1839	
158	Navarra, Pulaki			1280	Dec.14,1838	Lydia Navarra, Admx.
36	Owens, James J.			640	Jul. 5,1838	
52	Prewet, James			1280	Sep. 6,1838	
70	Preweet, Robert B.			1280	Aug. 1,1839	
	Powers, Andrew J.			1280	Dec.14,1839	
57	Powers, Lewis B.			640	Jul. 1,1838	
2	Robertson, John L.			640	Mar.15,1838	
32	Ridgeway, Wm. M.			1280	Jul. 5,1838	
33	Ridgeway, Jarret M.			1280	Jul. 5,1838	
49	Rizull, Henry			640	Sep. 5,1838	
89	Rogers, A. G.			640	Aug. ,1839	
77	Roberts Wm. W.			640	Aug. ,1839	

No.	Name	Lgs.	Lbr.	Acres	Date	Remarks
11	Springfield, James M.			640	May 3,1838	
40	Smith Franklin			640	Sep. 6,1838	
41	Shepherd, Charles			640	Sep. 6,1838	
53	Stroud, Lagan A.			640	Sep. 6,1838	
54	Stroud, Reden			640	Sep. 6,1838	
59	Shelton, A. M.			1280	Sep. 6,1838	
65	Stroud, S. M.			640	Aug. 4,1839	
66	Stroud, K.			640	Aug. 4,1839	
114	Seneli, Benjamin			640	Dec.14,1839	
19	Tytis, Robert M.			640	Jun. 7,1838	
57	Treadwell, John			1280	Sep. 6,1838	
58	Treadwell, Milton			1280	Sep. 6,1838	
49	Thompson, John S.			1280	Jul. 1,1839	
59	Thompson, Wm. G.			640	Jul. 1,1839	
54	Thompson, Robert			1280	Jul. 1,1839	
79	Underhill, John F.			1280	Aug. ,1839	
22	Vance, John			640	Jun. 7,1838	
48	Vaughn, Albert			1280	Sep. 6,1838	
6	Watson, John D.			640	May 15,1838	
23	Ward, Cyras T.			1280	Jun. 8,1838	
1	Watson, Wm. C.			1280	Mar.15,1838	
67	Ward, Jesse J.			640	Jul. 8,1839	
99	Ward, Wm. R.			640	Dec.14,1839	
133	Webb, Thos			1280	Dec.14,1839	
134	Webb, Morris			640	Dec.14,1839	
136	Webb, Edmund			640	Dec.14,1839	
43	York, II			640	Sep. 6,1839	
47	Young, Thomas			1280	Sep. 6,1839	

THIRD CLASS

No.	Name	Lgs.	Lbr.	Acres	Date	Remarks
12	Allen, John			320	Mar. 1,1839	
14	Buevell, William			640	Mar. 1,1839	
16	Bryant, Joseph			320	Mar. 1,1839	
28	Boon, Mordieai; Sr.			640	Apr. 4,1839	
29	Boon, Mordieai; Jr.			320	Apr. 4,1839	
42	Burns, James			640	Jun. 6,1839	
98	Bayne, William G.			320	Dec.14,1839	
127	Boon, Daniel			320	Dec.14,1839	
132	Brown, John A.			320	Dec.14,1839	
137	Broadwell, George M.			320	Dec.14,1839	
147	Burne, John			640	Dec.14,1839	
148	Burne, Isaac			320	Dec.14,1839	
31	Casey, John			340	Apr. 4,1839	
91	Caroll, John			320	Nov.25,1839	
102	Chambler, Robert			320	Dec.14,1839	

No.	Name	Lgs.	Lbr.	Acres	Date	Remarks
109	Cole, James			320	Dec. 1,1839	
115	Campbell, Squire			320	Dec. 1,1839	
130	Chambler, William			640	Dec. 1,1839	
131	Chambler, George W.			320	Dec. 1,1839	
138	Cavitt, Volney			320	Dec.14,1839	
149	Compton, Richard			320	Dec.14,1839	
156	Cobb, Pinckucy			320	Dec.14,1839	
1	Dawson, Henry			320	Mar. 1,1839	
73	Duncan, Thomas			320	Aug. 1,1839	
113	Davis, Eli			320	Dec.14,1839	
152	Duup, William C.			320	Dec.14,1839	
21	Ellison, Jesse			640	Apr. 4,1839	
69	Eaton, Samuel			320	Aug. 1,1839	
10	Finn, D.P.			320	Mar. 1,1839	
36	Flanigan, Robert E.			640	Apr. 4,1839	
145	Fitz, Hiram H.			320	Dec.14,1839	
146	Foster, William			320	Dec.14,1839	
104	Gragg, Thomas F.			320	Dec.14,1839	
108	Gleason, James M.			320	Dec.14,1839	
17	Harlin, William C.			320	Mar. 1,1839	
30	Higgs, George			640	Apr. 4,1839	
46	Hathaway, Roben C.			320	Jun. 6,1839	
80	Haywood, Henry			640	Aug. 1,1839	
92	Hill, Charles			320	Nov.25,1839	
94	Henry, Hugh E.			320	Nov.25,1839	
95	Henry, John D.			320	Nov.25,1839	
124	Hinson, David			320	Dec.14,1839	
136	Hewlett, James			320	Dec.14,1839	
84	Johnson, Joseph			320	Aug. 1,1839	
124	Jones, James A.			320	Dec.14,1839	
153	Jones, Hezekiah			640	Dec.14,1839	
141	Kerr, William			640	Dec.14,1839	
144	Kilgore, Charles			320	Dec.14,1839	
53	Love, A. C.			320	Jul. 1,1839	
107	Love, James M,			640	Dec.14,1839	
118	Lynde, John M.			640	Dec.14,1839	
142	Langston, Jacob			640	Dec.14,1839	
7	McMillan, George			320	Mar. 1,1839	
22	Martin, Bailey			320	Apr. 4,1839	
34	McCanless, John P.			320	Apr. 4,1839	
37	Mathews, Abner			640	Apr. 4,1839	
100	McCuistion, Noah			320	Dec.14,1839	
101	McMurty, James L.			640	Dec.14,1839	
105	Mallory Patrick			320	Dec.14,1839	
117	McKnight, Jonathan P.			320	Dec.14,1839	
128	Moss, Anson F.			320	Dec.14,1839	

No.	Name	Lgs.	Lbr.	Acres	Date	Remarks
69	Nanny, Charles			320	Aug. 1,1839	
126	Neville, William			320	Dec.14,1839	
5	Patton, E. L.			640	Mar. 1,1839	
36	Porter, Robert H.			640	Apr. 4,1839	
72	Prewett, Henry H.			320	Aug. 4,1839	
106	Pendergast, Luke R.			640	Dec.14,1839	
110	Pendergast, Samuel R.N.			320	Dec.14,1839	
139	Plummer, Jacob			640	Dec.14,1839	Nacissa Plummer Admx.
48	Patrick, Alexander			640	Jun. 6,1839	
32	Raymond, Charles H.			320	Apr. 4,1839	
93	Reed, Elijah			320	Nov.25,1839	
122	Rogers, Stephen; Jr.			320	Dec.14,1839	
2	Smith, William Q.			320	Mar. 1,1839	
4	Swinney, James			320	Mar. 1,1839	
20	Stokes, John			320	Apr. 4,1839	
35	Smith, John E.			320	Apr. 4,1839	
45	Sofield, James			640	Jun. 6,1839	
52	Stokes, Edward P.			320	Jul. 1,1839	
114	Stephens, A. D.			320	Dec.14,1839	
116	Scott, Ensey E.			320	Dec.14,1839	
143	Strother, John I.			320	Dec.14,1839	
119	Travis, Mathias			640	Dec.14,1839	
120	Travis, Alfred			320	Dec.14,1839	
129	Tredwell, William J.			320	Dec.14,1839	
47	VanZant, Neri			320	Jun. ,1839	
112	Vanhorn, Edgar R.			320	Dec.14,1839	
13	Ware, James B.			320	Mar. 1,1839	
87	Webb, James M.			320	Aug. 1,1839	
88	Webb, Joseph H.			320	Aug. 1,1839	
97	Wooburn, John			320	Nov.25,1839	
125	Wagener, Charles			320	Dec.14,1839	
140	West, Wilson			320	Dec.14,1839	
62	Webb, W. C.			320	Jul. 8,1839	

SABINE COUNTY

FIRST CLASS

No.	Name	Lgs.	Lbr.	Acres	Date	Remarks
21	Adams, James M.	1	1			William Defee, Admr.
33	Adams, John M.; Jr.	1/3				
79	Adams, John N.	1	1			
81	Adams, Joseph	1/3				John M. Adams, Admr.

No.	Name	Lgs.	Lbr.	Acres	Date	Remarks
137	Adams, Lewis H.	1	1			G. W. Slaughter, Admr.
627	Adams, John M.; Jr.	2/3	1			
161	Allison, E. C.		1			Received title league.
145	Angling, Drury	1	1			
5	Boren, Wm. W.	1	1			
49	Bailey, James	1	1			
61	Boren, Bazzel W.	1/3				
70	Benton, Jesse	1/3				
78	Brown, Daniel	1	1			
132	Brown, Edward	1	1			
135	Bensley, Seymour S.	1	1			
142	Boyd, John		1			
160	Burrow, John	1/3				
207	Benton, Dorothy	1	1			
208	Benton, Nathaniel	1	1			
174	Benton, Samuel	1	1			
147	Bullock, William	1	1			
640	Bateman, A. D.		1			
	Boyd, John; Jr.	1	1			
3	Caradine, Robert	1	1			
4	Cheveral, John S.	1	1			
22	Crenshaw, Thomas	1/3				Cornelius Crenshaw, Admr.
29	Copeland, John T.	1	1			
59	Clark, Henry	1	1			
62	Clark, Elijah	3/4	1			
63	Collins, Elisha M.		1			Has received a league.
86	Clayton, J. G. W.	1	1			
92	Chilers, John		1			Received title for a league.
95	Coneley, James	1/3				
96	Clark, William; Jr.	1	1			
114	Crenshaw, Cornelius	1	1			
127	Caradine, Isaac	1	1			
128	Christa, Rama	1	1			
168	Curny, James		1			Recieved title for league.
171	Clark, John		1			Recieved title for league.
203	Chisholm, Enoch P.	1	1			
213	Coulson, Wm. S.; Heirs of					Quantity not specified.
252	Crowder, John	1/3				William Isaacks, Admr.
141	Coughran, John	2/3	1			
175	Clark, Wm.; Sr.					2258,000 v'$: rec'd title for balance.

No.	Name	Lgs.	Lbr.	Acres	Date	Remarks
647	Crenshaw, Dan'l	1	1			
201	Cook, Green B.	1	1			Isaac Low,Admr.
489	Caldwell, A. C.	1	1			
53	Clark, James			369		
16	Defee, William					9,410,556 varas, and 1 labor.
58	Donoho, Hiram	1	1			
60	Donoho, William, Jr.	1/3				
84	Dikes, Dennis	1	1			
113	Davis, Cad. W.		1			Received title for a league.
254	Donaho, William		1			Received title for a league.
236	Davis, W.	1/3				
144	Duncan, Jane	1	1			
65	Earl, Matthew	1	1			
68	Eastep, Daniel	1/3				
123	Earl, William	1/3				
129	Eastey, James	1/3				
143	Evans, Joseph	1/3				Samuel D. Mc-Mahon.
628	Eastey, Daniel		1			
6	Easly, John			369		
15	Ford, William M.	1	1			
98	Forsyth, Thos. H. W.	1/3				
191	Frazer, W. B.	1/3				
200	Frazer, A. L.	1/3				
5	Frazer, Harman		1			
13	Grinage, Alvin M.	1	1			
47	Gellatly, Robert	1	1			
72	Gaines, E. P.	1	1			
149	Groce, Larkin		1			Received title for league.
155	Gaines, John B.	1/3				
624	Gibbons, John W.	1/3				
484	Gaines, James		1			
28	Gillaspie, George	1/3				
643	Gibbons, John W.	2/3	1			
7	Huffman, Michael S.	1/3				
34	Hall, Burgess G.	1/3				
44	Hughes, James	1/3				C. J. Williamson, Admr.
75	Hatton, Thomas J.	1/3				
97	Hill, Moses	1	1			
105	Hines, William	1	1			
139	Humphreys, Jesse C.	1/3				John Boya,Admr.
154	Huson, Charles B.	1/3				
192	Horton, John	1	1			
190	Horton, James	1/3				

No.	Name	Lgs.	Lbr.	Acres	Date	Remarks
189	Harris, Wm. H.	1	1			
220	Hyer, Absalom	1	1			
622	Hines, Elbert	1	1			
623	Hines, Davis	1/3				
642	Hathaway, Henry	1/3				
483	Hale, John C.	1	1			Samuel Davis, Admr.
165	Herring, William	1/3				
625	Hoket, E. W.		1			
629	Holt, Thomas	1/3				
621	Irvine, James T. P.		1			
156	Isaacs, William		1			Received title for league.
12	Joel, Richard R.	1	1			
26	Jackson, Curtis M.			369		
88	Jackson, Susannah	1	1			
103	Jackson, Thomas J.		1			Received title for league.
4	Jackson, Curtis M.	1/4				
640	Jacobs, John G.	1/3				
14	Knight, Frederick	1	1			
43	Kinght, Joseph	1/3				
37	Large, Jacob	1	1			
38	Large, Abraham	1	1			
40	Latham, Jerimiah		1			Received Title for league.
41	Love, Robert S.	1/3				
150	Lawson, John	1	1			
164	Low, Joel	1/3				
206	Low, Jesse	1	1			
137	Love, Joseph	1	1			
648	Low, Eli		1			
631	Latham, Lewis		1			Received title for league.
649	Laue, John	1/3				
648	Linsey, Owen II	2/3	1			
1	Low, Isaac H.	1/3				
3	Low, Isaac H.		15			
2	McKeane, John	1	1			
11	McCarter, John M.	1	1			
25	Martin, Henry	1	1			
30	Maxamillian, Joseph	1/3				
35	Maxamillian, John; Sr.	1	1			
42	Mason, James	1	1			
67	Maxamillian, John; Jr.	1	1			
66	Monette, Narciss	1	1			
80	Means, William		1			
82	Miller, Edward	1/3				John M. Adams, Admr.

No.	Name	Lgs.	Lbr.	Acres	Date	Remarks
87	Mariott, Joseph T.	1/3				
107	McMahen, James B.	1	1			
109	Mitchell, Moses	1	1			
111	Mason, John	1	1			
112	Mitchell, James M.	1/3				
115	McKim, James		1			Has received title for league
117	McKim, William	1/3				
121	McKim, Charles	1/3				
125	Mills, Granville	1	1			
130	Mason, William	1	1			
137	Means, Racgaek	1	1			
172	Melton, Elizabeth	1	1			
177	Morris, Alfred	1	1			
192	Mopping, Jesse	1	1			Luke J. Presnal Admr.
204	McCarter, S. M.	1/3				
205	McCarter, Winston H.	1/3				
249	Mason, Anna	1	1			John Mason,Admr.
250	McGee, A.		1			
235	Mackey, Naomi		9			Received title for 17 labors.
630	Mitchell, A. T.	1	1			
634	Miller, Leroy			369		
646	McKim, Charles	2/3	1			
2	Miller, Leroy	2/3	1			
9	Morgan, John F.; Dec'd.	1/3				Curtis M. Jackson, Admr.
244	McMahons, Samuel D.		1			
217	McCuller, B.	1/3				
54	McLane, Neill	1	1			
56	Murphrey, Willis		1			
251	Nichols, Henry		1			
626	Nichols, Robert	1/3				
76	Odom, Brittian		1			Received title for league.
100	O'Neill, William	1/3				
24	Presnal, Luke J.	1	1			
57	Parker, Moses L.	1	1			
64	Payne, Benjamin W.	1/3				
77	Price, Hardy W.	1/3				
159	Pace, John	1/3				
162	Payne, Epps D.	1	1			
163	Pace, Isaac F.	1/3				
190	Payne, John	1	1			
644	Pace, Isaac F.	2/3	1			
	Patterson, James					No. & qaun'y in orig'l ret'ns blank
7	Parker, Willis	1/3				Mathew Parker, Admr.

No.	Name	Lgs.	Lbr.	Acres	Date	Remarks
8	Parker, William S.			369		Curtis M. Jackson, Admr
308	Pace, William	1	1			Isaac F. Pace, Admr.
6	Randolph, L. C.	1	1			
19	Ryal, John J.	1	1			
20	Renfro, Isaac	1	1			
23	Ryans, James	1/3				
27	Ragsdale, William	1	1			
45	Russell, Jesse, Sr.	1	1			
46	Russell, Jesse, Jr.	1/3				
48	Russell, Jonathan	1	1			
52	Roberts, Sion	1	1			
85	Russell, Margarett	1	1			
93	Ragsdale, Peter C.	1/3				
106	Riddle, George			369		
120	Russell, Henry	1/3				
134	Richardson, Daniel		1			Received title for league.
151	Roberts, Charles, Sr.	1	1			
152	Richards, Francis	1/3				
158	Rowe, James	1	1			
178	Ragsdale, Nimrod	1	1			Peter C. Ragsdale, Admr.
179	Ragsdale, Edward B.	1/3				
209	Riley, James	1	1			
638	Renfro, David	1	1			
166	Robinson, William	1	1			
50	Smith, James M.	1/3				
89	Smith, Major		1			
99	Smith, F. L.	1	1			
101	Scurlock, William	1	1			
104	Sparks, William F.	1	1			
118	Slaughter, Geo. W.	1	1			
136	Slaughter, James W.	1/3				
138	Slaughter, William	1	1			
140	Smith, Marcus	1/3				John Boyd,Admr.
169	Smith, Robert	1	1			
193	Slaughter, Samuel	1/3				
222	Smith, Philip	1/3				
140	Smith, John		1			
235	Sturrock, William	1	1			Robert Gellaty, Admr.
72	Thomas, James		1			Received title for league.
90	Tippet, James	1	1			
91	Tines, Sylpha	1	1			
119	Tippet, Andrew	1/3				
148	Taylor, William	1	1			
176	Tippet, Robert	1/3				
194	Taylor, William	1/3				

No.	Name	Lgs.	Lbr.	Acres	Date	Remarks
221	Tippet, William	1/3				
645	Taylor, John		1			
55	Vickers, Harris	1	1			
1	Walker, Jacob; Dec'd.	1	1			Absalom Hyer, Admr.
9	Weatherred, Francis M.	1	1			
10	Weatherred, Wm. C.	1/3				
17	Walters, Anthony W.	1/3				
18	Walters, Alexander	1	1			
31	Weatherred, Banjn. F.	1/3				
32	Williams, Young	1	1			
51	Westover, Jonathan	1/3				
73	Williamson, Charles J.	1/3				
116	Williams, James W.	1	1			
126	White, Elizabeth	1	1			
131	Wilson, William	1/3				
133	Walker, Jessee	1	1			
193	Warren, Lewis			369		L. C. Randolph, Admr.
199	White, Martin D.		1			Has received title for league
197	Webb, William		1			G.W. Jones, Admr rec'd tit. for
210	Williams William	1	1			
211	White, Benajmin	1	1			
212	Weatherred, F. M.; Jr.	1/3				
230	Wilson, Jefferson		1			
143	Wingate, A. C.	1/3				
637	Williams, William H.	1/3				
424	Williams, Abner O.	1	1			
110	Yates, Thomas	1	1			
144	Young, Pleasant	1	1			

SECOND CLASS

No.	Name	Lgs.	Lbr.	Acres	Date	Remarks
	Banta, John			1280		
	Crawford, Jacob; Sr.			1280		
	Crawford, Jacob; Jr.			640		
	Chisholm, Joseph			640		
	Chancy, F. F.			640		
	Cole, John			640		
	Carter, E. M.			1280		
	Carter, Jesse M.			640		
	Campbell, John T.			1280		
	Cauble, John W.			640		
	Crawford, John F.			640		
39	Capps, Abiathar B.			1280	Jul. 4,1839	

No.	Name	Lgs.	Lbr.	Acres	Date	Remarks
44	Crawford, Samuel M.			640	Jul. 4,1839	
95	Champion, Elisha			640	Nov. 8,1839	
	Daimwood, David			640	Nov. 8,1839	
	Daimwood, Henry			640	Nov. 8,1839	
	Delany, James			1280	Nov. 8,1839	
	Davidson, Solomon			640	Nov. 8,1839	
	Derenny, Richard			640	Nov. 8,1839	
26	Dowell, James			640	Nov. 8,1839	
	Deoly, Mary			1280	Nov. 8,1839	
	Davis, John			1280	Nov. 8,1839	
	Devenny, Ebenezer			640		
94	Daimwood, John W.			640		
154	Daimwood, Henry, Jr.			640		
155	Daimwood, David			640		
	Estes, Bethlehem			1280		
	Frazer, M. G.			1280		
	Frazer, John			1280		
	Green, William			640		
	Gray, Amos H.			640		
	Gaines, F. T.			640		
	Gibson, R. T.			1280		
	Garrett, Howell			1280		
	Garrett, Scott			640		
	Gomer, James F.			1280		
18	Gann, John D.			640		
102	Griffin, Thos J.			640	Nov. 8,1839	
25	Hinkley, Walter			640		
29	Holbert, Joel			1280	Jun. 7,1839	
30	Holbart, Stephen			1280	Jun. 7,1839	
117	Harris, Ezekiah R.			640	Dec. 9,1839	
	Johnson, James H.			1280		
	Kendal, Almon			1280		
	Kendal, Christean			1280		
	Kendal, Conved			1280		
36	Lee, James A.			1280	Jun.20,1839	
378	Leagrone, Martin			640	Jan. 9,1840	
	Lowrie, William			1280		
14	Millican, Hugh			640		
	McRae, John H.			640		
	McCullock, H. E.			640		
	McDonald, Ira			1280		
	Mitchell, Seth W.			1280		
	Miers, Dennis			640		
	Melton, Geo. W.			640		
	McAdoo, Nancy			1280		

No.	Name	Lgs.	Lbr.	Acres	Date	Remarks
	Mitchom, James			1280		
	Mazy, Thomas			640		
4	McGuire, Lawrence			1280	Jun. 7,1839	
27	Norford, Gideon A.			640		
	Ogden, James S.			1280		
21	Packer, Joseph B.			1280		
46	Palmer, Wilson L.			1280		
86	Parker, James			1280		
	Renfro, William			1280		
28	Ridgeway, Johnathan			640		
	Sanford, Robert			1280		
	Southernor, John			1280		
	Sensabaugh, J.			640		
	Shermon, Jason			1280		T. Jackson,Admr
	Thompson, James H.			640		
	Temmenson, Taylor			640		
	Welch, David			1280		
	Wiagate, Sterne			1280		
	Wyche, John			640		
	Wyche, Wm. P.			1280		
	Westfall, Zachariah			1280		
75	Wilder, Edward			640	Sep. 6,1839	
153	Wingate, Stepehn			1280	Dec.17,1839	
196	White, Alexander			1280	Jan.13,1840	
196	Williams, Littleton R.			640		
	Young, Abner H.			1280		

THIRD CLASS

No.	Name	Lgs.	Lbr.	Acres	Date	Remarks
55	Ashmore, William			640	Sep. 6,1839	
57	Ashmore, Henry			640	Sep. 6,1839	
58	Ashmore, Paschal			320	Sep. 6,1839	
98	Ard, Neil			640	Nov. 8,1839	
100	Arnold, Benjamin			320	Nov. 8,1839	
101	Ashmore, Spencer			320	Nov. 8,1839	
115	Anding, Abraham			640	Dec. 9,1839	
173	Asken, Casey			320	Dec.19,1839	
178	Asken, Henry			640	Dec.19,1839	
195	Armstrong, James H.			640	Dec.20,1839	
259	Askew, William			320	Dec.26,1839	
292	Andees, James			320	Dec.30,1839	
364	Adams, Mary			640	Jan. 9,1840	
365	Adams, Joseph R.			640	Jan. 9,1840	
366	Adams, Hugh H.			320	Jan. 9,1840	

No.	Name	Lgs.	Lbr.	Acres	Date	Remarks
1	Brown, Thomas M.			320	May 23,1839	
2	Brown, Samuel P.			320	May 23,1839	
3	Bennett, Arlemas			640	May 23,1839	
5	Bishop, Oliver W.			640	Jun. 7,1839	
38	Burks, John P.			640	Jul. 4,1839	
41	Barnett, John C.			640	Jul. 4,1839	
50	Burks, Wm. B.			320	Sep. 5,1839	
77	Blackman, David			640	Oct. 3,1839	
78	Blackman, John			320	Oct. 3,1839	
88	Brown, James S.			320	Oct. 3,1839	
91	Brown, Joshua D.			640	Nov. 8,1839	
96	Bessonett, Wm. T.			320	Nov. 8,1839	
108	Barber, George			640	Nov. 8,1839	
109	Barber, Phineas W.			320	Nov. 8,1839	
114	Bott, James P.			640	Dec. 9,1839	
127	Boyd, George W.			640	Dec.14,1839	
145	Beth, Angus P. M.			640	Dec.17,1839	
163	Buchanan, John W.			320	Dec.18,1839	
169	Bradshaw, Enoch			640	Dec.19,1839	
179	Balance, Ragfold C.			640	Dec.19,1839	
183	Bliss, Patrick R.			320	Dec.19,1839	
198	Brinkley, Elisha			320	Dec.21,1839	
200	Baines, William C.			640	Dec.21,1839	
214	Barnett, S. Slade			640	Dec.21,1839	
219	Barnett, Wm. H. H.			320	Dec.23,1839	
222	Black, James M.			640	Dec.23,1839	
230	Benson, James			320	Dec.24,1839	
231	Benson, Alenson			320	Dec.24,1839	
232	Benson, Eden			320	Dec.24,1839	
276	Brown, William			320	Dec.28,1839	
279	Burt, John, Jr.			320	Dec.28,1839	
281	Burt, John, Sr.			640	Dec.28,1839	
286	Brown, David, Sr.			640	Dec.28,1839	
288	Brown, William			640	Dec.28,1839	
300	Burrough, Philip			320	Dec.30,1839	
315	Boothe, Abraham			640	Dec.30,1839	
316	Boothe, James			320	Dec.30,1839	
337	Burkes, James			320	Dec.31,1839	
343	Brown, Martin J.			640	Dec.31,1839	
367	Bennett, Mary			640	Jan. 9,1840	
368	Bennett, Daniel G.			320	Jan. 9,1840	
371	Brown, John F.			320	Jan. 9,1840	
372	Bass, Jordan			320	Jan. 9,1840	
263	Brighton, Margaret G.			640	Jan. 9,1840	
6	Carlton, James M.			640	Jun. 7,1839	
19	Cartrell, James			640	Jun. 7,1839	
42	Carpenter, Dangerfield			640	Jul. 4,1839	
43	Crenshaw, Nathaniel			320	Jul. 4,1839	
64	Cauble, John W.			640	Sep. 6,1839	
65	Carlton, John C.			640	Sep. 6,1839	
76	Coleman, Alexander			640	Sep. 6,1839	
92	Criswell, Thomas			320	Nov. 8,1839	

No.	Name	Lgs.	Lbr.	Acres	Date	Remarks
99	Cathey, John D.			320	Nov. 8,1839	
113	Cose, John L.			320	Dec. 9,1839	
159	Cansay, Solomon			320	Dec.18,1839	
223	Cooper, William			320	Dec.24,1839	
234	Carter, William			320	Dec.24,1839	
248	Collins, Seymour R.			320	Dec.26,1839	
251	Collins, Hiram			320	Dec.26,1839	
273	Corbett, Charles A.			640	Dec.27,1839	
287	Cooper, Carroll			320	Dec.28,1839	
297	Chaney, Loveless R.			320	Dec.30,1839	
296	Chaney, Asa N.			320	Dec.30,1839	
320	Carpenter, Andrew W.			320	Dec.31,1839	
321	Carpenter, William G.			320	Dec.31,1839	
329	Cobb, Lowrey			640	Dec.31,1839	
342	Cambern, James B.			320	Dec.31,1839	
370	Carter, William W.			320	Jan. 9,1840	
385	Campbell, DAvis			320	Jan.12,1840	
210	Cleaveland, Wm. H.			640	Dec.21,1839	
34	Dement, Robert H.			320	Jun. 7,1839	
112	Doen, Bennett, J.			320	Dec. 9,1839	
142	Dickerson, William			640	Dec.17,1839	
217	Davis, Burnham			320	Dec.21,1839	
243	Duncan, William R.			320	Dec.25,1839	
304	Duncan, David			640	Dec.28,1839	
307	Davis, Timothy H.			640	Dec.28,1839	
348	Dobson, William T.			320	Dec.31,1839	
374	Davis, Madison H.			320	Jan. 9,1840	
12	Estill, Jefferson			320	Jun. 7,1839	
119	Eddins, Theophilus			320	Dec.10,1839	
227	Ewing, Samuel			320	Dec.24,1839	
271	Easley, John B.			320	Dec.27,1839	
360	Eubanks, Hatch			320	Jan. 1,1840	
20	Flowers, Wm. O.			320	Jun. 7,1839	
47	Fort, Frederick			640	Aug. 1,1839	
59	Faircloth, Wiley			320	Sep. 5,1839	
61	Fearing, Frederick A.			320	Sep. 6,1839	
67	Fulgham, James H.			640	Sep. 6,1839	
70	Fulgham, Henry			320	Sep. 6,1839	
89	Fearing, Martin			640	Oct. 3,1839	
121	Franklin, William			320	Dec.13,1839	
137	Fuller, Henry			320	Dec.16,1839	
172	Fulgham, Ezekiel T.			640	Dec.19,1839	
176	Fulgham, Jesse			320	Dec.19,1839	
177	Fulgham, Robert C.			640	Dec.19,1839	
191	Ferguson, Roland			320	Dec.19,1839	
298	Filley, Peery			320	Dec.28,1839	
299	Filley, Levi C.			320	Dec.28,1839	
37	Gamblin, John			640	Jun.20,1839	
162	Green, Joseph W.			322	Dec.18,1839	

No.	Name	Lgs.	Lbr.	Acres	Date	Remarks
164	Green, Robert F.			320	Dec.18,1839	
190	Grimes, Thomas R.			320	Dec.19,1839	
218	Goodrich, John			320	Dec.21,1839	
239	Gaines, Benjamin J. H.			320	Dec.24,1839	
261	Gillaspie, John D.			640	Dec.26,1839	
305	Gordon, Thomas			320	Dec.28,1839	
10	Harris, William			640	Jun. 7,1839	
14	Harrison, Retemer			640	Jun. 7,1839	
24	Harrison, Albert A.			320	Jun. 7,1839	
26	Higgins, John			320	Jun. 7,1839	
27	Hester, Willis			640	Jun. 7,1839	
83	Hobbs, John			640	Oct. 3,1839	
84	Harris, Seabourn			640	Oct. 3,1839	
97	Huffman, Owen			320	Nov. 8,1839	
104	Hobbs, Preston W.			320	Nov. 8,1839	
110	Hinds, Homer			320	Nov. 8,1839	
116	Harris, John A.			640	Dec. 9,1839	
122	Harris, Ausborn			640	Dec.13,1839	
141	Hopson, Zachariah			640	Dec.17,1839	
143	Hadley, Simon P.			320	Dec.17,1839	
185	Harris, Hartwell G.			320	Dec.10,1839	
194	Hendson, Jackson			320	Dec.19,1839	
201	Harris, Theophilus			640	Dec.21,1839	
202	Harris, Wm. D.			320	Dec.21,1839	
204	Hokil, Richard			320	Dec.21,1839	
206	Harvey, John D.			640	Dec.21,1839	
207	Harvey, Robert S.			320	Dec.21,1839	
215	Haight, James L.			320	Dec.21,1839	
254	Harris, Jesse			320	Dec.26,1839	
263	Harris, Peter			320	Dec.26,1839	
340	Hardwick, James			320	Dec.31,1839	
345	Hampton, Anthony			640	Dec.31,1839	
346	Haughton, Kennedy			640	Dec.31,1839	
357	Harris, Matthew			320	Jan. 1,1840	
362	Harris, Sarah			640	Jan. 2,1840	
49	Huffman, Charles B.			640	Sep. 5,1839	
330	Herlock, Vincent			640	Dec.31,1839	
240	Huffman, Owen			320	Dec.24,1839	
21	Ivy, Micajak			640	Jun. 7,1839	
22	Ivy, Isaiah			640	Jun. 7,1839	
23	Ivy, Jeremiah			640	Jun. 7,1839	
31	Ivy, Isaiah, Jr.			320	Jun. 7,1839	
313	Irby, William B.			320	Dec.30,1839	
93	Jackson, John M.			320	Nov. 7,1839	
295	Jackson, Rufus			320	Dec.28,1839	
326	Jones, James M.			320	Dec.31,1839	
327	Jones, Joshua D.			640	Dec.31,1839	
328	Jones, John F.			640	Dec.31,1839	
339	Johnson, Benjamin C.			320	Dec.31,1839	

No.	Name	Lgs.	Lbr.	Acres	Date	Remarks
103	Kendal, Henry A.			640	Nov. 8,1839	
174	Kirkwood, George			640	Dec.19,1839	
220	Kilpatrick, Joseph N.			640	Dec.23,1839	
221	Kilpatrick, Wesley M.			320	Dec.23,1839	
233	Kelly, Joseph			320	Dec.24,1839	
256	Kelso, Andrew F.			320	Dec.26,1839	
293	King, Andrew C.			320	Dec.30,1839	
302	Knowles, Reuben			320	Dec.30,1839	
318	King, William			640	Dec.31,1839	
319	King, Miles			320	Dec.31,1839	
351	King, Davis			640	Dec.31,1839	
353	King, Madison			320	Dec.31,1839	
11	Latham, Beverly D.			320	Jun. 7,1839	
40	Low, John C.			320	Jul. 4,1839	
107	Lemore, Franklin M.			320	Nov. 8,1839	
120	Langford, Nicholas			320	Dec.13,1839	
156	Leher, John			320	Dec.18,1839	
165	Lott, Absalom			640	Dec.18,1839	
166	Lott, Jackson			640	Dec.18,1839	
175	Leonard, Washington			320	Dec.18,1839	
238	Loring, Henry W.			320	Dec.24,1839	
242	Lewis, Robert B.			640	Dec.25,1839	
312	Little, Matthew T.			640	Dec.30,1839	
325	Little, Moses			320	Dec.31,1839	
379	Leagrone, Washington			320	Jan. 9,1840	
380	Lathrage, Wm.; Dec'd.			320	Jan.13,1840	Luke Presnal, Admr.
7	McKay, Michael V. R.			320	Jun. 7,1839	
9	Martin, G. Lyeurqus			640	Jun. 7,1839	
15	Montgomery, Archibald			640	Jun. 7,1839	
16	Martin, George W.			640	Jun. 7,1839	
17	Martin, John D.			640	Jun. 7,1839	
52	Milford, John S.			640	Sep. 5,1839	
74	Mason, Job			320	Sep. 6,1839	
80	Mitchell, Ashur G.			640	Oct. 3,1839	
81	Merchant, Richard M.			640	Oct. 3,1839	
85	Meador, Silas			640	Oct. 3,1839	
123	Millican, Oliver H.			640	Oct.14,1839	
132	Miller, James R.			320	Dec.14,1839	
139	Morris, John W.			320	Dec.17,1839	
170	Milton, Jarriott E.			640	Dec.19,1839	
180	Massingale, John			640	Dec.19,1839	
181	Meador, Richard			640	Dec.19,1839	
187	Matlock, James M.			640	Dec.19,1839	
192	Martin, William			640	Dec.19,1839	
193	Martin, Thomas J.			320	Dec.20,1839	
212	Moseley, Daniel			640	Dec.21,1839	
246	Morton, Pleasant W.			320	Dec.25,1839	
252	McMahon, John B.			640	Dec.26,1839	
253	McAdoo, Samuel H.			320	Dec.26,1839	
280	Mixon, William			320	Dec.28,1839	

No.	Name	Lgs.	Lbr.	Acres	Date	Remarks
284	Middleton, William			640	Dec.28,1839	
290	Mitchell, John W.			640	Dec.28,1839	
306	Mitchell, Wm. W.			640	Dec.30,1839	
308	Mitchell, Alsbury H.			640	Dec.30,1839	
309	McCollum, Andrew J.			320	Dec.30,1839	
314	McGuire, Hamilton B.			640	Dec.30,1839	
338	Martin, Robert W.			640	Dec.31,1839	
350	Miller, Pleasant M.			320	Dec.31,1839	
352	McGown, George			640	Dec.31,1839	
354	McLester, James			320	Jan. 1,1840	
373	Melton, George			320	Jan. 9,1840	
376	Mackey, John F.			320	Jan. 9,1840	
382	Mulholland, Bunard			320	Jan.13,1840	
377	McCredice, John			320	Jan. 9,1840	
208	Northcott, Joel W. C.			640	Dec.21,1840	
211	Nickle, Thomas			320	Dec.21,1840	
369	Naylor, Archibald W.			640	Jan. 9,1840	
140	Owens, Owen M.			640	Dec.17,1839	
152	Oliphant, Alfred D.			320	Dec.18,1839	
157	Oliphant, Bluford A.			320	Dec.18,1839	
268	Oliphant, Hiram S.			320	Dec.26,1839	
291	Orr, William S.			640	Dec.30,1839	
341	Ogle, Michael			320	Dec.31,1839	
105	Palmer, William			640	Nov. 8,1839	
106	Potter, Benjamin D.			640	Nov. 8,1839	
128	Presnall, William			320	Dec.14,1839	
129	Partlow, Elijah			640	Dec.14,1839	
130	Phillips, Wm. M.			640	Dec.14,1839	
133	Partlow, Elijah J.			640	Dec.14,1839	
134	Partlow, Richard B. H.			320	Dec.14,1839	
135	Partlow, Wm. E. J.			320	Dec.14,1839	
144	Polley, Robert			640	Dec.17,1839	
146	Polley, John			320	Dec.17,1839	
147	Polley, Thomas F.			320	Dec.17,1839	
160	Penn, George F.			640	Dec.18,1839	
216	Painter, Wm. G.			640	Dec.21,1839	
225	Pearce, Winton D.			320	Dec.24,1839	
229	Petty, John M.			320	Dec.24,1839	
244	Payne, Augustus J.			640	Dec.25,1839	
247	Phinney, James			320	Dec.26,1839	
257	Pinnell, Ellen			640	Dec.26,1839	
275	Parsons, James C.			320	Dec.27,1839	
282	Price, Jackson			320	Dec.28,1839	
310	Patton, John A.			640	Dec.30,1839	Lawrence McGuire Admr.
347	Patterson, Pleasant W.			320	Dec.31,1839	
359	Pitts, Stephen			320	Jan. 1,1840	
375	Patterson, Harriet			640	Jan. 1,1840	
383	Payne, William M.			320	Jan.13,1840	
384	Powell, Tilman			320	Jan.13,1840	

No.	Name	Lgs.	Lbr.	Acres	Date	Remarks
311	Quartemus, Patrick			640	Dec.30,1839	
8	Randal, Leonard			640	Jun. 7,1839	
13	Ridgeway, Elizabeth			640	Jun. 7,1839	
25	Ridgeway, James H.			320	Jun. 7,1839	
48	Rash, Robert C.			640	Aug. 1,1839	
60	Ratcliff, Edward			640	Sep. 6,1839	
66	Ratcliff, William			640	Sep. 6,1839	
68	Ratcliff, James			320	Sep. 6,1839	
69	Ratcliff, Rufus K.			320	Sep. 6,1839	
136	Romtree, Robert			640	Dec.14,1839	
138	Rhodes, Nathaniel H.			640	Dec.17,1839	
148	Renfro,John F.			640	Dec.18,1839	
149	Renfro, Isaac S.			320	Dec.18,1839	
151	Reeves, George			320	Dec.18,1839	
203	Robinson, Harmon			640	Dec.21,1839	
205	Rasco, Laban			320	Dec.21,1839	
226	Roberson, John C.			320	Dec.24,1839	
260	Ross, Wm. M.			640	Dec.26,1839	
262	Robinson, Richard G.			320	Dec.26,1839	
264	Rucker, Richmond H. C.			320	Dec.26,1839	
265	Robbins, George			640	Dec.26,1839	
266	Ruckman, John			640	Dec.26,1839	
267	Robbins, Joseph			320	Dec.26,1839	
272	Roberts, Thomas J.			320	Dec.27,1839	
45	Speights, William M.			320	Jul. 4,1839	
54	Squyres, Lewis L.			640	Sep. 6,1839	
90	Skinner, Franklin			640	Nov. 8,1839	
118	Shelton, John			640	Dec. 9,1839	
158	Shepherd, Joseph J.			320	Dec.18,1839	
167	Sanggs, Jesse T.			640	Dec.19,1839	
188	Sandige, Thomas J.			320	Dec.19,1839	
189	Sterling, John			320	Dec.19,1839	
224	Story, Gibson			320	Dec.24,1839	
235	Smith, Henry			320	Dec.24,1839	
245	Smith, James			640	Dec.25,1839	
250	Stone, Erastus			322	Dec.26,1839	
255	Spears, Friend			320	Dec.26,1839	
258	Stivender, Washington			320	Dec.26,1839	
278	Seale, Joshua			640	Dec.28,1839	
283	Scott, Daniel			320	Dec.28,1839	
317	Slaughter, Benjamin			320	Dec.31,1839	
331	Samford, William D.			640	Dec.31,1839	
333	Smith, Philip			320	Dec.31,1839	
335	Scarborough, James			320	Dec.31,1839	
349	Sapp, Stratford H.			320	Dec.31,1839	
355	Simonton, Robert S.			320	Jan. 1,1840	
356	Simonton, Henry T.			320	Jan. 1,1840	
303	Scofield, William			640	Dec.30,1839	
274	Stockstill, Wm. C.			320	Dec.27,1839	
53	Turner, Edward			640	Sep. 5,1839	
56	Turner, John J.			320	Sep. 6,1839	

No.	Name	Lgs.	Lbr.	Acres	Date	Remarks
62	Taylor, Hugh A.			320	Sep. 6,1839	
63	Towner, Hiram V.			320	Sep. 6,1839	
124	Thompson, Charles			640	Dec.14,1839	
125	Tucker, John D.			320	Dec.14,1839	
186	Taylor, Joseph			640	Dec.14,1839	
209	Tanner, Abraham			640	Dec.21,1839	
228	Trutman, Adolph			320	Dec.24,1839	
285	Trull, Jesse			640	Dec.28,1839	
301	Turner, Edward B.			640	Dec.30,1839	
361	Thompson, William P.			320	Jan. 1,1840	
199	Turner, Robert			640	Dec.21,1839	
82	Voris, William H.			640	Oct. 3,1839	
168	Vining, Benjamin			640	Dec.19,1839	
171	Vining, Lewis M.			640	Dec.19,1839	
32	Waite, Andrew J.			320	Jun. 7,1839	
33	Williams, James W.; Jr.			320	Jun. 7,1839	
35	Winn, William			320	Jun.20,1839	
71	Ward, John			640	Sep. 6,1839	
72	Walker, John			640	Sep. 6,1839	
73	Walker, James B.			640	Sep. 6,1839	
79	Wall, George W.			640	Oct. 3,1839	
87	Wyche, Oscar D.			320	Oct. 3,1839	
126	Windham, John D.			640	Dec.14,1839	
131	White, William L.			640	Dec.14,1839	
150	Wright, Alonzo D.			320	Dec.13,1839	
161	Williamson, William R.			320	Dec.13,1839	
182	Walker, Henry			640	Dec.19,1839	
184	Walker, Silas J.			320	Dec.19,1839	
197	Williams, James T.			320	Dec.21,1839	
213	Weatherford, John			320	Dec.21,1839	
237	Whitney, Leonard			320	Dec.24,1839	
241	Wilson, Israel			320	Dec.24,1839	
249	Wickes, Albert			320	Dec.26,1839	
269	Walker, William			320	Dec.26,1839	
270	Whitesides, Quissenbury			320	Dec.27,1839	
277	Willingham, Archibald			640	Dec.28,1839	
289	Walker, Robert			320	Dec.28,1839	
294	White, Isaiah			320	Dec.30,1839	
322	Watson, William			640	Dec.31,1839	
323	Watson, Edwin H.			320	Dec.31,1839	
324	Watson, William C.			320	Dec.31,1839	
334	Wort, James			320	Dec.31,1839	
336	Williams, Andrew J.			320	Dec.31,1839	
358	Williams, George S.			640	Jan. 1,1840	

SAN AUGUSTINE COUNTY

FIRST CLASS

No.	Name	Lgs.	Lbr.	Acres	Date	Remarks
31	Aakin, Wm. S.	1/3				
45	Anderson, Holland	1	1			

No.	Name	Lgs.	Lbr.	Acres	Date	Remarks
48	Anderson, Vincent	1	1			Holland Anderso Admr.
52	Anthony, F.	1	1			
61	Anderson, Benjn.	1	1			
80	Anderson, John W.	1/3				
140	Anderson, Benjn.; Jr.	1/3				
194	Ayres, Henry C.	1/3				Hayden Arnold, Admr.
222	Anthony, Rhody	1	1			
244	Anderson, Bailey	1	1			
492	Anderson, Wm. G.	1	1			
499	Ayres, John	1	1			
541	Anderson, Timothy	1/3				Holland Anderso Admr.
620	Allen, William	1	1			
680	Abrams, A.	1/3				
1206	Alsten, Matthew	1	1			
1177	Anderson, John P.	1	1			
254	Allen, Samuel T.		1			Matilda F. Alle Admx.
141	Anderson, Charles	1/3				
644	Allen, Jarrett J.	1	1			
104	Augustine, H. W.		1			
5	Brown, Squire	1/3				
15	Bates, Tarlton F.	1	1			
19	Burleson, Joseph	1	1			
33	Bordin, Oliver H. P.	1/3				
37	Banks, Joel	1/3				
38	Barr, Alanson	1	1			
47	Burditt, Jesse	1	1			
49	Blount, Stephen W.	1/3				
85	Burch, James	1/3				
106	Brown, Lemuel B.	1	1			
115	Bordin, John	1	1			
135	Bowie, John			369		
138	Bloomfield, James T.	1/3				
144	Burditt, Newel W.	1/3				
147	Bridges, James		1			
170	Beathe, Eli A.	1/3				
195	Blythe, Champion	1	1			
217	Burch, Valentine	1/3				
242	Bridges, James	1	1			
249	Brownrigg, Geo. B.		1			
256	Bullock, James		1			
259	Benson, Wm. B.	1/3				
260	Border, John	1/3				
264	Burnes, Joseph	1	1			
286	Brown, David		1			
294	Bullock, Julius	1/3				
295	Bird, Daniel	1	1			
305	Bacon, Sumner	1	1			
385	Buckham, Wm. C.	1/3				
439	Banks, Salitha	1	1			

No.	Name	Lgs.	Lbr.	Acres	Date	Remarks
486	Boon, Hannah	1	1			
488	Baggett, William	1/3				
288	Bennett, Aaron	1	1			
289	Bennett, James	1	1			
523	Barns, Elizabeth	1	1			
674	Baterman, William	1/3				
677	Burch, Samuel	1	1			
896	Burdett, J. A.	1/3				
991	Baker, Ameziah E.	1				
1269	Booker, E. R.			359		A. G. Kellogg, Admr.
7	Burdett, Giles H.	1/3				
107	Bridges, James	1	1			
634	Baker, John W.	1	1			
255	Brown, Hiram		1			
98	Burnes, Sam'l L.	1/3				
130	Blair, John	2/3				
714	Brown, Lucretia		1			
614	Barnett, John	1	1			
996	Brewer, Erasmus	1	1			
955	Bowie, John	1/3				
924	Brighton, Jas. W.	1/3				Richard Haley, Admr.
683	Bridges, A.	1/3				Joseph Rowe, agent for heirs.
9	Cartwright, James	1/3				
25	Caldwell, Wiley	1	1			
27	Chamley, Thomas	1/3				
36	Corzine, H.	1/3				
41	Churmley, John	1	1			
50	Cherry, David	1	1			
56	Clark, John	1	1			
57	Cartwright, George W.	1/3				
60	Carpenter, Micher	1	1			
67	Cabler, Francis P.	1	1			
77	Cellum, James	1	1			
78	Cullen, Ezekeal W.	1	1			
99	Chatin, James	1/3				
117	Coulter, Carney H.	1/3				
118	Coulter, A. M.	1/3				
123	Coulter, Henson	1	1			
142	Carson, Thomas	1/3				
152	Carson, John	1	1			
206	Cunningham, David A.			369		
218	Cartwright, Robert G.	1	1			
219	Caldwell, Matthew	1/3				
220	Caldwell, John C.	1/3				
241	Crain, Rodan F.	1/3				
262	Corzine, Shelby					7,371,350 varas.
271	Canfield, A. W.		1			
275	Caldwell, Robert W.	1/3				
280	Campbell, Isaac	1/3				
309	Caldwell, John	1/3				
186	Carpenter, John W.	1	1			

No.	Name	Lgs.	Lbr.	Acres	Date	Remarks
323	Chumley, Armsted		1			
335	Caldwell, William	1	1			
339	Caldwell, John	1/3				
351	Cartwright, Matthew	2/3	1			
423	Caddell, Andrew		1			
426	Cartwright, John		1			
463	Collins, G.S.W.		1			Reduced from a league
500	Cole, John B.	1	1			
678	Campbell, James	1	1			Susanah Herton, Admx.
954	Chism E. P. G.	1/3				R. H. Hibbet, agent for heirs.
1495	Curry, Thomas		1			
1496	Curry, Wilson	1/3				
1167	Calvinton, James J.	1	1			
230	Caldwell, Mary	1	1			
204	Crain, Elizabeth	1	1			
4	Davis, Anna	1	1			
7	Davis, Jesse	1/3				
23	Daivin, Mary	1	1			
90	Daniel, James M.	1	1			
92	Dickey, M. D.	1	1			
97	Daily, Raimond	1	1			
102	Daniel, Wm.	1	1			
119	Dillard, Joseph	1/3				
124	Dillard, Allen	1	1			
126	Dillard, Green J.	1/3				
153	Davis, A. M.	1/3				
154	Davis, Jas. R.	1	1			
156	Doyal, Matthew	1/3				
212	Deen, Calloway	1	1			
225	Davis, Wm. M.		1			
226	Davis, Pleasant	1/3				
249	Davis, Edward B.	3/4	1			
291	Davis, Washington S.	1/3				
178	Davis, Sam'l. H.	1	1			
547	Davis, Warren	1	1			Edward Davis, Admr.
561	Douthet, Alfred	1/3				
897	Davis, Elias K		1			
8	Davis, Nancy		1			S.S. Davis, Admr.
10	Davis, William			369		S.S. Davis, Admr.
9	Davis, S. S.			369		
66	Dorsett, Susan	1	1			John Dorsett, Admr.
621	Dixon, Levi	1	1			
14	Ewing, Edfey		1			
69	Ellison, James	1	1			
71	Ellison, Jas. H.	1/3				
72	Ellison, John C.	1/3				

No.	Name	Lgs.	Lbr.	Acres	Date	Remarks
222	Eagles, Wm. D.	1/3				
340	Ewing, William	1/3				
445	Earl, Davis	1	1			Matthew Earl, Admr.
548	Edmundson, Samuel	1/3				Philip H. Edmundson, Admr.
724	Ewing, Wilson		1			
509	Ewing, W. E.		1			
21	Frazier, John W.	1	1			
26	French, Joseph		2			
141	Farris, James	1	1			
174	Fisher, William	1/3				
245	Foote, Robert H.			369		
200	Fox, John A.	1	1			
438	Foy, Frederick	1	1			
893	Farney, Samuel	1/3				John Webb,Admr.
457	Freeland, Kile	1	1			Richmond Daily, Admr.
1550	Fassel, George	1/3				B. J. Thompson, Admr.
13	Gainer, John N.	1/3				
32	Gilliland, Samuel	2/3	1			
58	Garish, James		1			
82	Greene, David G.	1	1			
103	Gainer, Sarah	1	1			
107	Greene, F. L.	1	1			
116	Garner, John	1	1			
163	Gilbert, David W.	1/3				
166	Graham, Harrison	1/3				Curtailed to one-third league.
302	Galloway, Peter		1			
296	Garrett, C.	3/4	1			J. Garrett,Admr.
310	Goodlow, Robert K.	2/3	1			
359	Garner, Sebastian C.	1/3				
479	Garner, Thomas H.		1			
489	Gray, Anthony	1	1			
110	Griffith, Horatio	1	1			
514	Gillaspie, John	1	1			
670	Garrett, Jacob		6			
774	Gallion, Eleanor	1	1			
899	Gregory, Patsey		1			
364	Gilbreath, Mary	1	1			
959	Gates, John	1	1			
162	Gilbert, John	1	1			
257	Gioce, Christian	1	1			
303	Goodlow, R. K.	1/3				H.H.Hall,assignee
293	Garrett, William	1	1			
11	Horton, Wade	2/3	1			
40	Hial, James	1	1			
51	Holman, W. W.	1/3				

No.	Name	Lgs.	Lbr.	Acres	Date	Remarks
54	Hale, A. G.	1/3				
63	Hail, Jonas		1			
83	Harvey, B. W.		1			
89	Hill, David	1	1			
91	Haut, Thomas	1/3				
75	Howard, Jonas	1/3				Joseph Rowe, Assignee.
100	Haynes, John T. C.	1/3				
134	Hanks, Thomas	1	1			
136	Herrin, John	1	1			
137	Hanks, Joshua B.	1/3				
143	Hafford, Charles			672		
159	Hendrick, Obadiah; Jr.	1/3				
165	Hall, H. H.	2/3				
175	Howard, Aaron W.	1/3				
182	Hendrick, John	1/3				
183	Hereford, Wm. H.	1	1			
188	Howard, Edward	. 1/3				
199	Houston, A.			615		
216	Hall, Henry	1/3				
238	Hanks, E. F.		1			
251	Hardin, John	1/3				
269	Hendrick, Thos. D.	1/3				
277	Hanks, Bird L.		1			
278	Hanks, Thomas J.	1/3				
298	Haggerty, Jefferson	1	1			
311	Horton, Alexander	3/4	1			
313	Hunt, Nathaniel		1			
314	Horton, Henry P.	1	1			
322	Holman, Sandford	1/3				
347	Holman, John W.			369		
358	Hennis, J. J.	1	1			
367	Hamilton, James		1			
370	Houston, Emery S.	1/3				
378	Hanks, Isabella		1			
382	Hanks, Wyatt		1			
376	Hubble, John	1	1			
399	Hendrick, Edwin	1	1			
420	Holloway, John	1/3				
461	Harris, David	1	1			
472	Hamilton, Sam'l W.		1			
485	Hendrick, Obadiah	1	1			
487	Horn, H. H.	1	1			
493	Hibbitts, Robert H.	1	1			
608	Higgerty, Dennis	1/2				
608	Holloway, Simpson		1			
672	Holman, Isaac	1	1			Shelby,Colby,Adm
681	Hunt, Thomas	2/3	1			
729	Hanks, W. W.	2/3	1			
894	Holloway, Lewis		1			
1270	Horton, Susuuah		1			
1306	Holman, Sandford	2/3	1			
1498	Hendrick, Henry	1/3				Obediah Hendrick Jun'r Admr.

No.	Name	Lgs.	Lbr.	Acres	Date	Remarks
342	Herrington, Peter	1	1			
367	Hamilton, Nathaniel			369		
609	Harris, John	1/3				
1323	Howard, Chas. C.	1/3				
441	Haley, R. B.	1	1			
513	Holly, John S.	1	1			
363	Hanks, James	1/3				John G. Love, Admr.
3	Iden, Thomas	1	1			
120	Irish, Milton	1/3				
192	Irvin, Wm. D.	1/3				
197	Irvin, Josephus S.	1/3				
315	Irvine, Jane	1	1			
958	Irvin, R. B.			369		
2	Irvin, Josephus	2/3	1			
6	Johnson, James		1			
8	Jordon, Samuel	1/3				
17	Jones, George W.	1	1			
84	Jefferson, Thomas	1/3				
87	Johnson, James; Jr.	1/3				
108	Jessup, Timothy	1	1			
114	Johnson, William			369		
180	Jordan, John F.	1/3				
214	Jones, William	1/3				
224	Johnson, Solomon		1			Zachariah C. Johnson, Admr.
227	Johnson, Zachariah C.		1			
343	Johnson, William	1/3				
344	Johnson, John		1			
352	Johnson, Joseph R.	1/3				
361	Jarmon, John	1/3				
383	Jessup, Curtis	1/3				
79	Kemberling, Benjn.	1	1			
18	Knighton, Hannah	1	1			
159	Kimbrough, William		1			
176	Kimberland, James	1	1			
337	Kellogg, A. G.			369		
495	Kenly, Thomas H.	1	1			
29	Lindell, John	1	1			
35	Lont, Bailey	1/3				
44	Lindville, David	1/3				
68	Lout, Pickney		1			John Bodin, Admr.
86	Lindsey, Isaac	1	1			
111	Lochridge, H. H.	1/3				W.D.Ratliff, Admr.
121	Lout, Martin V.	1/3				
127	Love, G. H.	1/3				
128	Love, John G.	1	1			
131	Love, David H.	1/3				
155	Lumpkin, Wm.	1	1			

No.	Name	Lgs.	Lbr.	Acres	Date	Remarks
164	Linsey, Owen H.			369		
200	Lucas, John		1			
290	Lucy, Martin	1/3				
326	Lakey, William		1			
332	Lockhart, Chas. M.	1/3				
362	Lakey, George W.	1/3				
381	Ledbetter, Sneed	1/3				Calloway Dean, Admr.
397	Loyd, Wm. M.	1/3				
424	Lawhon, John C.		1			
427	Love, James	1	1			
435	Lout, Martin, V	2/3	1			
440	Lane, John S.		1			
456	Lowery, Thomas	1	1			
458	Lindville, Richard		1			
459	Lindville, Worldly	1/3				
465	Lewis, Allison A.	1/3				
498	Lewis, Abel A.	1	1			Allison A. Lewi Admr.
667	Lansing, James	1	1			
673	Lindsey, Benjamin	1/3				
1294	Lewis, A. A.	2/3	1			
1411	Lewis, John H.	1	1			
1428	Lawhon, D. E.	1	1			
1484	Lane, Walter B.	1/3				
633	Linsly, Nathaniel	1	1			
132	Lout, John	1	1			Martin Parmer, Admr.
12	Martin, Thomas J.	1/3				
16	McDaniel, John B.	1/3				
42	McCoy, David		1			
64	Marrow, Martha G.	1	1			
65	Martin, Patrick C.	1/3				
88	McGraw, Daniel	1	1			
133	McGaha, Benjamin	1	1			
148	May, Morris	1	1			
158	Moore, John		1			
160	McGallon, Thomas		1			
168	Maxamillon, Antonio	1/3				
179	McGowan, A. J.	1/3				
181	McGowen, John	1	1			
201	McDaniel, Robert C.		1			
213	Moss, James			369		
239	McDougal, John	1/3				
265	McLaughlin, Alfred M.	1/3				
274	Malone, Wm. T.	1	1			
281	Mabbitt, L. H.			369		
282	Morgan, Henry	1/3				
297	Moore, Daniel S. D.		1			
304	Moses, David	1/3				Morris May, assignee.
306	Miller, Solomon			369		
320	McGinnis, John		1			

No.	Name	Lgs.	Lbr.	Acres	Date	Remarks
325	Martin, James	1/3				
345	McCade, Merideth	1/3				
386	Murchison, John	1/3				
387	McDonald, Donald		1			
418	Moss, Sam'l	1	1			Lewis Holloway, Admr.
419	Moss, James	2/3	1			
421	McFarland, Thomas S.	2/3	1			
540	McDaniel, John B.	2/3	1			
617	Meador, John	1/3				Alanson Barr, Admr.
682	Miller, M. S.			369		
1310	Martin, Thomas J.	2/3	1			
1145	McKee, John	1	1			
198	McCombs, Robert	1/3				
1131	Moore, Samuel T.	1	1			
1148	Morman, Adolphus	1	1			
1114	McDonough, William	1	1			
466	Moore, John	1	1			
193	Maza, Thomas	1/3				
292	McGowen, Samuel	1/3				
299	Nash, John D.		1			
324	Nash, William		1			
480	Narred, William	1/3				
892	Neily, John	1/3				Baily Anderson, Admr.
471	Norred, Martha	1	1			
1006	Orton, Willis	1	1			
2	Parks, Joseph B.	1	1			
32	Pierce, Lewis	1	1			
39	Parmer, Martin		1			
55	Payne, Jedediah	1/3				
94	Parker, Ira	1	1			
151	Payne, Thomas	1/3				
157	Parmer, Isham			370		
184	Pierce, Samuel	1	1			
221	Prather, Freeman	1	1			
231	Payne, Guillord	1/3				
350	Perkins, James		1			
432	Payne, Thomas		1			
433	Payne, Daniel	1/3				
94	Parmer, Thomas	1	1			
545	Patterson, John		1	1		
675	Peterson, Oliver		1			
336	Pate, Peter	1	1			
503	Phelps, Mason	1	1			
173	Payne, W. H.	1	1			
496	Quirk, Joseph	1/3				Raimond Daily, Admr.
451	Quirk, William	1	1			Raimond Daily, Admr.

No.	Name	Lgs.	Lbr.	Acres	Date	Remarks
34	Russell, Hiram H.	1/3				
53	Ruddell, John	1/3				
46	Rawls, Thomas	1/3				
167	Roberts, Henry	1/3				
169	Renfro, Peter F.	1/3				
196	Rugler, Solomon	1	1			
215	Rainer, Samuel M.	1	1			
252	Richards, Charles	1	1			
253	Richards, James	1/3				
254	Richards, John	1/3				
255	Ruddell, A.	1	1			Benjamin Lindsey, Admr.
261	Reilly, Bernard	1/3				
272	Russell, Aurillia	1	1			
353	Rowe, Joseph	1	1			
434	Russell, Robert B.			369		
669	Ratliff, Jane		1			
524	Roberts, Elisha		1			
725	Richards, William			369		
738	Rounds, Lyman F.	1/3				
1303	Roberts, William		1			Mary Roberts, Admx.
161	Roberts, Felix	1/3				
256	Rockwell, Chester	1/3				
330	Richards, William	2/3	1			
401	Ramsey, James G.	1	1			
101	Ratliff, W. D.	1	1			
30	Sugler, William N.		1			
43	Scurry, Richardson	1/3				
59	Stovall, George H.	1	1			
62	Sanders, Levi	1	1			
70	Scott, William	1/3				
74	Scott, Thomas M.	1/3				
81	Stovall, Francis M.	1/3				
28	Shepherd, William	1	1			
20	Smith, William J.	1	1			
105	Stevens, Samuel		1			
109	Sweedenburg, Frederick	1/3				
112	Shaw, Thomas J.	1	1			
122	Scott, Isaac	1	1			
146	Sanders, John	1/3				
177	Smith, Jordan	1/3				
185	Simpson, Dinsmore		1			
203	Smith, Jonas	1/3				
205	Smith, Edwin	1	1			
229	Steadham, Samuel	1	1			
237	Smith, James	1/3				
285	Scurlock, Mial	1/3				William Scurloc Admr.
301	Ship, Joseph		1			
307	Ship, William		1			
319	Simpson, James	1/3				
338	Sublett, Henry W.	1/3				

No.	Name	Lgs.	Lbr.	Acres	Date	Remarks
349	Stevenson, James P.	1	1			
360	Smith, Daniel	1/3				
380	Shields, Manson	1/3				Calloway Dean, Admr.
384	Sims, Joseph	1	1			
425	Stanley, Green B.	1/3				
437	Sanders, Charity	1	1			
460	Spear, Andrew		1			
461	Sowell, Ransom	1	1			
491	Sharpe, James	1	1			
898	Spears, John			369		
1202	Sanders, Levi	2/3	1			
1218	Shackleford, Jos. S.			369		
334	Sythe, Francis	1	1			
93	Stevenson, J. B.	1	1			
422	Scarbrough, Laurence	1/3				
308	Sneed, William J.	1	1			
1283	Ship, James	3/4	1			
462	Smith, Ephraim	1/3				
4	San Augustine Academy	4	4			
10	Thomas, John	1	1			
24	Thompson, W. A.	1	1			Phinety Thompson, Admr.
76	Turner, Elisha	1	1			
113	Tally, Ephraim	3/4	1			
129	Thomas, Shadrack D.	1	1			
130	Teal, Edward	1	1			John C. Brook, Assignee.
190	Trowbridge, Charles E.	1/3				
208	Thomas, Benjamin	1/3				
243	Thompson, Samuel	1	1			
246	Teal, Henry	1/3				Edward Teal, Admr.
247	Thomas, Jackson	1/3				
250	Thompson, Hiram	1/3				
270	Thompson, Charlton	1	1			
341	Thomas, Montgomery B.			369		
348	Thomas, James J.		1			
371	Thomas, Theophilus	1	1			
428	Thompson, John	1/3				
422	Thompson, Thomas W.	1/3				
429	Terry, Jesse	1	1			
484	Thompson, Burwell J.	1	1			
1285	Thompson, Wm. A.	1/3				
293	Thomas, J. D.		1			
294	Thomas, Mary		1			
98	Ussury, Nancy	1	1			
449	Ussery, Martin S.	1	1			
618	Ussery, Meriweather	1/3				
172	Voshary, John	1	1			
233	Vanbibber, Sidney	1/3				

No.	Name	Lgs.	Lbr.	Acres	Date	Remarks
276	Vivion, V. H.	1	1			William R.D. Ward, Admr.
266	Vivion, Benjamin S,	1/3				
284	Vivion, Thos, M.C.	1/3				
1	Warren, David O.	1	1			
66	Watson, H. E.	1	1			
73	Wallace, Lucinda	1	1			
95	White, Charles	1/3				
96	Ward, William R. D.	1	1			
125	Winn, Peter	1	1			
139	Wilson, Jane	1				
187	Wilson, Stephen P.	1	1			
191	Winn, John A.	1/3				
235	Ward, John	1/3				Mary Wárd, Admx.
236	Ward, Mary	1	1			
263	Walker, Philip	1/3				
330	White, William	2/3				
331	White, William	1/3				
357	Walker, Joseph	1	1			
366	Willingham, Edward	1	1			
442	Wright, Thomas	1	1			
470	Walker, Jesse	1	1			
481	Walker, William; Jr.	1/3				
490	Williams, Hiram H.	1	1			
497	Willmouth, Levi	1/3				
522	Watson Dexter	1/3				
606	Wood, Charles	1/3				
1254	Wood, R. D.		1			
590	White, Littleton	1	1			
249	White, A. H.	1/3				
149	Wilson, William	1/3				
503	Williams, William M.	1	1			
145	Yancy, Achilles	1/3				
629	York, Aaron	1	1			

SECOND CLASS

No.	Name	Lgs.	Lbr.	Acres	Date	Remarks
707	Adams, John S.			1280	Jun.23,1838	
905	Anderson, J. C.			1280	Jun.23,1838	
986	Anthony, Peter			640	Jul. 7,1838	
1149	Anderson, B.			1280	Oct.22,1838	
1304	Arnold, Rachael			1280	Nov. 8,1838	
1307	Ashmore, N.			640	Jan.10,1839	
1556	Anderson, Oliver			1280	Sep.14,1839	
1589	Arnold, M.			640	Nov. 7,1839	
1784	Andrews, G. H.			640	Dec.17,1839	
1836	Adams, Wyatt			640	Dec.21,1839	
731	Brown, Ezikiel W.	1/3			Jun.25,1838	
735	Broyle, Joseph	1/3			Jun.25,1838	
552	Barbee, E.			1280	Jun. 8,1838	

No.	Name	Lgs.	Lbr.	Acres	Date	Remarks
569	Bradley, J. R.			640	Jun. 8,1838	
687	Baker, L. D.			1280	Jun. 9,1838	
688	Brooks, F. N.			640	Jun. 9,1838	
692	Barnes, James A.			640	Jun. 9,1838	
721	Berry, J. G.			1280	Jun.23,1838	
904	Bryant, J.			640	Jun.23,1838	
966	Brown, Cathrine			1280	Jul. 7,1838	
974	Baker, N. F.			640	Jul. 7,1838	
975	Baker, A. L.			1280	Jul. 7,1838	
982	Brewer, Jackson			1280	Jul. 7,1838	
989	Brown, Mary			1280	Jul. 7,1838	
999	Brooks, J. A. G.			640	Oct.22,1838	
1151	Baker, W. W.			640	Oct.22,1838	
1157	Barrow, F. H.			1280	Oct.22,1838	
1159	Black, G. W.			640	Oct.25,1838	
1268	Brook, J. C.			1280	Oct.25,1838	
1284	Burns, Sam'l T.			640	Oct.25,1838	
1314	Blythe, A. W.			640	Jan.24,1839	
1584	Brooks, Samuel			1280	Oct. 7,1839	
1596	Blythe, N. J.			640	Nov. 7,1839	
1767	Beaty, John			1280	Dec.17,1839	
2058	Barrows, David			1280	Dec.26,1839	
2076	Baker, James			1280	Dec.26,1839	L.D.Baker,Admr.
558	Cannon, C. L.			640	Jun. 8,1838	
559	Cole, Jesse			1280	Jun. 8,1838	
576	Carson, Newton			640	Jun. 8,1838	
582	Cole, G. J.			1280	Jun. 8,1838	
695	Carter, A. B.			640	Jun. 9,1838	
698	Cuthbertson, Thos. N.			1280	Jun. 9,1838	
699	Cuthbertson, Jane			1280	Jun. 9,1838	
711	Chamberton, A. P.			1280	Jun.23,1838	
1156	Camron, A.			1280	Oct.22,1838	
1285	Cox, Wm. W.			640	Oct.25,1838	
1288	Cole, Levi			1280	Oct.25,1838	
1437	Cartwright, H.			1280	Apr.11,1839	
1510	Cochran, J.			640	Jun.30,1839	
569	Davis, Geo. W.			1280	Jun. 8,1838	
693	Davis, A. P.			640	Jun. 9,1838	
901	Durham, Elizabeth			1280	Jun.23,1838	
972	Davis, R. S.			640	Jul. 7,1838	
987	Durcan, Wm.			640	Jul. 7,1838	
1291	Duncan, J. H.			640	Nov. 8,1838	
1293	Durham, L. A.			1280	Nov. 8,1838	
2057	Dunn, John; Jr.			640	Dec.26,1839	
968	Duncan, Dan			1280	Jul. 7,1838	
714	Edgor, Nicholas			1280	Jun.23,1838	
903	Epps, Chs.			640	Jun.23,1838	
1193	Edy, H.			1280	Oct.23,1838	
1287	Evans, H. C.			640	Oct.25,1838	
1466	Evens, D. M.			640	May 2,1839	

No.	Name	Lgs.	Lbr.	Acres	Date	Remarks
713	Fuller, E. C.			640	Jun.23,1838	
909	Ford, Wm. J. B.			640	Jun.23,1838	
918	French, H. F.			640	Jul. 7,1838	
925	Fowler, A. J.			640	Jul. 7,1838	
1150	Funy, Mary			1280	Oct.22,1838	
1525	Frazier, G. H.			640	Jun.30,1839	
2055	Ford, John S.			1280	Dec.26,1839	
1327	Fry, Bartlett			1280	Feb.14,1839	
581	Fall, J. N.			1280	Jun. 8,1838	
727	Gilliam, L. W.	1	1		Jun. 8,1838	
578	Griffith, L. E.			640	Jun. 8,1838	
697	Gray, J. B.			1280	Jun. 9,1838	
705	Gray, Geo. S.			640	Jun.23,1838	
709	Griffin, P. J.			1280	Jun.23,1838	
717	Garrett, Jacob; Sr.			1280	Jun.23,1838	
902	Gray, W. W.			640	Jun.23,1838	
908	Greer, J. A.			1280	Jun.23,1838	
917	Griggs, D.			640	Jun.23,1838	
1152	Green, J. T.			640	Oct.22,1838	
1160	Greer, L. V.			640	Oct.22,1838	
1161	Greer, H. H.			640	Oct.22,1838	
1286	Grace, J.			1280	Oct.25,1838	
1398	Grier, B. F.			640	Apr. 4,1839	
1756	Gillbert, Milly			1280	Dec.17,1839	
1761	Gressham, Simon			640	Dec.17,1839	
1908	Gresham, John W.			640	Dec.26,1839	
553	Humil, A.			1280	Jun. 8,1838	
556	Humtill, Wm. J.			1280	Jun. 8,1838	
557	Hanil, S. H.			1280	Jun. 8,1838	
570	Humphrey, Jas.			1280	Jun. 8,1838	
702	Hughs, R.			640	Jun. 9,1838	
703	Hall, David			640	Jun.23,1838	
710	Hooker, J. W.			640	Jun.23,1838	
712	Hamilton, Mary			1280	Jun.23,1838	
716	Herayr, Berjn.			640	Jun.23,1838	
720	Humphins, Jesse			640	Jun.23,1838	
722	Herring, W. L.			1280	Jun.23,1838	
913	Hamilton, Jacob E.			640	Jun.23,1838	
922	Hamilton, Calvin			640	Jul. 7,1838	
967	Howard, Malinda			1280	Jul. 7,1838	
971	Halcombe, M.			640	Jul. 7,1838	
983	Herring, Sam'l			1280	Jul. 7,1838	
1000	Holland, Thomas J.			640	Jul. 7,1838	
1155	Hopkins, Sol			640	Oct.22,1838	
1162	Hopkins, J. H.			1280	Oct.22,1838	
1183	Hyde, J. G.			640	Oct.23,1838	
1192	Haystill, S.			640	Oct.23,1838	
1256	Hopkins, Levi			640	Oct.24,1838	
1305	Hall, J. M.			640	Jan. 3,1839	
1391	Huddlutton, Wm. M.			1280	Apr. 4,1839	
1424	Hirajr, B.			640	Apr.11,1839	
1470	Hale, Thos. B.			640	May 23,1839	

No.	Name	Lgs.	Lbr.	Acres	Date	Remarks
1508	Hyde, Samuel N.			640	Jun.30,1839	
1647	Hill, F.			1280	Nov.28,1839	
2936	Harriss, Luiry			640	Dec.26,1839	
912	Hamilton, Hans			1280	Jul. 7,1838	
963	Justice, J. M.	1			Jul. 8,1838	
689	Jessup, Inal			1280	Jun. 9,1838	
704	Jenks, H. B.			640	Jun.23,1838	
984	Johnson, R. J.			640	Jul. 7,1838	
1304	Jones, O. J.			640	Jan.10,1839	
1312	Jones, E.			1280	Jan.18,1839	
1313	Jones, J.			1280	Jan.24,1839	
577	Kellogg, Ebenezer			640	Jun. 8,1838	
1390	Killion, J. A.			1280	Apr. 4,1839	
1513	Kelly, Hugh			640	Jun.30,1839	
1528	Kellum, N. K.			640	Aug. 8,1839	
1645	Killian, Wm.			1280	Nov.28,1839	
726	Lucas, Geo. C.	1	1		Jun. 8,1838	
730	Lucas, Sam'l M.	1/3			Jun.25,1838	
565	Lamir, Asa H.			1280	Jun. 8,1838	
580	Lard, David			1280	Jun. 8,1838	
681	Lauders, F. G.			640	Jun. 8,1838	
985	Livimon, L. D.			640	Jul. 7,1838	
995	Lyddy, Wm.			1280	Jul. 7,1838	
1194	Lucas, D. C.			640	Oct.23,1838	
1199	Lucas, H. M.			640	Oct.24,1838	
1200	Lucas, David			1280	Oct.24,1838	
1265	Loyd, E. A.			640	Oct.25,1838	
1450	Lang, Wm. J.			640	Apr.25,1839	
1518	Littlefield, Wm. B.			640	Jun.30,1839	
1568	Lockhart, Wm. M.			640	Oct. 7,1839	
1934	Littlefield, J. G.			1280	Dec.26,1839	
665	Martin, Henry	1	1		Jun.21,1838	
567	McGrus, Wm. J.			640	Jun. 8,1838	
718	Mitchel, John			640	Jun.23,1838	
723	Mays, A.			1280	Jun.23,1838	
911	McFarland, Daniel C.			640	Jun.23,1838	
920	McKnight, J. H.			640	Jul. 7,1838	
978	Moses, Aaron F.			640	Jul. 7,1838	
980	Moses, N. H.			1280	Jul. 7,1838	
981	McKoy, Mack			640	Jul. 7,1838	
992	Marsh, Jos. M. S.			640	Jul. 7,1838	
1153	Mitchal, J. T.			1280	Oct.22,1838	
1163	Martin, G. W.			640	Oct.23,1838	
1190	Meredith, D.			1280	Oct.23,1838	
1191	Mastin, J.			640	Oct.23,1838	
1216	McAde, J. S.			1280	Oct.21,1838	
1290	Murphy, J. H.			640	Oct.25,1838	
1298	Martin, G. F.			640	Nov. 8,1838	
1302	Martin, J. F.			1280	Jan. 3,1839	

No.	Name	Lgs.	Lbr.	Acres	Date	Remarks
1388	Martin, R. H.			640	Apr. 4,1839	
1392	Morton, J. A.			1280	Apr. 4,1839	
1444	Moore, R. N.			640	Apr.25,1839	
1456	McGuin, Wm.			640	May 2,1839	Wm.Philips,Admr
1574	Mitchail, H.			640	Sep.14,1839	
2102	Morgan, Charles			640	Dec.26,1839	
923	Neighbors, A.			640	Jul. 7,1839	
1158	Needham, G.			640	Oct.22,1839	
549	Onill, Robert			640	Jun. 8,1839	
535	Polk, Chas.			1280	Jun. 8,1839	
550	Pulliam, B. B.			1280	Jun. 8,1839	
573	Powell, W. R.			1280	Jun. 8,1839	
579	Polk, John			1280	Jun. 8,1839	
671	Purse, S. G.			640	Jun. 8,1839	
700	Payon, G. N.			640	Jun. 9,1839	
701	Payon, Z.			640	Jun. 9,1839	
708	Purdy, Miles			640	Jun.23,1839	
719	Pigg, Alpud			1280	Jun.23,1839	
724	Payne, Robert			1280	Jun.23,1839	
979	Perkins, J. R.			640	Jul. 7,1839	
994	Philips, J. F.			1280	Jul. 7,1839	B.L.Hanks,Admr.
1154	Patton, A. B.			640	Oct.22,1839	
1267	Parker, Wm. W.			640	Oct.25,1839	
1393	Philips, Wm.			640	Apr. 4,1839	
2077	Phelps, Augustus			640	Dec.26,1839	
1326	Platt, Thos.			1280	Dec.26,1839	
536	Polk, Alfred			1280	Jan. 7,1839	
1409	Perry, Thos			640	Apr. 4,1839	
736	Reynolds, Isaac	1	1		Jun.25,1838	
964	Rogers,Wilin	1/3			Jul. 7,1838	
895	Rimbro, Neily	1/3			Jul. 6,1838	
574	Reyler, Solomon			1280	Jun. 8,1838	
1261	Rowark, A.			640	Oct.25,1838	
1266	Rowe, A. W.			1280	Oct.25,1838	
1296	Ruth, Silas			640	Nov. 8,1838	
1300	Rankin, J. M.			1280	Jan.18,1839	
1513	Relly, Hugh			640	Jun.30,1839	
732	Smith, Wm. D.	1	1		Jun.30,1839	
733	Smith, Andrew J.	1	1		Jun.30,1839	Wm.D.Smith,Admr
551	Smith, Wajer S.			1280	Jun. 8,1838	
555	Smith, Frarar			1280	Jun. 8,1838	
566	Saxton, Saml			1280	Jun. 8,1838	
568	Sanders, Jacob			640	Jun. 8,1838	
571	Sumpter, Nancy			1280	Jun. 8,1838	
575	Still, Joel H.			1280	Jun. 8,1838	
686	Shanks, Jos. S.			640	Jun. 9,1838	
706	Shryock, M. H.			640	Jun.23,1838	
914	Starke, J.			1280	Jun.23,1838	
926	Sharp, J. M.			1280	Jul. 7,1838	

No.	Name	Lgs.	Lbr.	Acres	Date	Remarks
965	Smith, Adam			640	Jul. 7,1838	
969	Stoddard, J. B.			1280	Jul. 7,1838	
970	Stevens, E. A.			640	Jul. 7,1838	
976	Smith, M.			1280	Jul. 7,1838	
993	Spain, R. D.			1280	Jul. 7,1838	
998	Shelton, Wm. D.			640	Jul. 7,1838	
1196	Sansom, G. W.			640	Oct.24,1838	
1197	Sanson, Wm.			1280	Oct.24,1838	
1198	Sanson, R. P.			640	Oct.24,1838	
1217	Sanson, S. D.			640	Oct.24,1838	
1259	Smith, J. C.			640	Oct.25,1838	
1292	Smith, J.			1280	Nov. 8,1838	
1297	Shofner, Wm.			1280	Nov. 8,1838	
1299	Shoffner, J. N.			640	Nov. 8,1838	
1300	Shouffner, A.			640	Nov. 8,1838	
1308	Spain, L. B. B.			640	Jan.18,1839	
1443	Sansone, J. W.			640	Apr.25,1839	
1462	Sherar, H. R.			640	May 2,1839	
1610	Smith, John S.			1280	Nov. 7,1839	
1658	Smith, Wm.			640	Nov.28,1839	
1704	Straccner, Benj.			1280	Dec. 5,1839	
1325	Shell, M. H.			1280	Feb.14,1839	
563	Thompson, N. B.	1/3			Jun. 8,1838	
562	Tanner, Wm. B.			640	Jun. 8,1838	
564	Thomaston, David			1280	Jun. 8,1838	
685	Talidy, Stephen			640	Jun. 9,1838	
691	Thomas, Nath'l			1280	Jun. 9,1838	
696	Tilly, Thos.			1280	Jun. 9,1838	
907	Temple, L. A.			1280	Jun.23,1838	
910	Thompson, Sam'l			1280	Jun.23,1838	
1262	Thompson, Sam'l			1280	Oct.25,1838	
1482	Thurwan, J. M.			640	Jun. 6,1839	
1260	Ubanks, J.			640	Oct.25,1838	
977	Valmer, Jos. F.			640	Jul. 7,1838	
988	Vincent, A.			1280	Jul. 7,1838	
1001	Whitehurst, John H.	1/3			Jul. 7,1838	
554	Walliny, N. D.			1280	Jun. 8,1838	
572	Woodworth, J. B.			1280	Jun. 8,1838	
694	Walker, Thos. R.			640	Jun. 9,1838	
714	Wiggins, Thos. S.			1280	Jun.23,1838	
915	Whiteman, J. S.			640	Jun.23,1838	
919	Wright, L. W.			640	Jul. 7,1838	
921	White, Chas. C.			640	Jul. 7,1838	
927	Webb, John			1280	Jul. 7,1838	
1195	Willmouth B.			640	Oct.21,1838	
1201	Wyatt, Elijah			640	Oct.21,1838	
1215	Warren, J. W.			640	Oct.21,1838	
1257	Wood, Richard			1280	Oct.25,1838	
1258	Wallace, W.			640	Oct.25,1838	
1263	Walker, R. M.			640	Oct.25,1838	

No.	Name	Lgs.	Lbr.	Acres	Date	Remarks
1426	Wright, J. A.			1280	Apr.14,1839	
1638	Walker, Milton			1280	Nov.28,1839	
1644	Watson, L.			640	Nov.28,1839	
1783	Webb, D. F.			640	Dec.17,1839	
1975	Watson, Locy			1280	Dec.17,1839	
2103	Wallace, Benjamin R.			640	Dec.26,1839	
1289	York, L. L.			640	Oct.25,1839	

THIRD CLASS

No.	Name	Lgs.	Lbr.	Acres	Date	Remarks
1401	Arnold, James			640	Apr. 4,1839	
1461	Alexander, J. L.			320	May 2,1839	
1467	Alexander, Horatio Gates			640	May 2,1839	
1526	Allen, Farnel			320	Jun.30,1839	
1527	Allen, J.J.			640	Jun.30,1839	
1558	Allen, John			640	Sep.14,1839	
1553	Anderson, W. S. B.			640	Sep.14,1839	
1571	Anderson, R. L.			640	Oct. 7,1839	
1650	Allen, Burton			640	Nov.28,1839	
1641	Allen, Jesse			640	Nov.28,1839	
1713	Alexander, John			320	Dec. 5,1839	
1745	Anderson, George R.			320	Dec. 5,1839	
1891	Anderson, William			640	Dec.26,1839	
1955	Anderson, Wm. T.			320	Dec.26,1839	
2035	Adams, B. F.			320	Dec.26,1839	
2050	Avery, Calm R.			320	Dec.26,1839	
1407	Barkley, R. H.			320	Apr. 4,1839	
1413	Brockwell, J.			640	Apr. 4,1839	
1432	Bail, D. M.			320	Apr.11,1839	
1449	Bonner, Nancy			640	Apr.25,1839	
1474	Browning, A.			320	May 30,1839	
1475	Barber, David			320	May 30,1839	
1493	Braden, A. G.			640	Jun.14,1839	
1500	Billingsly, W. B.			320	Jun.14,1839	
1515	Briggs, R.			640	Jun.14,1839	
1534	Brown, R. O.			640	Aug. 8,1839	
1607	Burtly, N.			640	Nov. 7,1839	
1617	Barrett, Sarah D.			640	Nov. 7,1839	
1618	Barrett, Thos. C.			320	Nov. 7,1839	
1619	Barrett, J. J.			320	Nov. 7,1839	
1686	Baym, G. H.			640	Dec. 5,1839	
1691	Brooks, T. G.			640	Dec. 5,1839	
1695	Bacon, Thomas			640	Dec. 5,1839	
1739	Bradford, John R.			320	Dec. 5,1839	
1759	Ballbridge, James W.			640	Dec.17,1839	
1760	Ballbridge, Thos. A.			320	Dec.17,1839	
1775	Bain, Alexander			320	Dec.17,1839	
1776	Brily, John			320	Dec.17,1839	Shadrick Bruy, Admr.
1781	Bill, Thomas W.			320	Dec.17,1839	
1791	Britney, James			320	Dec.17,1839	

No.	Name	Lgs.	Lbr.	Acres	Date	Remarks
1801	Boarman, Richard			320	Dec.17,1839	
1827	Bell, John S.			640	Dec.21,1839	
1847	Barton, Moses			320	Dec.21,1839	
1863	Bales, Andrew W.			320	Dec.24,1839	
1896	Butler, Charles			640	Dec.26,1839	
1897	Bohanan, Mary F.			640	Dec.26,1839	
1904	Burditt, H. N.			320	Dec.26,1839	
1923	Baker, John			320	Dec.26,1839	
1927	Bumpuss, William			320	Dec.26,1839	
1932	Bently, L. Meno			320	Dec.26,1839	
1936	Bennett, Samuel			320	Dec.26,1839	
1948	Boon, John			640	Dec.26,1839	
1957	Byers, William W.			640	Dec.26,1839	
1972	Burks, N. W.			320	Dec.26,1839	
1976	Berry, Morgan			640	Dec.26,1839	
1977	Berry, William			640	Dec.26,1839	
1981	Bigby, William C.			320	Dec.26,1839	
1984	Berryett, James C.			320	Dec.26,1839	
1998	Brown, Samuel			320	Dec.26,1839	
2000	Burrows, B. M. D.			640	Dec.26,1839	
2002	Blidsoe, William			640	Dec.26,1839	
2008	Batts, Robert			320	Dec.26,1839	
2015	Barkley, Robert			640	Dec.26,1839	
2028	Berry, John			640	Dec.26,1839	
2029	Burt, Henry			320	Dec.26,1839	
2030	Berry, Andrew J.			320	Dec.26,1839	
2031	Berry, James A. P.			320	Dec.26,1839	
2048	Butler, Thomas H.			320	Dec.26,1839	
2063	Berey, Edward			320	Dec.26,1839	
2065	Bryan, Robert H.			320	Dec.26,1839	
2066	Button, R. S.			320	Dec.26,1839	
2073	Barrows, Milton			320	Dec.26,1839	
2078	Bell, B. W.			640	Dec.26,1839	
2097	Brooks, H.			640	Dec.26,1839	
2100	Betts, Thomas			640	Dec.26,1839	
2108	Blass, Gideon			320	Dec.26,1839	
2109	Benerd, Sipeo M.			320	Dec.26,1839	
2122	Bueford, William			320	Dec.26,1839	
2129	Bolling, Thadeus			640	Dec.26,1839	
1445	Caldwell, R. F.			320	Apr.25,1839	
1451	Carl, Kinehen			320	Apr.25,1839	
1480	Cooper, A. H.			320	Jun. 6,1839	
1502	Caldwell, S. W.			320	Jun.14,1839	
1505	Cyrus, Jesse			320	Jun.30,1839	
1507	Caldwell, John			322	Jun.30,1839	
1555	Cole, C. L.			320	Sep.14,1839	
1582	Carrington, D. C.			320	Oct. 7,1839	
1586	Craig, Samuel			640	Oct. 7,1839	
1588	Crain, Joseph L.			640	Oct. 7,1839	
1592	Compton, W. D.			640	Oct. 7,1839	
1613	Croach, C. W.			640	Oct. 7,1839	
1637	Calhoun, William H.			320	Oct. 7,1839	
1655	Coatney, John			320	Oct.28,1839	

No.	Name	Lgs.	Lbr.	Acres	Date	Remarks
1656	Campbell, A. C.			640	Oct.28,1839	
1733	Cartwright, Robert H.			320	Dec. 5,1839	
1739	Cooke, D. P.			320	Dec. 5,1839	
1762	Cumly, Bird			320	Dec.17,1839	
1785	Cooble, Peter			640	Dec.17,1839	
1800	Cannon, Lawson R.			320	Dec.17,1839	
1814	Childrass, H. C.			640	Dec.17,1839	
1842	Crow, Preston T.			320	Dec.21,1839	
1850	Calhoun, Duncan			320	Dec.22,1839	
1872	Craggs, Richard			320	Dec.24,1839	
1884	Crawfer, John F.			320	Dec.26,1839	
1901	Crow, James M.			320	Dec.26,1839	
1921	Christion, John C.			320	Dec.26,1839	
1926	Coobieniss, C. A.			320	Dec.26,1839	
1944	Crow, Alen			320	Dec.26,1839	
1945	Caubler, Butler			320	Dec.26,1839	
1964	Cassay, Eli			640	Dec.26,1839	
1971	Calloway, James			320	Dec.26,1839	
1988	Crawford, Jesse			320	Dec.26,1839	
1989	Crawford, Rheubin			320	Dec.26,1839	
1996	Coleman, Matthew M.			320	Dec.26,1839	
1997	Coleman, Stephen			640	Dec.26,1839	
2003	Crice, L. W.			320	Dec.26,1839	
2012	Chambers, C. P.			320	Dec.26,1839	
2016	Connel, John E. O.			320	Dec.26,1839	
2019	Coonlen, Thomas O.			320	Dec.26,1839	
2034	Cooke, William			320	Dec.26,1839	
2061	Cockran, William			320	Dec.26,1839	
2080	Caldwell, Matthew			320	Dec.26,1839	
2130	Canklin, John			320	Dec.26,1839	
2133	Crump, Wm. G.			320	Dec.26,1839	
2090	Coleman, James H.			320	Dec.26,1839	
1452	Dewitt, William J.			320	Apr.25,1839	
1492	Davis, John			640	Jun. 6,1839	
1549	Daniel, J. P.			640	Sep.14,1839	
1578	Dickinson, James			640	Oct. 7,1839	
1579	Donaldson, Stephen			640	Oct. 7,1839	
1590	Donaldson, E.			640	Nov. 7,1839	
1688	Dell, James M. O.			640	Dec. 5,1839	
1757	Dixon, Francis D.			320	Dec.17,1839	
1779	Donly, S. P.			640	Dec.17,1839	
1792	Duffield, William C.			640	Dec.17,1839	
1824	Demoss, Lewis			320	Dec.17,1839	
1829	Dunlan, William			320	Dec.21,1839	
1876	Darnell, Nicholas H.			640	Dec.25,1839	
1942	Driver, Samuel			320	Dec.26,1839	
1984	Davidson, A. M.			640	Dec.26,1839	
1987	Davis, Henry S.			640	Dec.26,1839	
1995	Davis, Ashburne			640	Dec.26,1839	
2017	Davis, Jacob			320	Dec.26,1839	
2032	Dalliard, H. H.			320	Dec.26,1839	
2044	Daugherty, James			320	Dec.26,1839	
2060	Delany, Jeremiah			320	Dec.26,1839	

No.	Name	Lgs.	Lbr.	Acres	Date	Remarks
2064	Davidson, Samuel			320	Dec.26,1839	
2079	Deans, D.			640	Dec.26,1839	
2111	Dickey, Charles			320	Dec.26,1839	
1602	Edwards, Daniel			320	Nov. 7,1839	
1621	Eaker, William A.			320	Nov. 7,1839	
1622	Eaker, W. H.			320	Nov. 7,1839	
1623	Eaker, John			320	Nov. 7,1839	
1639	Edwards, Esther			640	Nov. 7,1839	
1649	Elkison, D. W.			320	Nov.28,1839	
1692	Edgar, William			320	Dec. 5,1839	
1700	Elkius, N. H.			640	Dec. 5,1839	
1810	Ellis, George L.			320	Dec. 7,1839	
1832	Evans, Samuel Dale			320	Dec.21,1839	
1841	Elkins, Benet			640	Dec.21,1839	
1983	Edwards, William			320	Dec.26,1839	
2013	Elkius, Eiasmus			320	Dec.26,1839	
2042	Evans, A. J.			320	Dec.26,1839	
2070	Estill, Milton			640	Dec.26,1839	
2118	Eubanks, H.			320	Dec.26,1839	
2123	Elgin, William			320	Dec.26,1839	
1415	Flanagan, C.			320	Apr. 4,1839	
1471	Fitzallen, O.			320	May 16,1839	
1514	Fruit, James			640	Jun.30,1839	
1541	Fuller, W. S.			320	Sep.14,1839	
1569	Fowler, Littleton			640	Oct. 7,1839	
1594	Foote, William			320	Nov. 7,1839	
1595	Foote, John			640	Nov. 7,1839	
1744	Fitzgerald, John C.			320	Dec. 5,1839	
1747	Fitzgerald, Christopher			320	Dec. 5,1839	
1748	Fitzgerald, Jackson			640	Dec. 5,1839	
1749	Fitzgerald, William			640	Dec. 5,1839	
1750	Fitzgerald, James N.			640	Dec. 5,1839	
1753	Fulton, Alexander			320	Dec. 5,1839	
1789	Floyd, James M.			320	Dec.17,1839	
1790	Floyd, Andrew J.			320	Dec.17,1839	
1837	Farman, G. L.			320	Dec.21,1839	
1845	Fergerson, Wm. A.			320	Dec.21,1839	
1848	Fergerson, John L.			320	Dec.21,1839	
1849	Fergerson, Isaac			320	Dec.21,1839	
1886	Fisher, Orenith			320	Dec.26,1839	
1954	Fry, Robert			320	Dec.26,1839	
1968	Flatt, James			320	Dec.26,1839	Clerk's returns say Platt.
2005	Farris, Andrew			320	Dec.26,1839	
2025	Fitts, John			320	Dec.26,1839	
2026	Fitts, Oliver H.			320	Dec.26,1839	
2083	Floyd, S. C.			320	Dec.26,1839	
2088	Frizzell, W. W.			320	Dec.26,1839	
1463	Gainer, William			320	May 2,1839	
1464	Gainer, J. H.			320	May 2,1839	
1519	Groce, George			640	Jun.30,1839	

No.	Name	Lgs.	Lbr.	Acres	Date	Remarks
1532	Griffith, J. S.			640	Aug. 8,1839	
1566	Gilbreath, J. A.			320	Oct. 7,1839	
1574	Gregory, John			640	Oct. 7,1839	
1575	Gregory, Richard; Jr.			320	Oct. 7,1839	
1577	Gregory, Richard			640	Oct. 7,1839	
1597	Gilbert, J. C.			640	Nov. 7,1839	
1631	Garrett, C. S.			320	Nov.28,1839	
1646	Griffith, M. B.			640	Nov.28,1839	
1652	George, James J.			640	Nov.28,1839	
1676	Garner, N. B.			320	Dec. 5,1839	
1711	Gilley, Charles			320	Dec. 5,1839	
1712	Gilley, John			320	Dec. 5,1839	
1769	Gainer, John			320	Dec.17,1839	
1798	Gilbert, L. A.			320	Dec.17,1839	
1803	Gayne, H. W.			640	Dec.17,1839	
1811	Greer, David			640	Dec.17,1839	
1812	Greer, Andrew			640	Dec.17,1839	
1813	Greer, Joseph			640	Dec.17,1839	
1816	Greer, R. J.			320	Dec.21,1839	
1910	Galespie, John L.			320	Dec.26,1839	
1911	Galespie, Samuel			640	Dec.26,1839	
1920	Garrett, Richard			320	Dec.26,1839	
1924	Gary, Benjamin F.			640	Dec.26,1839	
1938	Green, A. J.			320	Dec.26,1839	
1952	Grayham B.			320	Dec.26,1839	
1966	Grigson, Jacob			320	Dec.26,1839	
1986	Gormly, James S.			320	Dec.26,1839	
2014	Graves, Elizabeth			640	Dec.26,1839	
2128	Green, M.			320	Dec.26,1839	
1768	Gainer, Charles C.			320	Dec.17,1839	
1524	Gillian, W. P.			320	Jun.30,1839	
1399	Harris, Travis			640	Apr. 4,1839	
1402	Harris, Hmos			320	Apr. 4,1839	
1416	Horton, S. W.			640	Apr. 4,1839	
1425	Ham, Orange			320	Apr.11,1839	
1430	Hinds, H.			320	Apr.11,1839	
1457	Hays, D.			320	May 2,1839	
1472	Hart, Wm. M.			640	May 16,1839	
1497	Hendrick, B. D.			320	Jun. 6,1839	
1509	Hyde, A. J.			320	Jun.30,1839	
1537	Hampton, J. I.			320	Aug. 8,1839	
1570	Hunt, H.			320	Oct. 7,1839	
1580	Hew, J. W.			640	Oct. 7,1839	
1628	Hauld, R. A.			640	Nov.28,1839	
1670	Hunt, John			320	Nov.28,1839	
1679	Higgins, James			640	Dec. 5,1839	
1694	Horn, Wm. B.			320	Dec. 5,1839	
1706	Howell, Alexander G.			320	Dec. 5,1839	
1707	Harges, Joseph			640	Dec. 5,1839	
1730	Holland, Mark P.			640	Dec. 5,1839	
1738	Hanks, Jobn B.			320	Dec. 5,1839	
1788	Holland, Bird			320	Dec.17,1839	

No.	Name	Lgs.	Lbr.	Acres	Date	Remarks
1802	Higgins, Wm. P.			320	Dec.17,1839	
1818	Hudson, Lewis			320	Dec.17,1839	
1861	Hagler, John			320	Dec.22,1839	
1883	Hamil, Robert C.			320	Dec.25,1839	
1890	Hale, John B.			320	Dec.26,1839	
1731	Harten, B. T.			320	Dec. 5,1839	
1905	Horton, Wm. E.			320	Dec.26,1839	
1909	Haggerty, Elizabeth			640	Dec.26,1839	
1924	Houston, J. T.			320	Dec.26,1839	
1930	Haden, L. B.			320	Dec.26,1839	
1931	Hinds, Bolafox			320	Dec.26,1839	
1937	Horn, John			320	Dec.26,1839	
1941	Handeder, J. E.			320	Dec.26,1839	
1946	Hughes, Robert			640	Dec.26,1839	
1950	Horris, Jackson			320	Dec.26,1839	
1969	Hawkins, Brehon			320	Dec.26,1839	
2009	Hotchkiss, Lester			320	Dec.26,1839	
2014	Hobson, Samuel			320	Dec.26,1839	
2043	Howe, H. W.; Dec'd.			320	Dec.26,1839	B.I.Hauke,Admr.
2045	Hill, J. R.			320	Dec.26,1839	
2052	Hausoetine, James			320	Dec.26,1839	
2086	Harding, D. G.			320	Dec.26,1839	
2096	Hester, Ralph			640	Dec.26,1839	
2105	Hobson, Tesherner			320	Dec.26,1839	
2134	Hatcher, Solomon W.			320	Dec.26,1839	
1491	Iver, James			320	Jun. 6,1839	Clerk's returns say McIver.
1854	Irvin, Lockhart J.			320	Dec.22,1839	
2101	Ivins, John			320	Dec.26,1839	
1468	Johnson, Samuel			640	May 16,1839	
1523	Jackson, Wm. T.			320	May 16,1839	
1583	James, J. M.			640	Oct. 7,1839	
1598	Johnson, James B.			320	Nov. 7,1839	
1754	Joseph, Thomas M.			320	Dec.17,1839	
1755	Jackson, Edward T.			320	Dec.17,1839	
1787	Jones, Robert P.			320	Dec.17,1839	
1865	Jackson, Moses			640	Dec.24,1839	
1929	James, Jesse			320	Dec.26,1839	
2006	Jones, John			320	Dec.26,1839	
2027	Johnson, Lewis			320	Dec.26,1839	
2046	Johnson, Thomas			640	Dec.26,1839	
2087	Johnson, R. B.			320	Dec.26,1839	
2112	Jewett, Samuel G.			320	Dec.26,1839	
2126	Johnson, M. T.			640	Dec.26,1839	
1591	Janett, M.			320	Nov. 7,1839	
1587	Kenley, David			640	Oct. 7,1839	
1599	Killion, Perry			320	Nov. 7,1839	
1710	King, Wm. H.			640	Dec. 5,1839	
1717	Killion, Goodwin			640	Dec. 5,1839	
1725	Kittlewell, Jonathan			640	Dec. 5,1839	

No.	Name	Lgs.	Lbr.	Acres	Date	Remarks
1806	Kizzin, Benjamin G.			320	Dec. 7,1839	
1807	Kizzin, John			640	Dec. 7,1839	
1417	Lee, Linsly			640	Apr. 4,1839	
1479	Lane, George			320	Jun. 6,1839	
1499	Lucas, E. W.			640	Jun. 6,1839	
1538	Loggins, W. H.			320	Aug. 8,1839	
1542	Lovell, Felix G.			640	Sep.14,1839	
1546	Lindsly, Thomas Sherod			320	Sep.14,1839	
1601	Loggins, Samuel			640	Nov. 7,1839	
1718	Loggins, J. P.			640	Dec. 5,1839	
1740	Loudour, Martin			640	Dec. 5,1839	
1741	Lang, Robert			320	Dec. 5,1839	
1742	Lang, John; Sr.			640	Dec. 5,1839	
1796	Laing, John			320	Dec.17,1839	
1864	Lewis, Joel			320	Dec.24,1839	
1881	Larkman, Saniey			320	Dec.25,1839	
1887	Lewis, Johnson			320	Dec.26,1839	
1900	Louis, M. O.				Dec.26,1839	No quantity give
1949	Lucas, Charles			640	Dec.26,1839	
2001	Leaaise, V. B.			640	Dec.26,1839	
2018	Love, Wade			640	Dec.26,1839	
2020	Love, John			320	Dec.26,1839	
2021	Love, David			320	Dec.26,1839	
2038	Lively, Philip			320	Dec.26,1839	
2095	Loyd, A. M.			320	Dec.26,1839	
2127	Loggins, C. M.			640	Dec.26,1839	
2131	Leggins, Greenbury			320	Dec.26,1839	
1777	Linson, John			320	Dec.17,1839	
2113	Lee, Thomas			320	Dec.26,1839	
1403	McNeil, Neil			640	Apr. 4,1839	
1406	Mann, Washington P.			640	Apr. 4,1839	
1419	McDonald, James			640	Apr.11,1839	
1429	Mortin, John			640	Apr.11,1839	
1433	McAdoo, R. G.			320	Apr.11,1839	
1438	Montieth, Mary			640	Apr.11,1839	
1439	Montieth, J.			320	Apr.11,1839	
1440	Montieth, Daniel			320	Apr.11,1839	
1441	Montieth, J.			320	Apr.11,1839	
1442	Massey, W. T.			640	Apr.11,1839	
1447	Martin, Benjamin			320	Apr.25,1839	
1448	Martin, Susanah			640	Apr.25,1839	
1460	McAnnally, Elizabeth			640	May 2,1839	
1476	Moore, John			640	May 16,1839	
1501	McCosly, William			320	Jun.14,1839	
1512	McMahoon, William			320	Jun.30,1839	
1522	McShan, William B.			320	Jun.30,1839	
1529	McAnally, John			640	Aug. 8,1839	
1530	Montgomery, William			320	Aug. 8,1839	
1540	McAlexander, J.			320	Sep.14,1839	
1552	McIntosh, Joshua			320	Sep.14,1839	
1559	McDaniel, William			640	Sep.14,1839	
1560	McDaniel, J. S.			320	Sep.14,1839	

No.	Name	Lgs.	Lbr.	Acres	Date	Remarks
1608	Matthews, M.			320	Nov. 7,1839	
1609	Matthews, William G.			320	Nov. 7,1839	
1611	Matthews, J. F.			320	Nov. 7,1839	
1612	Martin, J. B. B.			320	Nov. 7,1839	
1643	Moore, Frankey			640	Nov. 7,1839	
1674	Maner, William			320	Nov.28,1839	
1680	McKnight, J. H.			320	Dec. 5,1839	
1681	McDonald, D. R.			320	Dec. 5,1839	
1682	Martial, John			320	Dec. 5,1839	
1683	Meader, Jasen			640	Dec. 5,1839	
1698	Meek, Wm. D.			640	Dec. 5,1839	
1699	Meek, A. J.			320	Dec. 5,1839	
1708	Matthews, Mays			640	Dec. 5,1839	
1719	Meban, Allen			640	Dec. 5,1839	
1736	McDougall, A. L.			320	Dec. 5,1839	
1743	Morris, Samuel			320	Dec. 5,1839	
1746	McKay, John L.			320	Dec. 5,1839	
1751	McRay, Jno. C.			640	Dec.17,1839	
1758	Martin Noah			640	Dec.17,1839	
1765	Marchison, John			640	Dec.17,1839	
1766	Menihue, Geordon T.			320	Dec.17,1839	
1772	McFarland, James A.			320	Dec.17,1839	
1773	McKnight, William			320	Dec.17,1839	
1774	McKnight, H. W. N.			320	Dec.17,1839	
1780	Matlock, William			320	Dec.17,1839	
1782	McLamore, William			320	Dec.17,1839	
1794	Mosely, Elisha			640	Dec.17,1839	
1799	Mallory, Stinson R.			320	Dec.17,1839	
1823	Montgomery, Thomas C.			320	Dec.17,1839	
1825	McClannell, William B.D.			640	Dec.17,1839	
1826	Montgomery, John			640	Dec.21,1839	
1843	McKinney, Henry			640	Dec.21,1839	
1851	Miller, Stewart A.			320	Dec.22,1839	
1858	McRoy, George			640	Dec.22,1839	
1859	Montgomery, R. C.			320	Dec.22,1839	
1868	McAda, James			640	Dec.24,1839	
1870	McFarland, Lewis J.			640	Dec.24,1839	
1871	McMeen, Ebenezer			640	Dec.24,1839	
1877	McKnight, Anne N.			640	Dec.25,1839	
1879	McKnight, John O.			320	Dec.25,1839	
1915	McCarter, James			320	Dec.26,1839	
1918	Maies, Andrew			320	Dec.26,1839	
1925	McIntyre, Hugh C.			320	Dec.26,1839	
1928	McGill, A. J.			320	Dec.26,1839	
1935	Mason, James			640	Dec.26,1839	
1936	McWhorter, A.			640	Dec.26,1839	
1957	McWhorter, James H.			640	Dec.26,1839	
1959	McWhorter, John R.			640	Dec.26,1839	
1960	McWhorter, Wm. P.			320	Dec.26,1839	
1961	McWhorter, Adam F			320	Dec.26,1839	
1963	McWhorter, Aniziah A.			320	Dec.26,1839	
1973	Malown, James			640	Dec.26,1839	
1974	Malown, Ebenezar			320	Dec.26,1839	
1990	McRay, Samuel D.			320	Dec.26,1839	

No.	Name	Lgs.	Lbr.	Acres	Date	Remarks
1991	McRay, John R.			320	Dec.26,1839	
1992	McRay, Alexander			640	Dec.26,1839	
1999	McGuin, George A.			640	Dec.26,1839	
2004	Morris, James			640	Dec.26,1839	
2033	McCauly, James			640	Dec.26,1839	
2056	Moore, Elisha			640	Dec.26,1839	
2067	Messitt, John R.			320	Dec.26,1839	
2069	Morgan, H. S.			320	Dec.26,1839	
2075	Moore, Jesse			320	Dec.26,1839	
2121	Mize, W. D.			640	Dec.26,1839	
1728	Mason, Lewis			320	Dec. 5,1839	
1614	Matthews, George			640	Nov. 7,1839	
1615	Matthews, James			320	Nov. 7,1839	
1616	McCoy, John			320	Nov. 7,1839	
1446	Needham, Samuel			640	Apr.25,1839	
1520	Nicholson, John			640	Jun.30,1839	
1603	Nutt, Walter			320	Nov. 7,1839	
1606	Norwood, W. C.			320	Nov. 7,1839	
1627	Nicks, G. W.			640	Nov.28,1839	
1720	Norwood, Alfor			320	Dec. 5,1839	
1722	Norwood, Wm.			640	Dec. 5,1839	
1814	Norwood, Daniel			320	Dec.21,1839	
1869	Nation, Fred. W.			320	Dec.24,1839	
1902	Norriss, Aguilla			640	Dec.26,1839	
2072	Nations, Sally			640	Dec.26,1839	
2115	Nemmon, O. H.			320	Dec.26,1839	
1563	O'Daniel, Thomas			320	Sep.14,1839	
1585	Oliphant, Margaret			640	Dec. 7,1839	
1797	Overton, John F.			320	Dec.17,1839	
1808	Oliver, Andrew			320	Dec.17,1839	
1943	Osburne, Elizabeth			640	Dec.26,1839	
2049	Olephant, John			320	Dec.26,1839	
1410	Pool, A. N.			320	Apr. 4,1839	
1434	Polk, John			640	Apr.11,1839	
1454	Payne, J. W.			640	Apr.25,1839	
1459	Phisbus, James			320	May 2,1839	
1477	Patterson, J. T.			640	Jun. 6,1839	
1531	Powell, R. E.			640	Aug. 8,1839	
1533	Parker, Thomas			640	Aug. 8,1839	
1545	Parr, George			320	Sep.14,1839	
1557	Parker, David			640	Sep.14,1839	
1573	Payne, Wm. R.			320	Oct. 7,1839	
1581	Patterson, W. B.			640	Oct. 7,1839	
1672	Patton, Samuel, M.			640	Nov.28,1839	
1693	Pierce, John A.			320	Dec. 5,1839	
1716	Platt, Radcliffe			320	Dec. 5,1839	
1721	Poe, Stephen			320	Dec. 5,1839	
1793	Pearson, Alexander G.			320	Dec.17,1839	
1805	Pucket, Montgomery			320	Dec.17,1839	
1895	Parker, John			640	Dec.26,1839	

No.	Name	Lgs.	Lbr.	Acres	Date	Remarks
1899	Poll, Wm. H.			320	Dec.26,1839	
1913	Penington, Philip T.			640	Dec.26,1839	
1917	Peterson, P.			320	Dec.26,1839	
1939	Parsons, H. K.			320	Dec.26,1839	
1940	Paton, Elis			320	Dec.26,1839	
1970	Pugh, M. H.			320	Dec.26,1839	
2037	Payton, Elijah			640	Dec.26,1839	
2039	Payton, Wm. H. M.			640	Dec.26,1839	
2059	Phifer, Silas			640	Dec.26,1839	
2081	Payne, Charlton			640	Dec.26,1839	
2092	Polk, L. B.			320	Dec.26,1839	
2093	Polk, James W.			320	Dec.26,1839	
2094	Polk, Benjamin			640	Dec.26,1839	
1965	Quirl, Martha C.			640	Dec.26,1839	
1408	Rawis, J. T.			640	Apr. 4,1839	
1414	Rast, Joseph			320	Apr. 4,1839	
1421	Robinson, A.			640	Apr.11,1839	
1422	Robinson, William L.			320	Apr.11,1839	
1431	Row, Isiah			640	Apr.11,1839	
1458	Robinson, M. C.			320	May 2,1839	
1506	Roberts, George			640	Jun.30,1839	
1511	Ritchie, E. P.			320	Jun.30,1839	
1565	Roberts, Isaac			320	Oct. 7,1839	
1572	Riley, Miles T.			320	Oct. 7,1839	
1576	Rawles, Robert			320	Oct. 7,1839	
1626	Ray, J. W.			320	Nov.28,1839	
1632	Rankin, Samuel			320	Nov.28,1839	
1633	Rankin, D. H.			320	Nov.28,1839	
1653	Ritchie, Stephen D.			320	Nov.28,1839	
1654	Ritchie, James W.			320	Nov.28,1839	
1677	Rankin, C. P.			320	Dec. 5,1839	
1678	Rush, Philip			320	Dec. 5,1839	
1681	Roach, Jackson			640	Dec. 5,1839	
1702	Roberts, J. J.			320	Dec. 5,1839	
1703	Roberts, Thomas B.R.			320	Dec. 5,1839	
1714	Reed, David			320	Dec. 5,1839	
1715	Reed, Joel; Jr.			320	Dec. 5,1839	
1795	Rannon, Mary			640	Dec.17,1839	
1816	Rhodes, John P.			640	Dec.17,1839	
1831	Russell, Gibson			320	Dec.21,1839	
1834	Rodin, John			640	Dec.21,1839	
1835	Rodin, Aaron C.			320	Dec.21,1839	
1856	Ridens, John			320	Dec.22,1839	
1866	Richie, E. P.			320	Dec.24,1839	
1882	Rielley, Jeremiah			640	Dec.25,1839	
1883	Russell, B. N.			320	Dec.25,1839	
1889	Ray, Robutus R.			320	Dec.26,1839	
1898	Roland, James S.			320	Dec.26,1839	
1947	Raubun, Robert S.			640	Dec.26,1839	
1951	Rice, James			640	Dec.26,1839	
1978	Runnill, James			320	Dec.26,1839	
2071	Robinson, John H.			320	Dec.26,1839	

No.	Name	Lgs.	Lbr.	Acres	Date	Remarks
2091	Rutledge, Thomas J.			320	Dec.26,1839	
2117	Rollins, Mark			320	Dec.26,1839	
2119	Right, H. H.			320	Dec.26,1839	
1409	Smith, Samuel			640	Apr. 4,1839	
1427	Smith, William L.			640	Apr.11,1839	
1469	Slaughter, William H.			640	May 16,1839	
1478	Stark, J. T.			320	Jun. 6,1839	
1503	Scales, J. H.			320	Jun.30,1839	
1516	Smith, A. J.			320	Jun.30,1839	
1536	Shanks, Charles			320	Aug. 8,1839	
1551	Sorsaman, Jacob			640	Sep.14,1839	
1562	Stockton, T. J.			640	Sep.14,1839	
1604	Spain, M.			320	Nov. 7,1839	
1620	Sorsaman, H. C.			320	Nov. 7,1839	
1629	Swain, William			320	Nov.28,1839	
1630	Swain, A. G.			320	Nov.28,1839	
1657	Standfer, L. C.			320	Nov.28,1839	
1671	Smith, Henry			320	Nov.28,1839	
1675	Sims, R. J.			320	Dec. 5,1839	
1698	Sadler, George M.			320	Dec. 5,1839	
1697	Sadler, Jeremiah			320	Dec. 5,1839	
1709	Smithson, Henry			320	Dec. 5,1839	
1727	Smith, David H.			320	Dec. 5,1839	
1734	Spain, B. S. D.			320	Dec. 5,1839	
1764	Spidle, Jacob			640	Dec.17,1839	
1778	Steel, James R.			320	Dec.17,1839	
1804	Smith, H. T.			320	Dec.17,1839	
1809	Smith, Edwin F.			320	Dec.17,1839	
1819	Stepp, Phebe			640	Dec.17,1839	
1820	Stone, Stephea			640	Dec.17,1839	
1822	Stepp, William			640	Dec.17,1839	
1828	Smith, E. C.			320	Dec.21,1839	
1830	Strocher, Henry R.			320	Dec.21,1839	
1857	Steel, Henry			640	Dec.22,1839	
1903	Slivers, William			640	Dec.26,1839	
1906	Stepp, Jane			640	Dec.26,1839	
1907	Sanders, John J.			640	Dec.26,1839	
1967	Strode, William			320	Dec.26,1839	
2022	Searcy, Robert; Jr.			320	Dec.26,1839	
2024	Searcy, Robert; Sr.			640	Dec.26,1839	
2051	Strahon, Thomas			320	Dec.26,1839	
2053	Strahon, Mathew			640	Dec.26,1839	
2054	Strahon, David			320	Dec.26,1839	
2068	Scurry, William R.			320	Dec.26,1839	
2082	Shelby, Evan W.			320	Dec.26,1839	
2084	Smith, P.			640	Dec.26,1839	
2089	Stokes, W. B.			320	Dec.26,1839	
2098	Stewart, John			640	Dec.26,1839	
2104	Shank, John			320	Dec.26,1839	
2107	Sullivan, David			320	Dec.26,1839	
1815	Simpson, Thomas			640	Dec.17,1839	
1404	Thacker, J. B.			320	Apr. 4,1839	
1423	Thompson, John			640	Apr.11,1839	

No.	Name	Lgs.	Lbr.	Acres	Date	Remarks
1465	Thompson, William			320	May 2,1839	
1483	Thurman, Thomas J.			640	Jun. 6,1839	
1567	Talbot, M.			640	Oct. 7,1839	
1659	Talbot, John D.			320	Nov.28,1839	
1687	Thurmond, Thomas R.			320	Dec. 5,1839	
1705	Truit, A. M.			320	Dec. 5,1839	
1729	Thompson, William R.			320	Dec. 5,1839	
1838	Thacker, J. R.			640	Dec.21,1839	
1839	Thacker, Sanders J.			320	Dec.21,1839	
1852	Taylor, Isaac			640	Dec.22,1839	
1853	Taylor, Cyrus R.			320	Dec.22,1839	
1855	Taylor, John D.			320	Dec.22,1839	
1892	Thayes, Elizabeth			640	Dec.26,1839	Clerk's returns say Keyes.
1893	Thayes, James			320	Dec.26,1839	Clerk's returns say Keyes.
1916	Thornton, George W.			320	Dec.26,1839	
1919	Thornton, Aziett			320	Dec.26,1839	
1953	Thacker, Isaac H.			320	Dec.26,1839	
2007	Thompson, Thomas			640	Dec.26,1839	
2023	Taft, James F.			320	Dec.26,1839	
2040	Taber, James			640	Dec.26,1839	
2041	Terill, George W.			320	Dec.26,1839	
2047	Terill, R. A.			320	Dec.26,1839	
2114	Thornton, Amelia			640	Dec.26,1839	
2124	Tidwell, Samuel			320	Dec.26,1839	
2125	Tidwell, Peter			320	Dec.26,1839	
2116	Turner, Charles			320	Dec.26,1839	
1412	Vaughn, H.			640	Apr. 4,1839	
1543	Vandosin, J. M.			320	Sep.14,1839	
1821	Vining, Casley			640	Dec.17,1839	
1405	Whitson, G. N.			320	Apr. 4,1839	
1418	Weeks, James			640	Apr.11,1839	
1420	Wofford, M. D.			320	Apr.11,1839	
1435	Wilson, H. A.			320	Apr.11,1839	
1436	Wofford, J. B.			320	Apr.11,1839	
1455	Wyatt, A. B.			320	Apr.25,1839	
1481	Weeks, W. A.			320	Jun. 6,1839	
1486	Waggoner, R.			320	Jun. 6,1839	
1504	Wisehart, Isaac			320	Jun.30,1839	
1521	Watson, Benjamin			320	Jun.30,1839	
1535	Williams, Edward J.			640	Aug. 8,1839	
1539	Ware, N. W.			640	Aug. 8,1839	
1544	Wood, H.			320	Sep.14,1839	
1547	Williams J.			640	Sep.14,1839	
1550	Wilson, E.			320	Sep.14,1839	
1554	Watson, M.			640	Sep.14,1839	
1561	Walker, R. H.			640	Sep.14,1839	
1598	Williams, M. P.			320	Nov. 7,1839	
1600	Wilson, A. T.			640	Nov. 7,1839	Clerk's returns say 320 acres.
1605	Wilson, R. P.			640	Nov. 7,1839	
1624	Wilson, John			320	Nov. 7,1839	
1634	Wilson, Daniel			320	Nov.28,1839	

No.	Name	Lgs.	Lbr.	Acres	Date	Remarks
1636	Wilson, Cyrus W.			320	Nov.28,1839	
1648	Williams, Jeptha			640	Nov.28,1839	
1673	Wright, Henry			320	Nov.28,1839	
1685	Worden, John			320	Dec. 5,1839	
1701	Walker, Joel; Jr.			320	Dec. 5,1839	
1723	Walker, James G.			320	Dec. 5,1839	
1724	Walker, Pleasant A.			320	Dec. 5,1839	
1735	Wing, William J.			320	Dec. 5,1839	
1752	Wallridge, Elbridge			320	Dec.17,1839	
1833	Wallace, Willis S.			640	Dec.21,1839	
1862	Waddell, John C.			320	Dec.24,1839	
1867	Watson, Thomas			640	Dec.24,1839	
1873	Wilson, Morgan			320	Dec.24,1839	
1874	Wilson, Francis			640	Dec.25,1839	
1875	Woods, John			640	Dec.25,1839	
1878	Wheely, Charles			320	Dec.25,1839	
1880	Wittlesey, Ralph			640	Dec.25,1839	
1888	Williams, Samuel A.			320	Dec.25,1839	
1894	West, R. R.			320	Dec.25,1839	
1912	Williams, John R.			320	Dec.26,1839	
1914	Williams, James A.			320	Dec.26,1839	
1933	Wheeler, Royal T.			640	Dec.26,1839	
1979	Watson, Lewallen			320	Dec.26,1839	
1980	Watson, James			320	Dec.26,1839	
1985	Whetherhead, James M.			640	Dec.26,1839	
1993	Watkins, James			320	Dec.26,1839	
1994	Watkins, Robert			640	Dec.26,1839	
2010	Whiteman, James S.			320	Dec.26,1839	
2106	Wilkins, L. S.			320	Dec.26,1839	
2062	Worden, John			640	Dec.26,1839	
2085	Woods, J. A.			320	Dec.26,1839	
2099	Wells, Robert B.			320	Dec.26,1839	
1860	Yeaney, James A.			640	Dec.22,1839	
1840	York, Aaron			640	Dec.21,1839	
1625	Yandle, M.			320	Nov.28,1839	
1770	Youngblood, Seth H.			320	Dec.17,1839	
1771	Youngblood, Nath'l G.			320	Dec.17,1839	
1962	Yargin, Baylam			320	Dec.26,1839	

SHELBY COUNTY

FIRST CLASS

No.	Name	Lgs.	Lbr.	Acres	Date	Remarks
38	Ashabranner, Henry	1	1			
5	Amosen, Jossey	1	1			
136	Askins, Charles	1	1			
77	Anderson, Baily	1	1			
101	Anderson, Jonathan	1	1			
138	Askins, James	1/3				
29	Alford, James	1	1			
140	Archer, John	1/3				

No.	Name	Lgs.	Lbr.	Acres	Date	Remarks
214	Anderson, Wiet	1/3				
275	Asher, James	1/3				
272	Asher, Thomas	1	1			
328	Aldereta, Benneta	1	1			
78	Anderson, Hampton	1/3				
347	Anderson, Grudy	1/3				
348	Anderson, Baily; Jr	1/3				
345	Applegate, John	1	1			
346	Anderson, Hazard	1	1			
498	Asher, Robertson	1	1			
497	Ashabran, George J.	1/3				
350	Anderson, Fryet; Dec'd	1	1			Jonathan Anderson Admr.
	Adams, James; Jno. Graves, Admr.	1/3				Proven for 1 L & 1 Lab; ent to 1-3
	Adams, James; Jno. Graves, Admr.	1	1			Provën before District Court.
58	Beauchamp, J. R.	2/3				
157	Burk, John C.	1	1			
9	Bradley, John M.	1	1			
163	Butler, George		1			
61	Barnes, John D.	1/3				
150	Barnes, P. P.	1	1			
116	Brandin, William M.	1	1			
17	Bowlin, James	1	1			
95	Blankenship, David	1	1			
71	Bigger, Mary	1	1			
72	Bigger, Richard S.	1/3				
52	Butler, A.	1	1			
144	Buckley, John	1	1			
222	Byfeel, Homes	1	1			
150	Bittick, Jonathan			3279		
132	Burk, Arthur	1/3				
315	Bowler, John	1/3				
209	Bankenship, S. B.	1	1			
304	Bougus, Franklin	1	1			
44	Beck, John	1/3				
44	Bowman, Joseph	1/3				
448	Bowman, Eli A.	1				
456	Buckner, John W.	1	1			Elizabeth Buckner, Admx.
484	Buckley, Tyre	1/3				
485	Briston, Thomas	1/3				
166	Bradley, John	1/3				
526	Butler, Joseph		1			
542	Berryhill, William	1	1			
	Bailey, Oliver; J. J. Cravens, Admr.	1/3				Given for a league, entit. to 1/3.
201	Bowlin, S.		1			L. Willis, Executor.

No.	Name	Lgs.	Lbr.	Acres	Date	Remarks
23	Castleberry, Aaron	1	1			
69	Crofford, William C.	1	1			
179	Cronk, John W.	1	1			
113	Castlebury, Wm. H.	1	1			
31	Crane, William J.					
155	Clark, William	1	1			
231	Cliver, Robert	2/3	1			Has obtained a patent for 1/3.
206	Carr, Anastacio	1	1			
12	Castleberry, Aaron	1/3				
213	Cook, William R.	1/3				
261	Carroll, Elizabeth	1	1			
330	Carr, Anthony		1			
329	Carr, Mosseir	1/3				
333	Corder, William	1	1			
334	Corder, Reuben T.	1/3				
392	Chapel, Sarah	1	1			
508	Castleberry, Aaron T.	2/3	1			
501	Castleberry, James C.	1/3				
582	Choat, Bedman		1			
	Cravens, James J.	1/3				
	Crosby, James B.	1/3				
372	Carsennarver, Estevan	1	1			
185	Critchfield, John	1/3				
314	Clighon, John W.	1	1			
18	Dunnagan, Isaac	1	1			
113	Dunn, Henry C.	1/3				
2	Davis, Nathan	1	1			
111	Davis, Samuel	1	1			
112	Dunn, William H.	1/3				
88	Dunn, Kisiah	1	1			
331	Duel, Joseph	1/3				Obtained ord. fo leag.; ent. to 1/3.
414	Dunn, James M.	1/3				
514	Duncan, Martha	1	1			
494	Dunman, Amy	1	1			
513	Douatill, Henry	1/3				
57	Davis, Harrison	1	1			
161	Davis, Eliza	1	1			
37	David, Patrick M.	1/3				O. McDavid.
86	English, Stephen	1	1			
54	English, William D.	1/3				
133	English, Sarah	1	1			
75	English, Richard B.	1/3				
56	English, William	1	1			
67	English, Joseph	1	1			
169	English, George			370		
30	English, James	1	1			
172	English, James; Jr.			370		
120	English, Joshua	1	1			
196	Elder, James	1/3				Applied for L.; entit. only to 1/3.

No.	Name	Lgs.	Lbr.	Acres	Date	Remarks
131	English, John	1/3				
115	English, William	1/3				
440	English, Elizabeth	1	1			
192	English, A. H.	1/3				
326	English, Jonas	1	1			
39	English, John	1	1			
62	Forsyth, John	1	1			
98	Forsyth, James	1	1			
165	Frisiman, Dan'l M.	1	1			
239	Ferguson, Joseph		1			
241	Ferguson, David	1/3				
240	Ferguson, John	1/3				
264	Finley, John	1	1			
117	Forrester, James		1			
439	Forsyth, James	1	1			
573	Friley, Elizabeth	1	1			
742	Fryer, William W.	1/3				
478	Ferguson, Aiston	1/3				
73	Gates, Greenberry	2/3	1			
153	Graves, Elizabeth	1	1			
48	Graves, Philip	1	1			
264	Goodwin, George	1	1			
495	Gray, Thomas	1	1			
507	George, Hezekiah	2/3	1			
503	Goodwin, Sherly	1	1			
535	Graves, Joseph	1/3				
49	Gray, Ann	1	1			
456	Goodbread, Joseph G.	1	1			
635	Glass, Nancy	1	1			
220	Goodwin, William	1/3				
148	Heath, John F.	1	1			
85	Hooper, Richard	1	1			
182	Hughes, Thomas M.	1	1			
42	Humphreys, Squire	1/3				
162	Hinton, Z.	1	1			
10	Haley, Richard	1/3				Ap. for 1 L. & 1 lab. ent. to 1/3.
109	Huphres, Bryant	1/3				
28	Holman, Jeremiah H.	1/3				
245	Haley, Thomas	1	1			
160	Haley, Mark	1/3				
292	Hargroves, John	1/3				
283	Howard, Hartwell	1	1			
282	Haley, Richard; Sr.	1	1			
285	Haley, John R.	1/3				
30	Haley, Charles Q.	1/3				
141	Hodges, Neal C.		1			Received title for league.
344	Holmes, Stephen	1/3				
387	Hooper, Franklin	1/3				Ap'd for 1 L. & 1 lab; ent to 1/3

No.	Name	Lgs.	Lbr.	Acres	Date	Remarks
386	Hooper, James M.	1/3				
407	Hooper, John J.	1	1			
371	Hill, Wesley	1	1			
415	Hooper, G. W.	1/3				Proved 1 L. 1 la ent to 1/3.
516	Hinton, James	1/3				
513	Hunley, John	1/3				
529	Haley, John	1/3				
533	Husmands, John	2/3	1			
561	Harrison, Jonas	1	1			Eleanor Harrison Admx.
	Hopson, Henry	1/3				
665	Hawkins, Thomas N.	1/3				Proved 1 L. 1 la ent. to 1/3.
746	Hammonds, John J.	1	1			
580	Hooper, Richard	1	1			Admr. of W. H. Saunders.
219	Haley, Marian	1	1			
244	Humphreys, William	1	1			
419	Howard, C. H.	1/3				
399	Husbands, John	1/3				
256	Humphreys, William		1			
411	Haley, Allen	1/3				
361	Howell, Nelson; Dec'd.	1/3				John M. Bradley, Admr.
280	Humphreys, George	1/3				Elizabeth Neil, Admx.
	Hooper, Benjamin F.	1	1			Proved before District Court.
	Haley, Mark	1	1			Proved before District Court.
3	Inman, John	1	1			
220	Irvin, Robert	1	1			
281	Inman, Hiram	1/3				
774	Irvan, William A.	1	1			
636	Johnston, James	1/3				Proved 1 L. 1 la ent. to 1/3.
108	Johnson, Alvey R.		1			
19	Jones, William	1/3				Admr. of Thos. Lewellen
43	Jordain, Redding A.	1/3				
33	Kelley, Thomas	1	1			
223	Kellogg, John	1/3				
215	King, William	1	1			
453	King, James H.	1/3				
394	Kimbro, Samuel	1/3				Obtained head-right for 1 L. ent to only 1/3
657	Kennedy, Cyzenia	1	1			
70	Kelvey, Jesse M.	1/3				See M's.
53	Kelvey, James M.	1	1			See M's.

No.	Name	Lgs.	Lbr.	Acres	Date	Remarks
36	Lindsey, Pennington	1	1			
35	Lindsey, Micajah	1	1			
83	Landrum, W. H.	1	1			
156	Latham, Louis		1			Received title for league.
46	Latham, John	1	1			
191	Lusk, R. O.	1	1			
216	Latham, King	1	1			
212	Lankford, G. F.	1	1			
174	Lagroon, William O.	1	1			
173	Lagroon, Adam	1	1			
242	Lindsey, Samuel	1/3				
196	Lowry, Aaron	1/3				
170	Lindsey, Thomas	1/3				
257	Lindsey, Charles	1	1			
263	Lankford, Asa	1/3				
265	Lewin, Bluford	1/3				
278	Louis, Barbary C.		1			
105	Lowry, John L.	1/3				
252	Lusk, G. V.	1	1			
1	Little John		1			
340	Little, Samuel	1	1			
342	Lindsey, Isaac		1			
341	Lindsey, Alfred	1/3				
74	Loute, Alfred	1	1			
515	Lindsey, Claiborne B.	1/3				
301	Little, William	1	1			
107	Lital, John	1/3				
84	Luce, Jesa	1	1			
258	Loury, Evin; Jas. English, Admr.	1	1			To the heirs of C. Choat.
564	Lavina, Joseph	1	1			J. Forthith, Admr.
19	Lewellen, Thomas	1/3				William Jones, Admr.
345	Lindsey, John		1			William Watson, Admr.
37	McDavid, Patrick	1/3				Or M. P. David.
102	McFadden, Samuel	1	1			
104	McFadden, Jonathan	1/3				
143	Mason, Reddin	1	1			
70	McKelveys, Jesse	1/3				See K's.
53	McKelveys, James	1	1			
94	Mags, Robert	1	1			
25	Merchant, Edward A.	1	1			
114	Mann, Winney	1	1			
139	Morris, Abner	1/3				Proven up 1 L; ent. only to 1/3.
117	Martinez, Augustine	1	1			
316	Merchant, John D.	1	1			
249	McCelvey, Susannah	1	1			
274	Miller, William		1			
27	Merchant, Berry	2/3	1			

No.	Name	Lgs.	Lbr.	Acres	Date	Remarks
332	McKelvy, Hezekiah	1	1			
336	McFadden, Andrew	1	1			
121	Martin, Daniel		1			
152	McCitrick, Francis	1/3				
367	McFadden, William	1/3				
546	McFadden, John	1/3				
	Murray, James H.	1/3				
581	Mann, Lindsey	1/3				
769	Merchen, James S. M.	1/3				
749	Mason, Philip	1	1			
753	Moody, Miles W.	1/3				
57	Matthews, James	1	1			
774	McConnick	1/3				
398	Masrika, Philip	1	1			
190	McFadden, William	1	1			
235	McGrew, John B.	1/3				
291	McFadden, Bailey	1/3				
404	Magehee, Henry	1/3				
554	Moss, John	2/3				
20	Nale, Andrew	1	1			
226	Nale, Abner	1	1			
280	Neil, Elizabeth	1/3				Admx. of Geo. Humphreys.
288	Neil, William	1	1			
423	Nail, George, or Vail	1/3				
	Nail, Hariet; J. M. Bradley, Admr.	1				Proved before District Court.
60	Odie, Benjamin	1/3				J. R. Beauchamp, Admr.
319	Obanion, Sherwood	1	1			
319	Ostane, Jose	1	1			
745	O'Neil, Francis	1	1			
433	Prewet, Josiah	1	1			
355	Porter, William	1/3				
164	Posey, D. B.	1/3				Proved up 1 L & 1 lab; ent to 1/3
32	Porter, Samuel	1	1			
137	Parmer, William	1	1			
92	Parmer, John	1	1			
64	Payne, John C.	1	1			
224	Peoples, Joshua		1			Proved up 1 L, & 1 lab; ent. only to 1 labor.
208	Pesekone, Ruth	1	1			
217	Parmer, Robert	1/3				
238	Payne, Matthew	1/3				
293	Parmer, John	1	1			
271	Page, John	1/3				
266	Payne, Homer	1	1			
299	Page, David		1			

No.	Name	Lgs.	Lbr.	Acres	Date	Remarks
488	Petit, Walker		1			Received title for 1 league.
524	Page, Jackson	1/3				
515	Pettyjohn, Joshua	1/3				
743	Pettyjohn, Joshua	2/3	1			
438	Polk, Mary	1	1			
	Pierce, William	1/3				
167	Pennington, Sidney O	1/3				Wm. Watson,Admr.
40	Roberts, Moses F.	1	1			
150	Rains, P. P.	1	1			
147	Rains, Joel D.	1	1			
164	Rains, E.					Received title for league.
93	Rowhus, Mary	1	1			
190	Reel, Alfred	1/3				
541	Reel, Daniel D.		1			
540	Reel, Henry A.	1/3				
539	Reel, James	1/3				
425	Riddle, William	1	1			
408	Ritter, Everett	1	1			
496	Reynolds, Matilda	1	1			
531	Reed, Isaac H.		1			
171	Robeson, William	1	1			
279	Roberson, Edward	1/3				Applied for L. & lab.; ent to 1/3.
498	Robertson, Asher	1	1			
96	Smith, James	1	1			
178	Sheals, Jackson	1/3				
16	Scritchfield, Polly		1			Received title for a league.
145	Smith, Manan	1	1			
185	Scrutchfield, John		1			
55	Stricklin, David	1	1			
119	Stricklin, Mary	1	1			
120	Stricklin, Amos	1	1			
90	Stockmin, Hancock	1	1			
34	Stricklin, Henry	1/3				
194	Standfield, Wm. W. O.	1	1			
11	Shawn, Thomas J.	1/3				
250	Scritchfield, Henry	1/3				
248	Smith, William	1	1			Nancy Smith,Admx.
106	Shoemaker, Ivin		1			Received title for league.
270	Sultins, Jesse	1	1			
290	Sticklin, James	1	1			
248	Smith, Arcable	1	1			
277	Satus, Cornelius	1/3				
45	Stricklin, Samuel	1	1			
356	Scarberough, John	1/3				
499	Shadowen, James	1	1			
523	Stockman, Henry J.	1/3				
534	Sharp, Jane	1	1			Or Tharp.

No.	Name	Lgs.	Lbr.	Acres	Date	Remarks
536	Stockwell, Jesse	1	1			John Little,Admr.
663	Smith, Jackson	1	1			
192	Smith, John	1	1			
244	Strickland, Sam	1	1			
267	Strickland, Benjamin	1/3				Amos Strickland, Admr.
99	Story, Rachael	1	1			
382	Santos, Jose; Sr.	1	1			
384	Scott, James	1	1			
548	Shoemaker, John G.	1/3				
359	Story, Ephraim; Dec'd.	1	1			John M. Bradley, Admr.
497	Smith, Samuel	1	1			Joshua English, Admr.
580	Saunders, William H.	1	1			Richard Hooper, Admr.
	Scott, George W.	1/3				Dist. Court. Jas W. Hail, As'g.
176	Tutle, Daniel	1	1			
24	Thomas, James H.	1/3				
89	Thomas, William	1/3				
87	Thomas, Hezekiah	1	1			
94	Todd, William	1	1			
253	Thomas, James M.	1/3				
276	Timmons, Thomas		1			
337	Thompson, Edinton	1/3				
330	Trittle, Daniel	1/3				
376	Taylor, Charles	1/3				
416	Tutt, James E.	1/3				
393	Todd, Samuel	1/3				
50	Tutt, Clement	1	1			
430	Tucker, James R.	1	1			
511	Timmon, James F.			'370		
530	Timmons, Felix G.	1/3				Thos. Timmons, Admr.
	Tipton, William	1/3				
269	Thomas, Eliza C.	1/3				
187	Usrey, John	1	1			
207	Ussrey, Meriweather	2/3	1			Obtained title for 1/3 league.
236	Ussrey, Nancy S.	1	1			
186	Vardeyman, Henry W.	1/3				
175	Vaun, Willis	1	1			
443	Vanwicken, John	1	1			
540	Vann, William	1/3				
8	Vann, Mason	1	1			
22	Watkins, William	1/3				Louis Watkins, Admr.
154	Wooten, Moses	1	1			

No.	Name	Lgs.	Lbr.	Acres	Date	Remarks
47	Woodfin, William D.	1/3				
180	Wells, William J.	1	1			
	Wilkinson, David	1	1			
125	West, Hampton	1	1			
124	West, James	1	1			
162	Walker, Z. C.	1	1			
14	Wiggins, Harburd L.	1	1			
181	Woodfin, Joshua	1	1			
82	Whetstche, Anderson	1/3				
81	Whetstone, Peter	1	1			
243	Watson, W. H.		1			Received title for league.
63	Willis, Arthur	1/3				
221	Walters, Isaac	1	1			
345	Watson, Wm.; admr of J. Lindsey					Qauntity not given.
363	Wiggins, Roderick		1			
201	Willis, L.		1			Exee'y of S. Bowlin.
441	Watson, Thomas	1/3				
542	Watson, George W.	1	1			
518	West, Larkin	1/3				Wm. Pierpont, Admr.
151	Watson, William	1	1			
338	Wornick, Jacob	1/3				
522	Watson, William H.	1/3				
	Weeks, John	1	1			
21	Watkins, Lewis	1	1			
579	Waling, Nelson D.	1	1			
124	West, James	1	1			

SECOND CLASS

No.	Name	Lgs.	Lbr.	Acres	Date	Remarks
118	Allen, Elija			1280	Sep. 1837	
158	Addington, Arastus			1280	May 1837	
218	Adams, Clement F.			1280	Sep. 1837	
74	Ashton, Henry C.			1280	Sep. 8, 1838	
78	Ashton, Chancer			640	Sep. 8, 1838	
77	Ashton, Joseph			640	Sep. 8, 1838	
51	Albread, Elijah			640	Sep. 6, 1838	
172	Andrews, William			640	Sep. 1837	No quantity given
246	Brewster, Asa W.			640	Jul. 1836	
154	Bagby, Aaron			1280	Apr. 1837	
155	Bagby, Leroy			1280	Apr. 1837	
160	Boyden, Thomas			640	Sep. 1837	
241	Bustin, Ben P.			640	Jun. 1836	
190	Barnes, Thomas			640	Sep. 1837	
213	Buckey, Thomas			1280	Feb. 1837	
214	Ball, Edward			1280	Feb. 1837	
186	Bowden, Bennett H.			1280	Sep. 1837	
215	Bonfield, John			1280	Feb. 1837	
217	Ball, John			1280	Feb. 1837	

No.	Name	Lgs.	Lbr.	Acres	Date	Remarks
216	Batles, William			1280	Feb. 1837	
313	Bell, Daniel			640	Aug. 1836	
314	Bell, Stephen			1280	Aug. 1836	
315	Brown, William			640	Aug. 1836	
10	Black, Kinnel			1280	May 9,1838	
21	Britten, Wm. B.			1280	Aug. 3,1838	
22	Britton, John W.			640	Aug. 3,1838	
34	Britton, Wm. M.			640	Aug. 3,1838	
35	Britton, Thos. F.			640	Aug. 3,1838	
43	Bolwer, Oliver T.			1280	Aug. 3,1838	
55	Belt, Thos			1280	Aug. 3,1838	
69	Britton, James			640	Aug. 3,1838	
86	Beavers, Joseph			1280	Oct. 4,1838	
91	Brewton, Sam'l			1280	Oct. 9,1838	
201	Camnadd, Frederick			1280	Nov. 1837	
117	Cunningham, Sam'l			1280	Nov. 1837	
118	Cunningham, John P.			640	Nov. 1837	
119	Cunningham, Wm. L.			640	Nov. 1837	
136	Cunningham, John A.			1280	Jul. 1837	
145	Chambers, John			640	May 1837	
224	Chambers, William A.			640	May 1837	
166	Caunon, R. W.			1280	Nov. 1836	
185	Castlebury, Sarah C.			1280	Sep. 1837	
183	Cunningham, James			1280	Sep. 1837	
379	Cox, John M.			640	Mar. 1837	
237	Carnes, Philip			640	Jun. 1836	
15	Castlebury, Stephen			1280	May 19,1838	
16	Choat, Thos. B.			640	Jul. 8,1838	
19	Connor, James			640	Jul. 7,1838	
44	Clark, Thos. B.			1280	Aug. 3,1838	
45	Clark, John Westly			640	Aug. 3,1838	
38	Culver, William B.			1280	Aug. 3,1838	
71	Clifton, John M.			1280	Sep.11,1838	
84	Cannon, D. K.			1280	Oct. 4,1838	
92	Carter, Charles			1280	Oct. 4,1838	
298	Davidson, Henry			640	Jun. 1836	
52	Davis, John E.			640	Sep. 1837	
53	Davis, Elibu S.			640	Sep. 1837	
141	Dyson, Isaac C.			640	Jul. 1837	
230	Daggett, Ebenezer			640	Jul. 1837	
171	Dillon, Levi H.			1280	May. 1837	
174	Donald, John B.			640	Jan. 1837	
181	Dunian			1280	Sep. 1837	Mary Dunian,Admx
296	Dunnaho, Suanson			1280	Jul. 1836	
297	Dillard, Reuben			640	Jul. 1836	
	Davis, E.			1280	Dec. 1839	John E. Davis, Admr.
8	Davinport, James			1280	May 5,1838	
41	Denton, James T.			1280	May 19,1838	
39	Dial, John			1280	Aug. 3,1838	
40	Dial, Joseph			640	Aug. 3,1838	

No.	Name	Lgs.	Lbr.	Acres	Date	Remarks
82	Dillard, Howard			1280	Oct. 4,1838	
81	Dillard, Martha			1280	Oct. 4,1838	
206	Evans, Lorenzo			1280	Apr. 1837	
211	Evans, Jesse			1280	Feb. 1837	
316	Evans, Horace			1280	Feb. 1836	
317	Evans, Hiram			640	Feb. 1836	
318	Everly, Augustus			640	Feb. 1836	
17	Edwards, L. W.			640	Jul. 6,1838	
48	English, Wm.			640	Sep. 6,1838	
73	Ellis, George			1280	Sep. 8,1838	
292	Foster, Ira H.			640	Aug. 1836	
293	Fowler, Asa H.			1280	Aug. 1836	
294	Ferguson, Henry			640	May 1836	
236	Foster, Henry			1280	Jun. 1836	
115	Farrar, Samuel			1280	Sep. 1837	
153	Fuquey, Alanson P.			1280	Apr. 1837	
187	Forbes, Reuben S.			1280	Nov. 1836	
291	Forbes, Benjamin			640	Aug. 1836	
292	Foster, Ira H.			640	Aug. 1836	
295	Flint, Reuben			640	May 1836	
319	Farmer, Henry			640	May 1836	
42	Fuller, Calvin			640	Aug. 3,1838	
43	Fuller, Pontiff			640	Aug. 3,1838	
57	Fain, Messer			1280	Sep. 6,1838	
196	Gillespie, Thomas			640	May 1837	
209	Gibsen, Allen			1280	Mar. 1837	
239	Garrison, Stephen			1280	Jun. 1836	
126	Gibbs, Vastie			1280	Aug. 1837	
24	Gage, Benjamin			1280	Aug. 3,1837	
27	Gibs, E. W.			640	Aug. 3,1837	
47	Graves, John			1280	Sep. 6,1838	
49	Graves, Samuel J.			640	Sep. 6.1838	
93	Gates, Henry			1280	Oct. 5,1838	B. Ogden, Admr.
98	Gwin, John			1280	Oct.15,1838	
265	Gester, Thomas			640	Jul. 1837	
231	Haley, Joseph W.			640	Jun. 1837	
227	Hurd, Hugh W.			1280	Sep. 1837	
223	Horne, Wm.			640	Sep. 1837	
127	Hawkins, Pinckethman C.			640	Feb. 1837	
103	Humphries, Betty			1280	Apr. 1837	
183	Houston, John			640	Feb. 1837	
191	Hinds, Mathias			640	Sep. 1837	
200	Hardin, John D.			1280	Jul. 1837	
202	Hardin, Lion			1280	Apr. 1837	
114	Holbert, Joel			1280	Sep. 1837	
51	Hill, Massanon			640	Mar. 1837	
125	Howell, Sarah			1280	Aug. 1837	
128	Hanks, George			1280	Dec. 1836	
129	Hanks, Hansford			1280	Apr. 1836	

No.	Name	Lgs.	Lbr.	Acres	Date	Remarks
240	Hannible, Marcus			640	Jun. 1836	
244	Hawkins, Pinkney			640	Jul. 1836	
9	Hughes, Sarah			1280	May 9,1838	
12	Hall, Sam'l P.			640	May 19,1838	
36	Humphries, Joseph			1280	Aug. 3,1838	
38	Hicks, Wm. B.			1280	Aug. 3,1838	
40	Hughs, Wm.			640	Aug. 3,1838	
41	Hughs, Thomas			640	Aug. 3,1838	
50	Holbert, James			1280	Sep. 6,1838	
52	Harris, John			1280	Sep. 6,1838	
66	Hall, James N.			1280	Sep. 6,1838	
75	Harvey, Pearl W.			1280	Sep. 3,1838	
76	Hanks, George			1280	Sep. 3,1838	
69	Hudson, Peter			1280	Oct.14,1838	
70	Hudson, Howell			1280	Oct.15,1838	
67	Hall, Sam'l			1280	Jun. 2,1839	
99	Hughs, John			1280	Jun. 2,1839	
103	Head, Sason			1280	Jun. 5,1839	
170	Hassell, Daniel			640	Sep. 1837	
355	Howell, Martha Ann			640	Sep. 1837	
233	Hodges, Neil			640	Jun. 1837	
89	Ingram, Wily			1280	Oct. 4,1838	
158	Joice, Wm. N.			1280	May 1837	
162	Joice, Absalom P.			640	May 1837	
132	Johns, James F.			640	May 1837	
265	Jestor, Thomas			640	Jul. 1837	
195	Jennings, Edward			640	Jul. 1837	
166	Jackson, Charles W.			1280	Dec. 1837	
281	Jenkins, Peter H.			1280	Jul. 1836	
282	Jenkins, Wilson A.			640	Jul. 1836	
283	Jenkins, Samuel			640	Jul. 1836	
284	Jones, Stephen			640	Jul. 1836	
299	Jennings, James M.			640	Jul. 1836	
18	Johnson, Elisha D.			640	Jul. 7,1838	
62	Jackson, John			1280	Sep. 7,1838	
61	Jackson, Samuel			1280	Sep. 7,1838	
64	Jackson, Aaron			1280	Oct. 4,1838	
90	Jarvis, R.			1280	Oct. 4,1838	
91	Jolly, B.			1280	Oct. 5,1838	
192	Kelly, Richard			640	Jun. 1837	
285	Kelly, William			640	Jul. 1836	
32	Kely, Abraham H.			640	Aug. 3,1838	
55	Kutch, Daniel			1280	Sep. 6,1838	
26	Kennedy, James M.			640	Aug. 3,1838	
245	Luthur, M.			640	Jul. 1836	
286	Lowe, Wm.			1280	Jul. 1836	
287	Lowe, Samuel			1280	Jul. 1836	
288	Larkin, Simon			640	Jul. 1836	
289	Lowe, James			640	Jun. 1836	

No.	Name	Lgs.	Lbr.	Acres	Date		Remarks
290	Larkin, Stephen			640	Jun.	1836	
194	Long, James T.			640	Apr.	1837	
204	Lockey, John P.			1280	Apr.	1837	
149	Lewellin, Anion			1280	Dec.	1836	
225	Lyle, Robert S.			1280	Jun.	1837	
108	Maice, William			640	Feb.	1837	
	Manning, Joseph			1280	Nov.	1838	By act of Congress.
120	Maise, M.			1280	Sep.	1837	Jane Maise, Admx.
112	McFaddin, Wm.			640	Oct.	1836	J.S. McNombre, Assignee.
164	May, John			1280	Oct.	1836	
222	Mitchell, Alexander F.			1280	Jul.	1837	
226	Morton, Alexander A.			640	Sep.	1837	
300	Miller, Benj. P.			1280	Aug.	1836	
147	Martin, Edward S.			1280	Jun.	1839	
165	Miller, Frederick H.			1280	Sep.	1837	
144	Myrick, H. W. K.			1280	Nov.	1836	
145	Myrick, John			1280	Nov.	1836	
173	Middleton, John W.			1280	Jun.	1837	
182	Martin, Andrew			640	Apr.	1837	
189	Milliner, James			640	Dec.	1836	
219	Miller, Lemuel			1280	Feb.	1837	
220	Miller, Caleb			1280	Feb.	1837	
221	Miller, Wm.			1280	Feb.	1837	
29	Murphy, Thomas			1280	Aug. 3,	1838	
37	Midlin, George B.			1280	Aug. 3,	1838	
51	Mathews, Jacob			1280	Aug. 3,	1838	
72	Mann, Charles L.			640	Sep. 8,	1838	
97	Myrick, John E.			1280	Oct. 9,	1838	
23	McKee, Thomas J.			1280	Jun. 25,	1839	
14	McClellan, Hugh			640	May 19,	1838	
280	Norton, Wm. G.			640	Jul.	1836	
193	Neighbors, Lewis			640	May	1837	
198	Notions, Edward			640	May	1837	
199	Notions, Nathaniel			640	Mar.	1837	
276	Nelson, Wm.			1280	Aug.	1836	
277	Nelson, John			640	Aug.	1836	
279	Normon, Joseph			1280	Aug.	1836	
311	Nobbs, Allen			640	Aug.	1836	
312	Norman, Absalom			640	Aug.	1836	
275	Oakley, Franklin			640	Jun.	1836	
274	Oldham, Drary			1280	Jun.	1836	
273	Oldham, David			640	Jun.	1836	
272	Oakley, Wm.			1280	Jun.	1836	
210	Owens, Abraham			1280	Feb.	1837	
197	Oliver, Wm.			640	Mar.	1837	
271	Oneill, Daniel			1280	Nov.	1836	
79	Obonnon, J. W.			1280	Sep. 8,	1838	

No.	Name	Lgs.	Lbr.	Acres	Date	Remarks
114	Patterson, Geo. R.			640	Sep. 8,1837	Jett Street,Admr.
207	Patille, Geo			1280	Mar. 1837	By H. McClellan, Attorney.
110	Phillips, Nathaniel B.			640	May 1837	
134	Porter, Benj. P.			1280	Sep. 1837	
150	Parish, Wm. G.			1280	Apr. 1837	
268	Prewet, Wm. K.			1280	Jul. 1836	
269	Prewet, Samuel			640	Jul. 1836	
270	Prewet, Levi			640	Jul. 1836	
320	Power, Lemuel G.			1280	Aug. 1836	
59	Powdril, Thomas			1280	Sep.11,1836	
238	Rhodes, Wm.			640	Jun. 1836	
230	Robertson, Arthur			640	Jun. 1837	
113	Robertson, Elizabeth			1280	Jun. 1837	
195	Russell, Thomas			640	Apr. 1837	
203	Roan, Woodward			1280	Apr. 1837	
140	Reed, Wm.			1280	Jun. 1837	
150	Runnels, Henry			1280	Sep. 1837	
151	Runnels, Wm. G.			640	Sep. 1837	
262	Rowland, John			1280	Jun. 1836	
264	Rowland, James			640	Jun. 1836	
263	Rowland, Samuel			640	Jun. 1836	
265	Russell, John			1280	Jun. 1836	
266	Russell, Daniel			640	Jun. 1836	
267	Russell, James			640	Jun. 1836	
301	Randle, John			1280	Jul. 1836	
302	Randle, Thomas			640	Jul. 1836	
303	Randle, John H.			640	Jul. 1836	
37	Rodes, Wm. R.			640	Aug. 3,1836	
44	Rogers, D. F.			1280	Aug. 3,1836	
63	Reaves, John B.			1280	Sep. 7,1838	
104	Rains, Geo. R.			1280	Jun. 5,1839	
250	Shoon, David			640	May 1836	
249	Shorter, Daniel			1280	May 1836	
248	Smith, Wm. W.			640	Jun. 1836	
247	Sanders, Margard			1280	Jun. 1836	
240	Snell, Margaret			1280	Jun. 1836	
168	Smithers, Stephen W.			1280	Jun. 1836	
111	Shields, Lucinda			1280	Sep. 1836	
159	Stewart, Bently			640	Mar. 1838	
121	Shields, James			640	Nov. 1836	
189	Smithers, Reuben			1280	May 1836	
190	Smithers, Thomas			1280	May 1836	
59	Sublitte, Benj. B.			640	Dec. 1837	
162	Shields, David			640	Sep. 1837	
234	Sewells, Martin			640	Mar. 1836	
224	Sherwood, Charles			640	May 1837	Justus Sherwood, Admr.
402	Sherwood, Justus			640	May 1837	
5	Smith, Edward			1280	May 1837	
33	Steward, John			640	Aug. 3,1837	
255	Thornton, Stephen			1280	May 1836	

No.	Name	Lgs.	Lbr.	Acres	Date	Remarks
254	Tolly, Henry			1280	May 1836	
253	Turner, Hiram			640	Jun. 1836	
252	Turner, Samuel G.			640	Jun. 1836	
208	Thompson, Wm. D.			1280	Mar. 1838	
212	Thorp, Ann			1280	Feb. 1837	
251	Turner, James S.			1280	Jun. 1836	
13	Tipton, Wm.			640	Mar. 1837	J. J. Cravens, Admr.
309	Turner, Alfred			1280	May 1836	
310	Turner, Peter			640	Mar. 1836	
242	Vanwinkle, Arthur H.			1280	Jun. 1836	
158	Vaughan, James W.			640	Mar. 1837	
167	Vance, William C.			1280	Jul. 1836	
184	Vaughon, Abner			1280	Jun. 1837	
229	Wright, Henry			640	Jun. 1837	
228	Woods, Samuel			640	Sep. 1837	
161	Webb, James			640	Jun. 1837	
129	Walker, Simoon			1280	Jul. 1837	
152	White, Josiah			1280	Mar. 1837	
143	White, Martin			640	Mar. 1837	
254	White, Martin			640	May 1836	
256	White, Jeremiah F.			640	May 1836	
151	White, Joel			1280	Jun. 1837	
145	Warner, Russell			640	Sep. 1837	
130	Wood, Moses			640	Jan. 1837	
130	West, Martin			1280	Jan. 1837	
146	White, Wm. T.			640	Mar. 1837	
232	Winston, Kelly			640	Jun. 1837	
235	Walker, Nancy Jane			1280	Oct. 1836	
243	Wade, Alfred R.			640	Jul. 1836	
256	Wood, Wm. W.			1280	May 1836	
257	Wood, John H.			640	May 1836	
258	Wood, Samuel			640	May 1836	
259	Womick, Joseph H.			1280	Jun. 1836	
269	Womick, Robert			640	Jun. 1836	
261	Womick, Reuben			640	Jun. 1836	
304	Wornille, Lemuel			640	Jun. 1836	
305	Webb, Abner			640	Jul. 1836	
6	Weeden, Sam'l B.			640	May 4,1838	
7	Wray, John T.			640	May 4,1838	
13	Williams, Elisha			1280	May 19,1838	
16	Walker, Wm. C.			1280	May 19,1838	
30	Wilburn, Elisha T.			1280	Aug. 3,1838	
21	Walker, Wm. A.			1280	Aug. 3,1838	
46	Wisener, Wm.			1280	Aug. 3,1838	
39	Withers, Matthew R.			1280	Aug. 3,1838	
41	Williams, Wm.			1280	Aug. 3,1838	
42	Wharton, Clement L.			640	Aug. 3,1838	
43	Williams, Elija			640	Aug. 3,1838	
58	Williams, John			640	Aug. 3,1838	
65	Wolf, Hopkins			640	Sep.11,1838	

No.	Name	Lgs.	Lbr.	Acres	Date	Remarks
68	Williams, J. C.			640	Sep. 8,1838	
96	White, David			1280	Sep. 8,1838	
205	Young, Jesse			1280	Apr. 1837	
156	Yarborough, Wm.			640	May 1837	
139	Yarborough, Joel			1280	May 1837	
306	Young, Samuel			1280	May 1836	
307	Young, Wm.			640	May 1836	
308	Young, Daniel			640	May 1836	

THIRD CLASS

No.	Name	Lgs.	Lbr.	Acres	Date	Remarks
1	Ayres, Benjamin P.			640	Dec. 1837	
47	Anderson, Thomas			640	Nov. 1838	
147	Ashcroft, Levi H.			640	Jun. 1838	
199	Alrice, William C.			640	Jan. 1838	
299	Anderson, Perry			320	Dec. 1839	
386	Anderson, Lorenzo B.			320	Dec. 1839	
318	Barnes, John B.			320	Nov. 1838	
28	Barton, Samuel K.			640	Apr. 1838	
36	Brinson, Matthew			640	Jan. 1838	
41	Brock, Isaac			640	Dec. 1838	
130	Brice, Samuel			640	Dec. 1838	
44	Bell, Hannible			320	Dec. 1837	
58	Beeker, William			320	May 1839	
181	Bennett, Bass			320	Jul. 1839	
170	Baker, Jabu			640	Dec. 1837	
227	Baty, Isaah			320	Aug. 1838	
135	Bourin, James			320	Mar. 1839	
167	Brice, Wm. C.			640	Jan. 1839	
257	Borkley, Alfred			320	Apr. 1839	
155	Butler, John B.			320	Dec. 1837	
170	Barnes, Simon P.			320	Aug. 1839	
176	Borker, John			320	Jan. 1839	
263	Bradshaw, Josiah			320	Jan. 1839	
231	Buford, James M.			320	Mar. 1839	
202	Bullock, James			320	Jun. 1839	
191	Brockson, Charles J.			320	Oct. 1839	
309	Britton, William J.			320	Oct. 1837	
310	Britton, Robert T. D.			320	Sep. 1839	
315	Baily, Charles			320	Dec. 1839	
372	Beane, Ezekiel			640	Seo, 1839	
376	Ball, Wm. L.			640	Dec. 1839	
384	Brown, James W.			320	Apr. 1839	
381	Brown, Daniel			320	Dec. 1839	
87	Burgess, Hardin			640	Oct. 4,1838	
327	Beach, Philo W.			640	Dec. 1839	
119	Cowlin, William H.			640	Nov 1839	
235	Cannon, Henry B.			640	Oct. 1838	
130	Carlin, Hugh			640	Jul. 1839	

No.	Name	Lgs.	Lbr.	Acres	Date	Remarks
162	Choat, R. C.			320	Apr. 1839	
240	Craig, Joseph B.			640	Sep. 1839	
171	Cram John			640	Dec. 1838	
198	Chickester, Lemuel			320	May 1838	
207	Clark, James			320	Sep. 1839	
302	Cooper, Charles H.			640	Dec. 1837	
304	Carnes, Thomas			320	Dec. 1839	
295	Clarke, Simon B.			320	Aug. 1839	
296	Choat, Champion			640	Aug. 1839	
330	Collins, Wade			640	Dec. 1839	
331	Collins, Moses			320	Dec. 1839	
406	Cummings, Joseph			320	Dec. 1839	
402	Carpenter, Claiborne			640	Dec. 1839	
400	Cook, Milton H.			640	Dec. 1839	
122	Dial, Margaret			640	Oct. 1837	
33	Dial, Nathaniel G.			320	Oct. 1837	
32	Dial, Caleb			320	Oct. 1837	
25	Dobbyns, Walter K.			320	Apr. 1837	
45	Davis, Thomas			640	Feb. 1838	
261	Doggett, E. M.			320	Apr. 1838	
262	Doggett, Charles B.			320	Jun. 1839	
187	Duncan, John T.			640	Oct. 1839	
188	Duncan, William V.			640	Oct. 1839	
190	Domeron, Samuel			640	Aug. 1839	
219	Dupie, William L.			320	Apr. 1839	
282	Dodds, James J.			640	Mar. 1839	
284	Dunn, George S.			320	Apr. 1839	
288	Daniel, Henry			640	May 1839	
300	Daggett, Henry C.			320	May 1839	
385	Dysort, Eli B.			320	Dec. 1839	
83	Dillard, James			640	Oct. 4,1839	
53	Dockery, Matthew			640	Sep. 6,1839	
249	Edwards, Benjamin			640	Mar. 1838	
245	English, John D.			320	Feb. 1838	
132	Elliott, William			320	Feb. 1838	
232	Eitson, James			320	Mar. 1839	
189	Evans, Wm. M.			640	Oct. 1839	
277	Ellis, Stephen			640	Nov. 1839	
320	Edwards, Jefferson J.			320	Nov. 1839	
335	Ebbin, John W.			320	Dec. 1837	
31	Elliott, Humphrey			640	Jul. 1838	
130	Eakin, Wm.			640	Feb. 1838	
244	Forsyth, Jefferson			320	Aug. 1838	
29	Flerney, Gustavus A.			640	Mar. 1839	
141	Fellows, Reason G.			320	Apr. 1838	
169	Fisher, Robert H.			320	May 1839	
203	Ferguson, Elijah			320	Mar. 1838	
280	Fisher, Lampson D.			640	Oct. 1839	
287	Ford, Samuel C. T.			640	Jul. 1839	
293	Fellows, John M.			320	Apr. 1839	

No.	Name	Lgs.	Lbr.	Acres	Date	Remarks
324	Freeman, Ira M.			640	May 1839	
27	Grossvener, Sherman			640	Dec. 1838	
46	Golden, James N.			640	Jan. 1838	
55	Griswell, Elija W.			320	Dec. 1837	
255	Graham, G. L.			320	Dec. 1837	
142	Garrison, Michael			640	Jun. 1838	
178	Gellespie, W. C.			640	Dec. 1838	
264	Graham, James M.			640	Jan. 1838	
265	Graham, Andrew			640	Jan. 1838	
272	Glassgou, Polly			640	Apr. 1838	
291	Groves, George W.			640	Dec. 1838	
307	Groves, Robert A.			640	Jul. 1838	
301	Groves, Giles N.			640	Jun. 1838	
321	Gilbert, James H.			320	Dec. 1839	
225	Gillespie, Thomas			640	Dec. 1839	
226	Gillespie, William			640	Dec. 1839	
330	Gallion, Francis A.			640	Dec. 1839	
387	Gillespie, James			640	Dec. 1839	
388	Gray, William M.			320	Dec. 1839	
389	Glenn, Nathan			640	Dec. 1839	
4	Ganonoy, John			640	Apr.20,1838	
49	Graves, Samuel J.			640	Sep. 6,1838	
80	Gray, John			640	Oct. 4,1838	
102	Goss, Gideon			640	Jun. 5,1839	
10	Henning, Lewis			640	Feb. 1839	
35	Hansford, John M.			640	Jan. 1839	
128	Horkness, Benjamin			640	May 1839	
126	Hall, Amos			640	Jan. 1838	
179	Hall, Samuel			320	Jan. 1838	
184	Houston, Samuel A.			640	Mar. 1838	
228	Hicks, A. W. O.			640	Nov. 1838	
229	Hall, John			320	Jan. 1838	
180	Hall, Rebecca			640	Jan. 1838	
61	Houston, Walter			640	Dec. 1837	
246	Herriot, Robert			320	Jun. 1839	
134	Hammilton, Kelby			320	Feb. 1838	
148	Hanks, George W.			320	Mar. 1838	
151	Haynes, Gorlant			320	Sep. 1839	
259	Hortty, Elija			640	Jul. 1839	
205	Handley, A. E.			320	Oct. 1839	
260	Hall, Isaac			640	Jan. 1839	
88	Hargesda, S. N.			640	Oct. 4,1839	
106	Henderson, Ambrose			640	Jun. 5,1839	
186	Hammers, Elisha			640	Apr. 1839	
194	Hendrix, Arastus C.			320	Oct. 1839	
218	Howard, John			640	Feb. 1839	
220	Hignight, Samuel P.			320	Dec. 1838	
239	Hoislip, Calvin W. H.			320	Jul. 1838	
271	Hassell, Zacchus			640	Jul. 1838	
290	Hodges, Isaac			320	May 1839	
311	Hill, George D.			640	Oct. 1839	
312	Henderson, Samuel C.			320	Apr. 1839	

No.	Name	Lgs.	Lbr.	Acres	Date		Remarks
340	Hughes, Mary			640	Nov.	1839	
342	Hughes, James M.			320	Nov.	1839	
341	Hughes, John J.			320	Nov.	1839	
322	Henderson, Robert W.			320	Nov.	1839	
328	Houston, Rheufus W.			320	Dec.	1839	
343	Howard, Evan			320	Dec.	1839	
344	Howard, Allen			320	Dec.	1839	
354	Horton, John S.			320	Dec.	1839	
357	Henderson, John M.			320	Dec.	1839	
360	Howard, William			640	Dec.	1839	
395	Horinton, B. J.			320	Dec.	1839	
404	Hullen, Robert S.			320	Dec.	1839	
39	Hooper, Wm. M.			320	Apr.	1839	
278	Houly, George W.			640	Apr.	1838	
223	Irvin, James			640	Aug.	1838	
182	Jones, James A. S. F.			320	Jul.	1837	
211	Jennings, J. J.			640	Mar.	1838	Susan Jennings, Admx.
308	Jones, Thomas			640	Dec.	1838	
232	Johns, Micajo H.			640	Dec.	1839	
317	Jacobs, William			320	Sep.	1839	
407	Jones, Milton W.			640	Dec.	1839	
117	Kelly, Henry B.			640	May	1839	
168	King, John			640	Oct.	1839	
204	Kinedy, Thomas P.			320	May	1839	
283	King, Thomas			640	Nov.	1839	
238	Keley, Cyrus K.			640	Dec.	1839	
26	Kerby, David D.			320	Mar.	1838	
289	Kilgore, Thomas			640	Jul.	1839	
172	Luthur, Josiah			320	Sep.	1839	
252	Lamkins, Thomas C.			320	Sep.	1838	
285	Lee, Owen			640	Dec.	1839	
294	Ladd, Wm. J.			640	Oct.	1839	
312	Lower, Francis X.			640	Dec.	1839	
334	Landrum, Wm. P.			320	Dec.	1839	
350	Lee, James S.			320	Jul.	1839	
368	Lee, Wm. H.			320	Dec.	1839	
166	Mosely, Morrel H.			640	Sep.	1838	
6	McCrora, Allen			320	Mar.	1838	
224	Mathews, Nathan			640	Nov.	1838	
9	McClellan, Samuel K.			320	Jun.	1839	
18	Mason, John			640	Nov.	1837	
23	Moore, George S.			320	Oct.	1838	
167	Mosely, John H.			640	Oct.	1838	
236	McKee, Francis V.			320	Jun.	1839	
133	Mathews, Thomas D.			640	Jun.	1839	
24	Maise, Matthew			640	Jul.	1838	
165	Mears, Thomas P.			320	Jun.	1839	

No.	Name	Lgs.	Lbr.	Acres	Date		Remarks
201	Mayfield, Reuben A.			640	Oct.	1838	
185	Montgomery, William			320	Sep.	1839	
234	McFerson, Daniel			640	Sep.	1839	
193	Martin, Wm. W.			320	Oct.	1838	
196	Messick, Jane			640	May	1839	
201	Messick, Robert			320	May	1839	
212	McKee, Wm. A. G.			320	Apr.	1839	
274	Morgan, John			640	Apr.	1838	
281	Morris, Malinda			640	Nov.	1839	
298	Miller, John M.			320	Jul.	1839	
303	Maun, Neill			640	Dec.	1839	
305	McInnis, Daniel			320	Dec.	1839	
318	McImsey, George D.			320	Dec.	1839	
325	McClure, Chancey H.			320	Feb.	1838	
339	Moorman, Charles			640	Dec.	1839	
347	Muslin, Elisha			320	Dec.	1839	
361	Morgan, Jeremiah V.			640	Dec.	1839	
363	Morgan, Daniel			320	Dec.	1839	
364	Morgan, David L.			320	Dec.	1839	
365	Mascion, David			320	Dec.	1839	
205	Moore, John S.			320	Nov.	1838	
403	Morgan, Wm. R.			320	Dec.	1839	
337	Mooreman, Charles W.			320	Dec.	1839	
223	Norchart, N. W.			640	Nov.	1838	
253	Nelson, Samuel			640	Dec.	1837	
175	O'Neill, Charles			640	Sep.	1839	
378	Overton, James D.			320	Dec.	1839	
383	Overton, Daniel M.			320	Nov.	1839	
16	Pugh, Joseph E.			320	Oct.	1838	
37	Parker, Jeste			320	Mar.	1838	
116	Price, Richard E.			640	Apr.	1839	
122	Potts, Abington C.			640	Dec.	1838	
251	Potts, John T.			320	Dec.	1838	
152	Pierce, Jesse			640	Jan.	1838	
238	Phillips, S. A.			640	Dec.	1837	
275	Parker, Joseph A.			640	Dec.	1838	
276	Parker, Isaac G.			640	Dec.	1838	
279	Peoples, Thomas			320	Apr.	1839	
349	Pouns, Samuel J.			640	Oct.	1839	
352	Price, Nathaniel M.			320	Dec.	1839	
353	Price, Richard			320	Dec.	1839	
149	Plurmer, Charles E.			320	Aug.	1839	
2	Phillips, Piakney			640	Apr. 5,	1838	
17	Ryan, Richard			640	Nov.	1837	
19	Ryan, Augustus M.			320	Nov.	1837	
166	Reid, John A.			320	Feb.	1839	
137	Rogers, Alvin			320	Mar.	1838	
240	Roberts, John R.			640	Oct.	1839	
241	Roberts, Isaac H.			320	Oct.	1839	
270	Reamond, Emily			640	Apr.	1838	

No.	Name	Lgs.	Lbr.	Acres	Date	Remarks
306	Ross, William			320	Dec. 1839	
324	Renfroe, James M.			320	Dec. 1839	
359	Reed, Samuel A.			320	Sep. 1839	
394	Rowland, James			320	Dec. 1839	
3	Roun, John M.			640	Apr. 6,1838	
95	Ridgeway, L. S.			640	Oct. 5,1838	
12	Smith, John A.			640	Mar. 1838	
21	Snell, John W.			640	Mar. 1839	
30	Straw, Leonard			640	Oct. 1838	
38	Slaughter, Turner			320	Apr. 1838	
42	Smith, Buckner			640	Dec. 1837	
60	Smith, Benjamin J.			320	Mar. 1839	
160	Shields, William			320	Dec. 1837	
162	Spinney, Alva			320	Mar. 1839	
139	Straughn, John			320	Oct. 1838	
150	Stewer, John			640	Mar. 1839	
147	Stanford, John			640	Mar. 1839	
173	Sample, John			640	Apr. 1838	
206	Snider, William			640	Mar. 1839	
209	Snider, Susan			640	Mar. 1839	
148	Samford, Evan			320	Dec. 1837	
192	Slaughter, John			640	May 1837	
214	Snider, Samuel			640	Feb. 1837	
197	Snider, Sanford			640	Mar. 1839	
297	Sessums, Redding			640	Feb. 1839	
345	Sprowls, Samuel			640	Dec. 1839	
351	Sprowls, James M.			320	Jul. 1839	
346	Stillwell, Green S.			640	Dec. 1839	
348	Stillwell, John A.			640	Dec. 1839	
362	Starr, Thomas			640	Dec. 1839	
368	Samford, Elkand			320	Dec. 1839	
369	Samford, Elija			320	Dec. 1839	
370	Snider, Joel			640	Dec. 1839	
375	Samford, William			640	Dec. 1839	
371	Samford, Simon Z.			640	Dec. 1839	
373	Samford, George			320	Dec. 1838	
392	Samford, Samuel			640	Feb. 1839	
393	Samford, Thomas			320	Dec. 1839	
396	Samford, Absalom			640	Dec. 1839	
397	Samford, Coswell			320	Dec. 1839	
398	Samford, John			320	Dec. 1839	
399	Samford, Mary			640	Dec. 1839	
163	Sweet, Edward			320	Dec. 1838	
239	Storkey, John			320	Nov. 1839	
319	Snider, Jesse			640	Nov. 1839	
1	Shepherd, Wm.			640	Apr. 5,1838	
85	Short, Drawry			640	Oct. 4,1838	
336	Truitt, Isaac			640	Jan. 1839	
250	Turpin, Wm.			640	Jul. 1839	
131	Turner, John H.			640	Jul. 1839	
146	Thompson, Layfield			320	Nov. 1839	
292	Thompson, Benjamin C.			320	Sep. 1839	

No.	Name	Lgs.	Lbr.	Acres	Date		Remarks
138	Talbot, Joanna			640	Sep.	1838	
401	Tombs, Robert			640	Dec.	1839	
382	Tomey, Wm. B.			640	Dec.	1839	
5	Vanriper, John			640	Sep.	1838	
208	Vance, Lorenzo D.			640	Dec.	1837	
48	Wagstaff, James			640	Feb.	1838	
221	Watkins, L. T.; Dec'd.			640	Dec.	1837	Elizabeth Watkins, Admx.
222	Watkins, Berymin D. S.			640	Dec.	1837	
40	Watkins, Burnett R.			640	Feb.	1838	
178	Watkins, Israel P.			640	Apr.	1838	
37	Watkins, Benjamin E.			320	May	1839	
62	Whitaker, Robert			640	Nov.	1838	
63	Whitaker, James W.			320	Nov.	1838	
247	Wedgworth, David B.			640	Nov.	1838	
249	Williamson, James P.			640	Dec.	1838	
136	Wheeler, Ransem			640	Apr.	1839	
163	Waller, Jacob M.			640	Jun.	1839	
258	Williams, William			320	Jan.	1839	
200	White, Reuben B.			320	Jun.	1838	
176	Withers, Silas			320	Apr.	1838	
215	White, Henry H.			640	Nov.	1838	
219	White, William H.			640	Nov.	1838	
273	Wilkinson, John			640	Jun.	1839	
286	Waits, Bolin G.			320	Dec.	1839	
316	Wilbourn, James L.			320	Dec.	1839	
314	Wood, Thomas			640	Nov.	1839	
320	Wood, James P.			320	Nov.	1839	
339	Wood, Christopher G.			320	Nov.	1839	
332	Wright, Joshua			640	Dec.	1839	
358	Wright, Amos P.			320	Dec.	1839	
369	Weaver, Ezekiel			640	Dec.	1839	
390	Webb, Wm. D.			320	Nov.	1839	
391	Webb, Reuben			320	Nov.	1839	
380	Webb, Sarah			640	Dec.	1839	
54	Willis, Robert			640	May	1839	
168	Wood, John			320	Dec.	1837	
169	Wood, Solomon			320	Dec.	1837	
140	Willis, Theodore G. A.			320	May	1839	
94	Withers, Valentine			640	Oct.	5,1838	
20	White, Henly			640	Oct.	5,1838	
100	Withers, Horace			640	Jan.	2,1839	
101	Walker, Peter			640	Jan.	5,1839	
248	Yates, Joseph C.			640	Dec.	1838	
144	Yarborough, Asa			640	Dec.	1838	

VICTORIA COUNTY

FIRST CLASS

No.	Name	Lgs.	Lbr.	Acres	Date	Remarks
70	Allan, James C.	1/3				
9	Burns, Arthur		1			
14	Baxter, William		1			
15	Baxter, Henry	1/3				
45	Balfour, David H.	1/3				
66	Bracken, William	1				
91	Bryan, Morgan O.	1/3				
92	Bryne, James	1	1			
73	Burns, Robert	1/3				Arthur Burns, Admr.
10	Carlisle, Robert		1			
53	Clarke, John		1			
35	Dakes, Dávid	1/3				
36	Dowlau, Patrick	3/4	1			
44	Douglass, John	1	1			John McHenry, Admr.
52	Dunbar, Lavinia		1			
56	Driscoll, Daniel O.	1/3				
58	Duggen, Catharine		1			
69	Datton, Patrick	1/3				John McHenry, Admr.
72	Duggen, Michael	1/3				
132	Edmondson, James	1/3				
4	Farish, Oscar	1/3				
97	Fraser, Hugh	1/3				Rob't Carlisle, agent for exec'r.
16	Garrette, John	1/3				
204	Gamos, Mana Cutario	1	1			Widow of Saragossa Rios.
5	Hardy, Milton H.	1/3				
8	Hayes, John	1/3				
12	Hart, Mary; heirs of		1			By Bridget, Mary and Timothy Hart.
22	Hardy, William		1			Margaret Hardy, Admx.
32	Howard, Henry	1/3				
57	Hays, Thomas		1			
122	Hart, John		1			B. Hart, Admr.
203	Hernandez, Jose M'a.		1			
74	Keating, John		1			

No.	Name	Lgs.	Lbr.	Acres	Date	Remarks
23	Linn, John J.	1	1			
29	Latsche, John	1/3				
47	Linn, Charles	1/3				John L. Linn, Admr.
55	Linn, Edward			369		
55	Linn, John	1	1			
90	Lambert, Walker			369		
94	Leavy, Patrick O.	1/3				
3	McHenry, John		1			
7	Moody, James A.	1/3				
20	McCrabb, John	3/4	1			
34	Marvin, Seth	1/3				
46	Myers, John	1/3				Seth Marvin, Admr.
68	Morgan, Richard	1/3				
96	McAuley, Malcolm		1			
111	McFarlane, John W. B.	1/3				
120	Odium, Benjamin	2/3	1			
75	Perry, Edward		1			
85	Pollan, John		1			
2	Quinn, Patrick	1/3				
6	Quinn, James	1	1			
11	Quinn, Bridget		1			
71	Quinn, Patrick			369		
13	Ryan, James			369		
28	Ryan, Jacob	1/3				
39	Reynolds, James			369		Sylvanus Hatch, assignee.
82	Ryan, Patrick		1			
27	Ryan, Nicholas J.	1/3				James Kerr, Attorney
17	Trudo, Margaret		1			
30	Taylor, William R.		1			
38	Taylor, Josiah		1			Hepecbeth Taylo Heir.
24	Tumblinson, Joseph	3/4	1			
25	Taylor, Josiah	1/3				
95	Toole, Jeremiah O		1			
93	Teal, Rosa	1	1			Peter Teal,agen
26	Taylor, Creed	1/3				Joseph Tumlin-son,att'y in fa
37	Vickerry, Carmin W.	1/3				
98	Venabides, Ysidro		1			
178	Villa, Pecho		1			
21	Wright, James	1	1			
33	Wood, John H.	1/3				

No.	Name	Lgs.	Lbr.	Acres	Date	Remarks
48	Waldemyer, Antonio	1/3				John J. Linn, Admr.
51	Ware, Joseph			369		
104	White, John	1/3				John McCrabb, Executor.

SECOND CLASS

No.	Name	Lgs.	Lbr.	Acres	Date	Remarks
76	Barry, Thomas	1/3			Jul. 3,1838	
79	Buchanan, John	1	1		Jul. 3,1838	
185	Brown, Ervin			640	Jan. 3,1840	
112	Bromley, Benjamin			640	Sep. 6,1838	
86	Creanor, Charles M.			640	Sep.26,1838	
101	Cameron, Erven	1/3			Sep.26,1838	
108	Chamberlain, Henry	1/3			Sep. 6,1838	
117	Carrigan, John			640	Sep. 6.1838	
109	Dowess, Isaac	1/3			Sep. 6,1838	
110	Devine, John			1280	Sep. 6,1838	
107	Delmas, Charles F.	1/3			Aug. 2,1838	
100	Eakin, John J.			640	Jul.27,1838	
87	Fugett, Joel			640	Jul.26,1838	
191	Grammont, J. J. H.			640	Jul. 8,1840	
50	Harrison, John	1/3			Mar.15,1838	
59	Johnson, Malcolm N.	1/3			Mar. 2,1838	
88	Jones, Ebenezer R.	1/3			Jul.26,1838	
77	Kemper, John F.	1/3			Jul. 3,1838	
114	Lease, George			640	Sep. 6,1838	
84	Manning, James M.	1/3			Jul.26,1838	
99	McKee, George			640	Jul.26,1838	
106	Mahoney, Peter			1280	Aug. 2,1838	
113	Murphy, James			640	Sep. 6,1838	
144	McMin Neuna, Wm.	2/3	1		Sep.26,1838	
63	Parkinson, Millard M.	1/3			Mar.28,1838	
118	Price, John T.	1/3			Oct. 3,1838	
121	Palmer, David D.	1/3			Nov. 2,1838	
202	Punch, John			1280	Jan. 8,1840	Mary Odlum,Admx.
62	Solbery, John	1/3			Mar.28,1838	
105	Smith, John	1/3			Aug. 2,1838	
205	Sweeney, Thomas			1280	Jan. 8,1840	
80	Wenfield, Hammond	1/3			Jul.26,1838	

THIRD CLASS

No.	Name	Lgs.	Lbr.	Acres	Date	Remarks
148	Adams, Alexander			640	Dec. 4,1839	
175	Anderson, Henry			320	Jan. 4,1840	
197	Anderson, Ephraim D.			320	Jan. 9,1840	
136	Black, James E.			320	Jun.27,1839	
150	Brown, John Harrison			320	Dec.12,1839	
151	Black, John W.			640	Dec.16,1839	
158	Black, John M.			640	Dec.27,1839	
201	Browning, John S.			320	Jan.11,1840	
146	Converse, John			320	Oct.13,1839	
159	Cyrus, William			640	Dec.30,1839	
160	Cyrus, Nimrod			640	Dec.30,1839	
166	Collins, John			640	Dec.31,1839	
123	Davies, William B.			320	Apr. 4,1839	
149	Deen, John W.			320	Dec.11,1839	
155	Deen, Nancy			640	Dec.18,1839	
181	Daniel, John			320	Jan. 7,1840	
198	Erskin, William			320	Jan.10,1840	
199	Erskin, John P.			320	Jan.10,1840	
162	Fanow, John M.			320	Dec.30,1839	
172	Fitch, Dennis M.			320	Dec.31,1839	
196	Fanell, Griffin			320	Jan. 8,1840	
124	Griffiths, Edward			320	Apr. 4,1839	
133	Gaffeny, Owen			640	Apr. 6,1839	
156	Guthrie, George W.			320	Dec.26,1839	
129	Hamilton, Calvin S.			640	Apr. 4,1839	
137	Halpin, Paget			320	Jun.27,1839	
157	Hix, George W.			640	Dec.27,1839	
167	Hughes, Thomas			640	Dec.31,1839	
180	Hutchins, John H.			320	Jan. 6,1840	
192	Hall, Samuel			320	Jan. 8,1840	
169	Hanly, Martin			320	Dec.31,1839	
184	Irahem, George W.			320	Jan. 7,1840	
143	James, Ashbury			320	Sep.23,1839	
152	Kemplin, Nicholas			320	Dec.16,1839	
194	Kirvin, Peter			640	Jan. 8,1840	
211	Kerr, William P.			640	Jan.11,1840	
183	Lane, Cornelins			640	Jan. 7,1840	
130	McDaniel, John C.			320	Apr. 4,1839	
139	Munay, Adam			320	Jul.29,1839	
163	Miller, Jacob A.			320	Dec.30,1839	

No.	Name	Lgs.	Lbr.	Acres	Date	Remarks
170	McMuney, Charles F.			320	Dec.31,1839	
171	Moore, Henry J.			320	Dec.31,1839	
187	McCaleb, Ephraim			640	Jan. 7,1840	
190	Mosier, William H.			320	Jan. 8,1840	
193	McCaleb, Alson			320	Jan. 8,1840	
210	McKenzie, Joseph M.			640	Jan.11,1840	
213	May Patrick			320	Jan.11,1840	
195	Moore, Samuel			320	Jan. 8,1840	
161	Nelmes, Allenson			640	Dec.30,1839	
189	Neill, William H.			640	Jan. 7,1840	
153	Pleasants, John			320	Dec.18,1839	
209	Parker, William T.			320	Jan.11,1840	
141	Rawson, Philerman S.			320	Aug. 8,1839	
206	Richeson, Varland			320	Jan.11,1840	
208	Richardson, Benjamin			320	Jan.11,1840	
207	Reilly, James T. O.			320	Jan.11,1840	
127	Swain, Sterling H. L.			640	Apr. 4,1839	
128	Sapp, Abraham			640	Apr. 4,1839	
135	Stephens, Edward			320	May 27,1839	
142	Swift, Madison			640	Aug. 8,1839	
164	Smith, Joseph			320	Dec.30,1839	
165	Smith, Asa			320	Dec.30,1839	
173	Spier, John			640	Jan. 3,1840	
174	Spier, Samuel			320	Jan. 3,1840	
179	Santos, Manuel De Los			320	Jan. 4,1840	
182	Stanton, James M.			320	Jan. 7,1840	
188	Stills, Moses			640	Jan. 7,1840	
200	Stockman, Frederick			640	Jan.11,1840	
214	Soy, James			320	Jan.11,1840	
168	Spier, William			320	Dec.31,1839	
154	Tippo, Daniel			320	Dec.18,1839	
186	Tarpley, S. O.			640	Jan.11,1840	
212	Taylor, Allan			320	Jan.11,1840	
131	White, Andrew W.			320	Apr. 4,1839	

WASHINGTON COUNTY

FIRST CLASS

No.	Name	Lgs.	Lbr.	Acres	Date	Remarks
7	Allcorn, James	1	1			
4	Atkinson, Jesse B.	1	1			
74	Alexander, Daniel			369		
136	Armstead, Robert S.	1	1			
182	Allcorn, William E.		1			
306	Arrington, William W.	2/3	1			
432	Adams, John	1/3				

No.	Name	Lgs.	Lbr.	Acres	Date	Remarks
202	Adams, Benjamin F.	1/3				
440	Allcorn, John H.			369		
3	Buffington, Anderson	1	1			
6	Barnett, George W.	1	1			
9	Beauchamp, John	1	1			
20	Blue, Uriah	1/3				
38	Barcley, John A.	1/3				
52	Billings, Loring	1/3				C. B. Stewart, Assignee.
102	Byars, Noah T.	1/3				
107	Bright, John	1/3				
111	Bartlett, Joseph C.	1/3				
126	Bibb, Richard	1	1			
134	Bradberry, James	1	1			
159	Boatright, Friend		1			
178	Berry, Jackson	1/3				
181	Barnhill, Pleasant A.	1/3				
209	Boren, Matthew	1	1			
256	Bridges, William B.	1	1			
286	Baily, Edward	1/3				
288	Berry, John	1	1			
289	Berry, Joseph	1/3				
326	Beccam, Mary; and heirs	1	1			
360	Brown, Samuel P.		1			
391	Boatwright, Lewis	1	1			
399	Bibb, Dandridge J.	1/3				
405	Bain, Moses		1			
416	Boatwright, Willaby	1	1			
417	Balton, Seth T.	1	1			
447	Barton, John		1			
524	Blakey, Thomas W.		1			
544	Boatwright, Amy; Dec'd.		1			Thos. Boatwright, Assignee
555	Burke, Benijah B.; Dec'd	1/4				Thos. Gay, Admr.
569	Bullock, Jonathan C.	1/3				
584	Belcher, Barshibe		1			
168	Brisbum, William; Dec'd.	1	1			A. C. Delaplain, Admr.
480	Bartlett, Jesse; Dec'd		1			J. C. Bartlett, Admr.
28	Blyth, Sion	1	1			James W. Smith, Admr.
60	Brewster, Nathaniel R.	1/3				John R. Cummings, Admr.
149	Boatwright, William	1/3				
156	Boatwright, Levi	1/3				
427	Bruner, George C.	1	1			
284	Ballentze, J. J.	1/3				P. M. Mercer, Admr.
18	Caruthers, Young; Dec'd	1/3				Allen Caruthers, Admr.
28	Connell, Isaac	1	1			
`34	Crawford, Robert	1/3				

No.	Name	Lgs.	Lbr.	Acres	Date	Remarks
77	Collins, Jno. S.	1/3				B. B. Stewart, Assignee.
79	Clements, Lewis	1/3				
82	Clampitt, Nathan	1/3				
153	Caruthers, Ewing; Dec'd.			369		Allen Caruthers, Admr.
158	Cook, James R.	1	1			
167	Carmean, John	1	1			
187	Colvin, Aaron		1			
198	Coe, Philip		1			
212	Clements, Ira	1	1			
213	Chambers, Thomas	1	1			
221	Childs, Lewis L.			369		
222	Cole, John W.		1			
226	Clements, Austin	1/3				
229	Clampitt, F. G.	1/3				
233	Carmack, Alexander	1/3				
243	Covington, Hays			369		
244	Clark, James		1			
247	Covington, Charles	1	1			
260	Clark, Haner	1/3				James Clark, Admr.
295	Chance, Joseph B.		1			
329	Cole, William A.	1/3				
340	Cox, James		1			
341	Castleman, Jacob	1/3				
343	Chapman, Heman	1/3				
353	Castleman, John	1/3				
363	Crawford, John B.	1/3				
401	Cummins, Susanah		1			
424	Cox, John	1/3				
433	Cogswell, Mary	1	1			
492	Cartmell, Henry R.	1/3				
542	Chamberlin, Willard	1/3				
521	Coleman, Greta H.		1			
551	Carey, Wm. M.; Dec'd.	1/3				Wm. P. Smith, Admr.
558	Curd, Isaac F. W.	1/3				
578	Cummins, Moses		1			
579	Clampitt, Ezakial; Dec'd.		1			Moses Cummins, Executer.
364	Cooper, Alfred M.	1/2				A. Dillard, Assignee.
365	Cooper, Alfred M.	1/2	1			
346	Crunk, Nicholas S.	1/4	1			Rob't Stevenson, Assignee.
51	Chadoin, Thomas	1	1			
17	Clayton, Joseph A.	1/3				
45	Clemmons, James		1			
80	Charles, William T.	2/3	1			
109	Crunk, Nicholas S.	3/4	1			
192	Coles, John P.		1			
150	Charles, William T.	1/3				

No.	Name	Lgs.	Lbr.	Acres	Date	Remarks
151	Caruthers, Allen	1/3				
200	Cox, Euclid M.	1	1			
381	Cain, John	1/3				Joseph S. Martin Admr.
357	Clark, Abraham K.	1/3				
454	Charles, Rufus	1/3				
	Cobler, Edwin S.	1	1			Proved before District Court.
	Cartmell, Henry R.	2/3	1			Proved before District Court.
16	Dunham, Daniel T.	1/3				
33	Dallas, James L.	1/3				
61	Dallas, Elizabeth	1	1			
62	Dallas, Walter R.	1/3				
67	Davis, Abner C.; Dec'd.	1/3				Wm. P. Smith, Admr.
122	Dutcher, Alfred	1/3				
170	Delaplain, Absolam C.	1	1			
180	Dillard, Abraham	3/4	1			
183	Dillard, Joseph; Dec'd.	1	1			Susan Dillard, Admx.
193	Davis, Lee R.	1	1			
214	Dobbins, Sterritt	1	1			
216	Dobbins, John	1	1			
227	Davis, Hiram E.	1	1			
232	Dillard, Dan'l B.	1/3				
267	Dix, John	1	1			
294	Dunlap, John	1	1			
309	Davis, George W.		1			
313	Dair, George	1	1			
370	Dobbins, William S.	1/3				
398	Dunn, Mathew			369		
419	Davis, Moses H.	1/3				
422	Donoho, Charles		1			
478	Drinkard, John; Dec'd.	1/3				Jesse Bartlett, Admr.
495	Dallas, Alexander J.	1/3				
534	Dever, William		1			
570	Dees, Malcisso	1/3				
203	Dunn, Mathew	2/3	1			
213	Daniel, G. W.	1/3				Anthony Butler, att'y for heirs.
491	Davis, George W.	1/3				William Pettus, Admr.
18	Davidson, Albert B. C.	1/3				Wm. W. Grant, Admr.
11	Evens, Moses	1/3				
19	Evitts, Samuel, Sr.	1	1			
37	Edger, Joseph S.; Dec'd.	1/3				Wm. W. Grant, Admr.
87	Evitts, James H.	1	1			
88	Evitts, Samuel G.	1/3				

No.	Name	Lgs.	Lbr.	Acres	Date	Remarks
108	Early, Thomas	1/3				
132	Eldridge, Thomas			369		
359	Echols, John	1	1			
474	Early, James C.; Dec'd.	1/3				Moses T. Martin, Admr.
543	Evitts, Sam'l G.	1				Special Act.
574	Ellis, Willis L.	2/3	1			
173	Ellis, Willis S.	1/3				
438	Early, John	1	1			
445	Ellis, James	1/3				J. Ellis,att'y for Admr. J. Gregg.
175	Fulcher, James	1/3				
196	Franks, Littlebury B.		1			
203	Fulcher, John		1			
206	Furmash, Robert; Dec'd.	1/3				L. B. Franks, Admr.
263	Farmer, James	1	1			
270	Ferrell, William L.	1/3				
271	Friar, Daniel B.		1			
287	Fleming, Peter		1			
375	Furnash, Charles, Sr.		1			
376	Fleming, Robert	1/3				
378	Furnash, Charles, Jr.	1/3				
379	Furnash, Conrad	1/3				
382	Furnash, Jehu			369		L. B. Franks, Assignee.
477	Freed, Henry; Dec'd.	1/3				Jesse Bartlett, Admr.
485	Finney, Robert	1/3				
486	Furnash, John	1	1			
509	Floyd, Joseph	1/3				
514	Ferrell, John	1/6				
515	Ferrell, John	1/6				Jesse Bartlett,
517	Frost, David			369		Assignee.
533	Foster, James		1			
571	Furnash, Charles	2/3	1			John W. Porter,
332	French, John	1/3				Assignee.
502	Fitzgerald, Lankford	1	1			
63	Fisher, John	3/4	1			
444	Farney, Sam	1/3				J. Ellis Att'y for Admr. J. Gregg.
36	Gant, William W.	1/3				
57	Gilpin, Elins; Dec'd.	1	1			Rob't Stevenson, Admr.
83	Gates, Amos	2/3	1			
85	Gates, Samuel H.	1	1			
97	Gray, James	1/3				
120	Gosline, John	1/3				Z. N. Morrell, Assignee.

No.	Name	Lgs.	Lbr.	Acres	Date	Remarks
129	Gay, Thomas		1			
139	Gray, Cary D.	1	1			
147	Gilleland, Daniel		1			
211	Graham, Joshua	1	1			
240	Graham, John	1/3				
242	Gentry, Frederick B.	1/3				
366	Garza, Francisco	1/3				
500	Gates, Samuel; Dec'd.		1			A & C Gates, executors
523	Gee, Alfred		1			M. T. Martin Assignee.
552	Gwynn, J.; Dec'd.	1/3				Wm. P. Smith, Admr
327	Guthrie, John F.	1	1			
84	Gates, William		1			Amos Gates, Admr.
299	Grimes, Rufus	1/3				
	Garraty, Joseph W.	1	1			Proven before Dist. Court.
2	Hall, William G.	1	1			
8	Houston, Andrew D.	1				Robert Stevenson, Assignee.
14	Hiach, Michael H.	1	1			
24	Hughes, Bradford	1	1			
27	Hughes, Moses	1/3				
43	Hunt, John C.	1/3				
46	Hoxey, Asa	1	1			
49	Hughes, Thomas M.	1/3				
54	Henderson, Francis K.	1	1			
56	Hall, Jackson	1	1			
60	Harbour, Joseph		1			
68	Hensley, Johnson	1	1			
94	Hill, Jeffrey B.	1/3				
96	Hill, James M.	1/3				
103	Hall, James, Jr.		1			
104	Hall, John	3/4	1			
121	Hudson, H. C.	1/3				
127	Hardeman, John M.	1	1			
128	Hardeman, Blackstone	1	1			
163	Harbour, Geo, W.	1/3				
186	House, John P.	1	1			
204	Houston, Andrew D.		1			
210	Houston, David	1	1			
217	Hughs, John I.	1	1			
252	Hope, Richard	1/3				
354	Hill, Asa	1	1			
356	Hollingsworth, James			369		
358	Hope, Prosper	3/4	1			
384	Hughes, Talliferro S.	1	1			
392	Hickman, Samuel	1/3				
396	Hall, William A.		1			
403	Hall, James, 3rd		1			C. B. Stewart, Assignee
404	Hudson, Obediah		1			
409	Harbour, James M.	1/3				
412	Hawkins, William J.			369		

No.	Name	Lgs.	Lbr.		Date	Remarks
421	Hill, Thomas		1			
452	Harrald, Denis		1			
458	Hill, W. C. J.	1	1			
469	Harrel, Benjamin	1/3				
473	Hughs, Moses	1				M. Evans & R. R. Peebles, Assignee
475	Hill, William W.	1/3				
490	Hensly, Harmon		1			By E. Hensley, for heirs.
519	Hall, James		1			
531	Harvey, James	1/3				
537	Hill, William W.	2/3	1			
542	Hensley, Jackson	2/3	1			
549	Hawkins, William			369		
567	Heath, Sam'l; Dec'd.	1/3				J. Scott & J. H. Wood, Admr's.
573	Hollingsworth, James	2/3	1			
583	Hawkins, Isaac K.			369		
253	Harrington, Arabella		1			
53	Henderson, John	1/3				
161	Honeycut, Roland	1	1			Heirs of.
166	Harbour, Thomas S.	1/3				
245	Hatfield, B. M.		1			David Ayres, Assignee.
497	Hillhouse, Wm.	1	1			Wm. H. Steel, Admr.
498	Hillhouse, Eli	1/3				Wm. H. Steel, Admr.
503	Hudson, David	1/3				
504	Hensley, Charles			369		James Hughes, Assignee.
654	Hunter, Wm.	1/3				Alanson Ferguson Admr.
573	Hollingsworth, James	2/3	1			
127	Haggard, Morrel	1/3				James Haggard, Admr.
	Holtzelaw, Barnard W.	1	1			Proven before District Court.
205	Ingram, Allen	1/3				
13	Jones, William	1/3				
66	Jackson, Elisha D.		1			
165	Jones, Stephen		1			
394	Jones, John H.		1			
471	Jones, Marcella	1	1			
387	Jameson, John D.	1/3				Aaron Colvin, Assignee.
444	Jackson, Isaac; Dec'd.		1			
493	Jackson, Isaac	1				
492	Johnson, Nathan B.	1/3				Wm. Pettus, Admr.
462	Jones, William C.	1/3				

No.	Name	Lgs.	Lbr.	Acres	Date	Remarks
249	Kirkpatrick, J. D.	1/3				
291	Kerr, Wm. P.	1/3				
315	Kennerly, Overton	1	1			
352	Kerr, George A.	1	1			
439	Kiggins, James; Dec'd.		1			To Nancy Kiggins and heirs.
467	Kellogg, Ben.; Dec'd.	1	1			Geo. W. Davis, Admr.
572	Kenyon, Alfred, Dec'd.		1			
383	Kerr, Lucy		1			
26	Kerr, Augustus T.	1	1			
37	Kerr, John	1/3				Lucy Kerr, Admr.
330	King, Aaron B.	1/3				J.H.M. Davidge, Admr.
381	King, Amos	1/3				Littlebury B. Franks, Admr.
507	Kimble, George	3/4	1			Prudence Kimble, Admx.
44	Lawrence, Adam	3/4	1			
45	Lynch, Joseph P.	1	1			
78	Lott, John	1	1			
100	Lynch, James		1			
117	Long, John	1/3				
148	Lester, Josiah		1			
169	Lyford, John	1/3				
192	Lawrence, Samuel		1			
254	Lewis, William	1				Isaac E. Robertson, Assignee.
255	Lewis, William		1			
282	Lusk, Samuel	1	1			
303	Lawrence, Joseph	1/3				
306	Larbelletrier, Charles	1/3				
314	Lawrence, Daivd		1			
410	Lockhard, Sam'l, Dec'd.		1			Heirs of.
414	Lawrence, Claiborne	1				
415	Lawrence, Claiborne		1			C.B. Stewart, Assignee.
429	Lee, Hiram; Dec'd.			369		Sanford Woodward Admr.
446	Lopez, Pethro	1/3				
530	Lewis, William J.	1	1			
535	Lee, Abner		1			
559	Lynch, John L.	1	1			
562	Little, James	1/3				
128	Lee, Isaac		1			Sanford Woodward executor.
547	Lessessier, Alexander	1/3				Saul & Smith, Admr's.
1	Marshall, Elijah	1/3				
25	Merritt, Robert	1/3				
31	Miller, Andrew		1			
39	Morris, Spencer	1/3				

No.	Name	Lgs.	Lbr.	Acres	Date	Remarks
47	Morton, J. J.	1/3				F.W. Hubert, Assignee.
65	Marsh, Shubal	3/4				
73	McKay, Daniel	1/3				
110	McFaul, Samuel	1/3				
141	Mitchell, Nathan	1/3				
174	Moore, Lovich P.	1	1			
235	McCoy, Prospect	1/3				
250	McCoy, Green	1/3				
251	Moore, James W.	1	1			
259	Martin, Joseph S.	1/3				
265	Martin, Albert; Dec'd.	1/3				J.S. Martin, Admr.
304	Miller, Samuel S.		1			
312	Millican, James D.		1			
320	Millican, Deadem	3/4	1			
369	Mercer, Peter M.	1/3				
374	Moore, Morris			369		
380	Moore, Rebecca		1			
402	Mancha, Jose Fraucisco	1				John Allcorn, Assignee.
425	Mancha, Antonio		1			Thomas Gray, Assignee.
426	Mancha, Antonio		1			
435	Mitchell, Isaac R.	1/3				
454	Moss, Elibu		1			
456	Millican, Wm. T.			369		
460	Millican, Dan'l L.	3/4	1			
461	Morrison, Stephen; Dec'd.		1			Heirs of.
484	McFaddin, Nathan A.		1			
510	Millican, Elliott M.		1			
525	Morris, John			369		W.Y. McFarland, Assignee.
536	Millican John			369		
540	McGary, Edward			369		
545	McGary, Bridget		1			
550	McCleland, Ross	1/3				W. B. Smith, Admr.
556	Mott, John	1/3				
575	Monitt, Robert	2/3	1			
582	McCrocklin, Jesse L.		1			
385	Martin, Moses T.	1/3				
587	Mathers, Joseph	1/3				
538	McCorester, john	1/3				
19	Moorc, Azariah G.	2/3	1			
20	Mott, John	2/3	1			
22	McMahon, D. B.		1			
174	Millican, John H.	1/3				
175	Millican, Willis	1/3				
387	Miller, William G.	1/3				
155	Murphy, John	1/3				
300	Mancha, Argarbo	1/3				H. C. Hudson, Assignee.
321	Morris, Spencer, Sr.		1			John Morris, Admr.
5	Moseley, Robert J.		1			Robert Stevenson, Admr.

No.	Name	Lgs.	Lbr.	Acres	Date	Remarks
468	McCreery, H. L. D.	1/3				
518	McGuffin, William		1			
81	Numley, Andrew	1/3				
146	Numley, Archilaus	1	1			
228	Nimmo, James	1	1			
234	Newton, John	1/3				
278	Neal, John C.	1/3				
397	Newman, Jonathan		1			
505	Newner, Dyer	1/3				
506	Nash, Ira; Dec'd		1			To Prudence Kimble for heirs.
508	Nener, Wm. McM.	1/3				
576	Neal, John C.	2/3	1			
25	Nelson, Edward	1/3				Alanson Ferguso Admr.
12	Orick, Jas.; Dec'd.	1	1			Elizabeth Orick Admx.
479	Outlaw, Lucian B.	1/6				Jessee Bartlett Assignee.
513	Outlaw, Lucian B.	1/6				
532	Outlaw, Lucian B.	2/3	1			
115	Oldham, William	1/3				
21	Perry, Ducalion A.	1	1			
22	Perry, Sion W.	1/3				
64	Pitts, Obediah; Dec'd.		1			Shabal Marsh, Admr.
105	Pankey, James		1			
106	Perry, Albert G.		1			
171	Pillon, Richard	1	1			
177	Pruett, James	1	1			
179	Perry, Burrell		1			
197	Pryor, Mary		1			
220	Peake, Eliza		1			
236	Parker, Joshua		1			
257	Pitts, Levi	1/3				
258	Pitts, John G.	1/3				
292	Pinchard, Thornton W.	1	1			
293	Pankey, Mary Ann		1			
347	Petty, George W.	1	1			
351	Pills, John G.	2/3	1			
436	Powers, John	1	1			
465	Peebles, Richard R.	1/3				
130	Perry, Richardson	1/3				Burrell Pery, Admr.
21	Pendleton, Creed T.	1	1			Shubal Marsh, Admr.
	Parker, Gustavus A.	1	1			Proven before District Court.
29	Raney, Clement	3/4	1			
130	Rutland, John S.; Dec'd	1/3				Thomas Gay, Adm

No.	Name	Lgs.	Lbr.	Acres	DAte	Remarks
185	Reed, Elijah B.	1	1			
191	Robinson, S. W.; Dec'd	1	1			Mary Fulcher, Admr.
199	Reed, Joseph	1/3				
253	Rice, Alpheus	1	1			
261	Reese, Thos. B.; Dec'd.	1/3				James Reese, Admr.
274	Roberts, Reddin	1/3				
279	Robinson, Andrew; Jr.	1	1			
345	Reynolds, Lewis A.	1/3				
362	Roddy, Ephraim	1	1			
451	Robinson, William; Dec'd		1			Rob't Stevenson, Admr.
463	Roberts, William	1	1			
487	Reed, Jacob		1			J.W.Porter, Assignee.
491	Ruble, Feelden		1			
546	Robertson, Isaac E.	1/	1			
372	Richardson, James	1/3				Asa Mitchell, Assignee.
561	Rector, Jackson	1/3				
93	Reese, James	1	1			
67	Rice, Wate F.	1/3				
457	Raynolds, Lewis A.	2/3	1			
586	Reed, Harmon	1	1			J.P.Brown, Admr.
389	Roberts, Stephen R.	1	1			
30	Smith, William	1	1			
42	Smith, William P.	1	1			
55	Stephens, John M.	1/3				
89	Sypert, W. C.	1/3				J. C. Bartlett, Assignee.
98	Stevenson, Robert		1			
112	Sitton, Jesse	1/3				
135	Sherrod, William	1/3				
140	Simpson, Jeremiah W.	1/3				
143	Saunders, Benj. F.	1/3				
144	Swoap, Benj. F.	1/3				
159	Shapard, Thos. P.	1/3				
164	Smith, Nelson; Dec'd.		1			Dorcas Smith, Admr.
194	Swier, Geo. W.	1/3				
215	Smith, James H.	1	1			
218	Stephens, Thomas		1			
264	Swisher, Jas. G.	1	1			
269	Swisher, John M.	1/3				
272	Stephens, James R.	1/3				
283	Sessum, Nichael		1			
307	Saffell, John	1/3				
340	Swisher, Henry H.	1	1			
350	Saul, Thomas S.		2			
388	Sharp, John	1	1			
390	Shuff, Washington T.	1	1			
423	Slight, Cornelius A.	1/3				
442	Stevens, Jacob		1			

No.	Name	Lgs.	Lbr.	Acres	Date	Remarks
443	Steward, Jno. W.	1	1			James D. Allcorn Admr.
457	Sheils, Sam'l; Dec'd.	1	1			M & A Colvin, Admr.'s.
453	Sparks, E'd	1	1			
464	Sleight, John L.	1/3				
476	Smith, Joshua G.			369		Jesse Bartlett, Admr.
482	Sessum, Ellis	1/3				J. T. Eubanks & C. White, As'gs.
488	Smith, Benj.; Dec'd.		1			Catherine Smith, Admx.
520	Shepard, Thomas P.	2/3	1			
528	Sayres, John	1/3				
563	Stephens, James		1			
564	Shaw, John		1			
565	Smith, William H.	1/3				
568	Stevens, Madison M.		1			
580	Sutherland, Walter;Dec'd.		1			Moses Cummains, Admr.
400	Smothers, Archibald	1/3				
114	Stephens, John M.; Jr.	1	1			
324	Seward, Samuel		1			
176	Shoins, Ashley R.		1			Wm. H. Hawkins, Admr.
498	Shelton, James	1	1			
511	Smith, Francis; Dec'd.		1			John P. Coles, Admr.
285	Shellem, George A.	1/3				
385	Shelton, George W.	1/3				
333	Santer, William	1/3				
80	Tom, John F.	1/6				C. B. Stewart, Assignee.
162	Tumlinson, John	1/3				
176	Thompson, Thomas A.	1/3				
223	Tom, Charles	1/3				
302	Turnage, Shelby C.	1	1			
336	Tandy, Ralph	1/3				
337	Tandy, William M.	1/3				
338	Tandy, Albert M.	1/3				
331	Tumlinson, L. F.; Dec'd.	3/4	1			W. W. Arrington, Admr.
371	Tandy, Ralph; Dec'd.	1	1			Heirs of.
470	Thompson, David A.	1/3				
481	Tumlinson, William P.	1/3				
560	Thompson, David A.	2/3	1			
48	Tate, Elijah	3/4	1			
407	Tom, William	1				
408	Tom, William		1			Charles B. Stewa Assignee.
23	Wood, John L.	1	1			
26	Wood, Joseph H.	1	1			

No.	Name	Lgs.	Lbr.	Acres	Date	Remarks
35	Walden, Charles S.	1/3				
40	Walker, Asa; Dec'd.	1/3				W. W. Grant, Admr.
50	Walker, Saunders	1/3				Gail Borden, Assignee.
59	Wilhelm, Jas.	1/3				Rob't Stevenson Assignee.
92	Waters, George	1/3				
95	Williams, Charles J.	1/3				
113	Walker, John M.	1	1			
115	Walker, James	1	1			
116	Walker, William C.	1/3				
131	Woods, Noah	1/3				
133	Williamson John W.	1/3				
138	Woods, William R.	1/3				
142	Weeden, George	1/3				
145	Williams, John; Dec'd.	1	1			W. Y. McFarland, Admr.
201	Wells, Lewis	1/3				
237	Williams, Allen B.		1			
239	Williams, James	1/3				
241	White, Cary	1	1			
246	Woodward, Sandford		1			
276	Willson, William C.			369		
361	Wilkinson, James G.		1			
393	Wooton, Thos. J.		1			
395	Wooton, Greenville	1/3				
406	Walker, Gideon		1			C.B. Stewart, Assignee.
434	Walker, John	1/3				
437	Walker, James	1/3				Martin Clow & Co., Assignees.
449	Walker, Gideon	1/3				Rob't. Stevenson, Assignee.
472	Wyatt, Eliza (alias Santee)	1	1			
483	Williams, John	1/3				
489	Walker, Elizabeth	1	1			
494	Woodleiff, D. J.	2/3	1			Monroe Edwards, Assignee.
499	Willhelm, Richard; Dec'd.		1			Sarah Willhelm, Admx.
501	Wood, Alfred	1/3				
526	Wilson, William C.	2/3	1			
527	Williams, Christopher C.			369		
541	Wood, James T.		1			
566	Walker, Wm.	3/4	1			To Nancy Walker, heir.
581	Whiteside, George W.		1			
84	Whiteside, John T.		1			
	Williamson, Robert M.	10	10			10 Certif. numb'd from 87 to 96.
107	Waldon, Joseph B.	1	1			Charles S. Waldon Admr.
154	Williamson, H. J.	1/3				Thos. S. Saul Admr.

No.	Name	Lgs.	Lbr.	Acres	Date	Remarks
446	Walters, James		1			Jas. Gregg,Admr.
189	Williams, Henry	1/3				
280	Williams, Wm. M.	1/3				J.B.Chance,Admr.
296	Williamson, Hiram J.	1/3				Thos. S. Saul, Admr.
450	Walker, Gideon	2/3				
588	Wilson, Stephen R.	1/3				John P. Wyatt, Admr.
119	Young, William		1			
23	Yarborough, Swanson	2/3	1			

SECOND CLASS

No.	Name	Lgs.	Lbr.	Acres	Date	Remarks
69	Andrews, Robert H.			640		
124	Aldridge, Coleman			640	Oct. 1,1837	
8	Alexander, Robert			640		
44	Ammons, Jesse	1/3			Jul. 5,1838	
45	Anderson, Henry J.			1280		
73	Auritt, Philip			640		
122	Alsbrock, Wade			640	Jul. 4,1839	
139	Abney, Ira			640	Aug. 1,1839	
462	Arlett, W. A.	1/3			Dec.31,1839	Peter C. Hunter, Att'y for T. Arlett, Admr.
125	Ballard, Ryland C.			1280		
190	Brown, Wm. S.	1/3				
219	Burnett, Jacob	1/3				
29	Bone, John			640		
32	Baker, Wilson			640		
43	Bird, Isaac	1/3			Jul. 5,1838	
49	Barnes, Robert S.			640		
72	Butcher, Amos C.			640		
95	Brown, David M.			640		
100	Brown, John			640		
104	Baskin, Samuel P.			640		
105	Burchard, Barrett			640		
111	Bishop, John			640		
112	Buster, Claudius	640				
121	Butten, James R.	640				
128	Bush, Maples H.			640	Sep. 1838	
138	Bratton, Joseph			640		
146	Brent, William B.	1/3				Joseph B. Chance Admr.
157	Branch, William			640	Oct. 1838	
163	Buster, William W.			1280		
174	Browning, John H.			640	Jan. 1839	
175	Browning, Nathaniel P.			1280	Jan. 1839	
358	Burns, Leander			1280	Dec.23,1839	
223	Bridges, John	1/3				
325	Calicutt, James			640		
344	Cummins, John R.			640		

No.	Name	Lgs.	Lbr.	Acres	Date	Remarks
7	Crawford, Andrew			640		
24	Crawford, Joseph W.			640		
25	Cook, William H.	1/3				
33	Cleaveland, A. M.	1/3				
41	Chapman, William F.	1/3				
52	Case, Uriah F.			640		
58	Cole, James			640		
59	Chearics, William H.			640		
60	Cloud, Andrew J.			640		
66	Chappell, James			1280		
114	Cooke, John H.			640		John R. Cummins, Admr.
126	Craig, Benj. M.			640	Sep. 1838	
129	Cloud, James M.			1280	Sep. 1838	
153	Campbell, John			640	Oct. 1838	
164	Caunon, Edward J.			640	Dec. 1838	
168	Cobb, Clay			640	Dec. 1838	
170	Cobb, David			640	Dec. 1838	
177	Cooper, James			640	Jan. 1839	
8	Clayton, John S.			640	Mar.14,1839	
51	Chisum, Thomas			640	Apr. 4,1839	Joseph B. Chance, Admr.
105	Crittenden, Geo. B.			640	May 23,1839	
432	Charles, James			640	Dec.30,1839	
442	Castleman, James			1280	Dec.30,1839	
239	Clanton, Francis R.	1/3			Dec. 5,1839	
71	Crabtree, James B.	1/3				
30	Downs, John			640		
48	Dupuy, John B.	1/3			Jul. 6,1838	
74	Dorian, Joseph			640		
79	Davidge, J. H. M.			640		
90	Davis, Madison M.			640		
99	Duncan, Brice P.	1/3				
110	Darby, Arther M.			640		
137	Dennis, James H.	1/3			Sep. 1838	
142	Dupuy, John B.	2/3				
151	Deak, Jonathan A.			640	Oct. 1838	
7	Dick, Michael			640	Mar.14,1838	
301	Day, Henry			640	Dec.12,1838	
433	Demoss, George H.			640	Dec.30,1838	
2	Decockrille, Charles			640		
15	Evans, Charles T.			640		
318	Eldridge, Arther	1/3				
1	Eden, James			640		
15	Ewing, William H.	1/3				
97	Ewing, Samuel H.	1/3				
145	Evens, Eben. R.			640	Sep. 1838	Wilson Y. McFarland, Admr.
221	East, Edward W.			640	Dec. 5,1839	
271	Estes, Hannah			1280	Dec. 5,1839	
169	Ewing, Thomas J.			1280	Sep. 5,1839	

No.	Name	Lgs.	Lbr.	Acres	Date	Remarks
55	Fowler, Samuel	1/3				
86	Franklin, Josiah R.			640		
148	Furr, Henry H.			640	Oct. 1838	
178	Furgerson, Tyre G.			640	Jan. 1839	
403	Fisher, John			640	Dec.30,1839	
308	Giltner, Jacob	1/3			Feb. 8,1838	
319	George, Wiley			640		
53	Givens, George	1	1			
80	Gillespie, James F.	1/3				
169	Gilbert, William	1/3			Dec. 1838	Walker H. Gilber Admr.
106	Gordon, Wiley B.			640	May 27,1839	
149	Griffith, Jacob			640	Aug. 1,1839	
282	Gentry, George	1	1		Dec. 5,1839	
55	Gentry, George W.			640	Apr. 4,1839	
140	Gear, Nathaniel H.			1280		
10	Gaither, John S.			640		
99	Harris, S. B.			1280		
109	Heard, Thomas J.			640		
273	Hawkins, Timothy P.	1/3				
298	Hughes, Joseph			640	Feb. 1,1838	
316	Hudler, Joseph	1/3				
317	Hart, James			640		
19	Hayter, William			640		
24	Hughes, John			640		
38	Hardeman, William M.			640		
47	Hackworth, William W.			640		
77	Hendershott, John S.	1/3				
84	Haynes, Charles	1/3				
89	Harvey, Jno. H.			1280		
108	Huckerbee, James			640		
120	Hailey, Thomas J.			1280		
133	Herbert, Hardy H.			640		
139	Hunt, William			640	Sep. 1838	
143	Hunt, Fitch K.			640		
147	Houchin, John			1280	Oct. 1838	
150	Howard, Charles B.			640	Oct. 1838	
155	Harding, William			640	Oct. 1838	
156	Hoyt, John M.			640	Oct. 1838	
160	Holt, James H.			1280	Oct. 1838	
167	Hutchins, Meritt			640	Dec. 1838	
171	Heffington, James G.			640	Dec. 1838	
176	Horton, George W.			640	Jan. 1839	
441	Harding, Thomas B.			640	Dec.30,1839	
165	Irion, Van Ransseler			640	Dec. 1838	
141	Irvin, Thomas			640	Sep. 1838	
349	Irwin, Joseph S.			1280	Dec. 5,1839	
357	Irwin, Absolam			1280	Dec.23,1839	
359	Irwin, Kibble T.			1280	Dec.23,1839	

No.	Name	Lgs.	Lbr.	Acres	Date	Remarks
172	Johnson, Theodore F.			640		
323	Jones, Milborn			640		
96	Jones, Gilland			640		
19	Jennigen, Hardy R.			640		
123	Jenkins, James R.			640	Sep. 1838	
131	Johnson, Benedict			640	Sep. 1838	
112	Johnson, Jacob			640	May 31,1839	
475	Jones, James S.			640	Dec.31,1839	
39	Jacobs, Madison G.			640		
159	Johnson, Jonathan			640	Oct. 1838	
177	Keyes, Horatio			640	Sep. 7,1838	
206	Kennady, Robert			640	Oct. 3,1838	
275	Kuiger, Daniel J.			640		
11	Kelly, Robert P.	1/3				
40	Kerkam, Green	1/3				
68	Keesee, William			1280		
72	Loffin, T. B.			1280	May 2,1839	
5	Lahee, James	1/3				
87	Longley, Campbell	1	1		May 2,1839	
98	Lloyd, Washington			640		
342	Lott, Robert A.			1280		
76	Lile, Robert			1280		
172	Leach, James			640		Edwin S. Cobler, Admr.
328	Miller, Alsey S.			640		
4	Moffit, James P.	1/3				
6	Millbrook, Augustus			640		
16	McKissick, John W.	1	1			
20	Martin, Wilson A.			640		
31	McFarland, Wilson J.			640		
56	Mickelborough, Edward			640		
57	Mickelborough, Henry			1280		
67	McCreary, William A.			640		
70	Morrey, Edward			640		
71	Marsh, Richard			640		James Eden, Admr.
78	McCorran, Alfred			640		
83	Moore, Charles	1/3				Jerome B. Robertson, Admr.
88	Marley, William			640		
102	McKinnon, Murdoch			640		
115	McNuse, Parrot W.	1/3				
117	McCoy, Charles B.	1/3				
124	Manning, Charles G.			640	Sep. 1838	
134	McKean, John G.			1280		Betsey, McKean, Admr.
144	Munson, Ira			640	Sep. 1838	
154	Murray, John	1/3			Oct. 1838	
161	Mullen, Peter			640	Oct. 1838	
162	McCampbell, William B.			1280	Oct. 1838	
13	McDannell, James			640		
34	McDermott, Peter			1280		

No.	Name	Lgs.	Lbr.	Acres	Date	Remarks
86	Mitchell, James H.			640	May 2,1839	
108	Miller, George B.			640	Jun.10,1839	
150	McKay, Samuel M.			640	Aug. 5,1839	
281	Mayfield, Suthaland	1	1		Dec. 5,1839	
321	Mayfield, William			1280	Dec.12,1839	
450	McCown, Joshua W.			1280	Dec.31,1839	
24	McDaniels, Benjamin	2/3	1		Mar. 1839	
476	Newsom, Nathan			320	Dec.31,1839	Augmentation.
27	Ogborn, John C.	1	1			
497	Ostrander, Volny	1/3			Jan.11,1840	
301	Pate, William H.	1/3			Feb. 6,1838	Alanson Ferguso Assignee.
322	Palmer, Thomas			640		
3	Phillips, Wilson			640		
9	Parker, Dudly J.			1280		
37	Palmer, John C.			640		
54	Poole, Seymour S.			640		
113	Porter, Rezin			640		
136	Phillips, Benjamin			1280		
149	Porter, Sims B.			640		
27	Petty, Isham			640	Mar.19,1839	
166	Patterson, William B.			640	Sep. 6.1839	
181	Porter, John B.	1/3			Sep.12,1839	
238	Peters, William R.			640	Dec. 5,1839	
500	Porter, Reece A.	1	1		Jan.11,1839	
173	Riley, John	1/3				
12	Regan, Henry			640		
22	Richardson, William S.			640		
46	Roberts, Mark			640		
50	Robertson, Henry A.			640		
61	Ramsey, Robert D.			640		
75	Rice, Soloman C.			640		
91	Randolph, Harvey			640		1838
92	Randolph, Perry D.			640		
93	Randolph, John			1280		
418	Robertson, James			1280		
122	Royall, William B.	1/3				
127	Rice, William			1240	Sep. 1838	
158	Reittner, Christen			640	Oct. 1838	
13	Rice, John G.			640	Mar.14,1839	
14	Rice, James P.			640	Mar.14,1839	
43	Rutledge, William P.			640	Mar.20,1839	
507	Rice, Charles H.			640	Jan.11,1840	
107	Roberts, Luke			640	Jan.11,1840	
109	Ridley, Mark C.			640		
44	Stevens, Thomas			640	Mar.20,1839	Wm. P. Rutledge Admr.
170	Shaw, Jonathan			640	Sep. 5,1839	
409	Smith, Charles H.			1280	Dec.30,1839	

No.	Name	Lgs.	Lbr.	Acres	DAte	Remarks
86	Sims, James B.			640		
14	Stevens, John P.			640		
26	Saunders, Leonidas			640		
28	Stout, Berryman O.	1/3				
42	Stuteville, James C.	1/3				
85	Shelburn, John P.			640		
130	Smith, Henry			640		
135	Skorupski, John	1/3				
184	Thomas, Benjamin R.			640		
290	Thayer, William C.	1/3			FEb. 5,1838	
339	Tom, William C.			640		
17	Torrell, Lindsey T.	1/3				
65	Tully, William D.			640		
69	Trimmier, William			640		
101	Thompson, Thomas J.			640		
106	Taylor, Miles N.			1280		
132	Tivoy, Joseph A.			640	Sep. 1838	
199	Vezey, Wiley G.			640	Sep.28,1839	
62	Voilett, John			640		
18	Wohlers, Johann Anna			640		
73	Wiggins, W. W.			640	May 2,1839	
121	Whitaker, Meradeth			1280	Jul. 4,1839	
160	Wilson, John N.			640	Sep. 5,1839	
190	Wilson, Hugh			1280	Sep.18,1839	
272	West, George			1280	Dec. 5,1839	
167	Whiteside, Philip S.			640	Sep. 5,1839	
101	Wyatt, John P.	1/3				
230	Willis, Peter J.			640		
332	Williams, Henry B.	1/3				
35	Winsett, John			640		
63	Walker, Silas H.			640		
94	Williams, John C.			640		
103	Whitaker, Jno. M.	1/3			Dec. 1838	
166	Whitaker, Jno. M.	2/3	1		Dec. 1838	
173	White, Hardin			640	Jan. 1839	
51	Young, James	1/3				

THIRD CLASS

No.	Name	Lgs.	Lbr.	Acres	Date	Remarks
75	Alsobrook, W. H.			320	May 2,1839	
100	Armstrong, George			320	May 2,1839	
116	Allen, W. R.			320	Jun.28,1839	
141	Adams, Francis			320	Aug. 1,1839	
152	Arnett, John H.			320	Aug.22,1839	
350	Ashley, John P.			320	Dec.21,1839	
380	Ashley, William			320	Dec.23,1839	
464	Allen, Jesse J.			320	Dec.30,1839	
509	Atkins, John J.			320	Jan.11,1840	

No.	Name	Lgs.	Lbr.	Acres	Date	Remarks
16	Blessing, Henry			320	Mar.14,1839	
38	Bullock, Richard			640	Mar.20,1839	
52	Brake, Joseph			320	Apr. 4,1839	
66	Baker, George			320	May 2,1839	
76	Bishop, Wayne			320	May 2,1839	
99	Baltzar, William			320	May 2,1839	
102	Brotherton, Robert			320	May 2,1839	
114	Bartlett, Jesse			320	Jun.25,1839	
148	Bayley, Shepard			640	Aug. 1,1839	
159	Bigelow, James S.			320	Sep. 5,1839	
193	Brown, James			640	Sep.19,1839	
210	Brown, James			320	Oct. 4,1839	
230	Boston, James			640	Dec. 5,1839	
237	Boner, Christian			640	Dec. 5,1839	
248	Bruce, Wilson W.			320	Dec. 5,1839	
259	Blake, Edwin			320	Dec. 5,1839	
268	Briggance, Foster			320	Dec. 5,1839	
293	Benham, George W.			320	Dec.11,1839	
307	Buson, John W.			320	Dec.12,1839	
333	Baylor, Robert E. B.			320	Dec.12,1839	
338	Bedford, Seth			320	Dec.21,1839	
362	Boyd, Amon			320	Dec.23,1839	
364	Bell, Jacob			320	Dec.23,1839	
389	Brinnin, Kerr			320	Dec.30,1839	
415	Brown, Joseph G.			320	Dec.30,1839	
418	Brown, William A.			640	Dec.30,1839	
431	Barnds, Jacob			320	Dec.30,1839	
434	Browning, William A.			320	Dec.30,1839	
443	Bigham, Samuel; Dec'd.			320	Dec.30,1839	John Ellis, Admr
487	Bostwick, William			320	Jan.11,1840	
503	Bloodworth, James C.			640	Jan.11,1840	
516	Baldridge, James			320	Jan.11,1840	
518	Best, William			320	Jan.11,1840	
520	Billow, John			640	Jan.11,1840	
521	Billow, Thomas			320	Jan.11,1840	
1	Cook, Lazarus D.			320	Mar.14,1839	
35	Crosby, Mary			640	Mar.19,1839	
36	Clark, N. A.			640	Mar.19,1839	
42	Clark, James J.			320	Mar.20,1839	
104	Chambliss, Nathaniel			640	May 23,1839	
124	Cummings, John			320	Jul. 4,1839	
140	Cleary, Tresvant			320	Aug. 1,1839	
142	Cleary, Francis W.			320	Aug. 1,1839	
156	Cissna, Joseph			320	Sep. 5,1839	
204	Chappell, William			640	Oct. 3,1839	
214	Cannon, James M.			640	Oct.16,1839	
234	Clow, John J.			640	Dec. 5,1839	
235	Cook, Isaac J.			320	Dec. 5,1839	
319	Clark, David			320	Dec.12,1839	
331	Chance, William A.			320	Dec.12,1839	
342	Cloud, John C.			640	Dec. 5,1839	
343	Crook, James H.			320	Dec. 5,1839	

No.	Name	Lgs.	Lbr.	Acres	Date	Remarks
374	Childress, James W.			320	Dec.23,1839	
381	Chappell, Robert			320	Dec.23,1839	
384	Connell, Sampson, Jr.			320	Dec.30,1839	
412	Conn, Harvey D.			320	Dec.30,1839	
425	Collum, Morgan			320	Dec.30,1839	
427	Carlez, William			320	Dec.30,1839	
428	Croft, Jacob			640	Dec.30,1839	
469	Calvert, Hugh A.			640	Dec.31,1839	
472	Chappell, George T.			320	Dec.31,1839	
505	Crowder, Nathaniel			320	Jan.11,1840	
522	Cleveland, John M.			640	Jan.11,1840	
523	Cleveland, James			640	Jan.11,1840	
138	Dix, Sherman D.			320	Aug. 1,1839	
163	Dubose, Elias			640	Sep. 5,1839	
228	Dixon, George C.			320	Dec. 5,1839	
292	Dodd, John			320	Dec.11,1839	
323	Dowland, Henry			320	Dec.12,1839	
339	Dunlap, Hugh			320	Dec.21,1839	
397	Dobbins, Starritt J.			320	Dec.30,1839	
494	Davis, Campbell M.			320	Jan.11,1840	
77	Eastham, Wm.			640	May 2,1839	
135	Estis, Anson L.			640	Aug. 1,1839	
194	Eldridge, John			640	Sep.19,1839	
195	Eldridge, William			320	Sep.19,1839	
229	Ellis, John			320	Dec. 5,1839	
236	Emmory, James			320	Dec. 5,1839	
299	Estes, Edward T.			320	Dec.12,1839	
365	Elgin, John			640	Dec.23,1839	
411	Edney, Samuel			640	Dec.30,1839	
413	Edney, Newton J.			320	Dec.30,1839	
30	Ferrell, Jesse			320	Mar.10,1839	
31	Ferrell, James; Dec'd.			640	Mar.10,1839	Jesse Ferrell, Admr.
39	Frazer, George R.			320	Mar.20,1839	
54	Ferrell, John			320	Apr. 4,1839	
56	Fitch, C. H.			320	May 2,1839	
58	Fitch, Sterling C.			320	May 2,1839	
146	Frost, James			320	Aug. 1,1839	
172	Foley, John H.			640	Sep. 5,1839	
220	Fugua, Stephen			640	Dec. 5,1839	
224	Finley, Josiah B.			320	Dec. 5,1839	
274	Ferrell, McAmy W.			320	Dec. 5,1839	
315	Finley, Wm. M.			320	Dec.12,1839	
326	French, James E.			320	Dec.12,1839	
377	Farmer, Willis H.			320	Dec.23,1839	
463	Farrell, Mahala			640	Dec.31,1839	
490	Foreman, John			320	Jan.11,1840	
46	Goodenow, Sarah			640	Mar.20,1839	
50	Gorman, Olvier			640	Apr. 4,1839	
64	Gilmore, Milford			640	May 2,1839	

No.	Name	Lgs.	Lbr.	Acres	Date	Remarks
207	Gibson, Isham			640	Oct. 3,1839	
222	Greer, Gilbert			320	Dec. 5,1839	
250	Griffen, John, Sr.			640	Dec. 5,1839	
251	Griffen, John; Jr.			320	Dec. 5,1839	
317	Gibbs, Arion C.			320	Dec.12,1839	
327	Greenwood, John			640	Dec.12,1839	
328	Greenwood, Beverly C.			320	Dec.12,1839	
329	Greenwood, Hudson A.			320	Dec.12,1839	
355	Gammon, Samuel			640	Dec.23,1839	
356	Gammon, George			320	Dec.23,1839	
361	Gentry, James R.			320	Dec.23,1839	
375	Goodwin, John W.			320	Dec.23,1839	
387	Griffen, Allen			320	Dec.30,1839	
480	Goodwin, George			320	Jan.11,1840	
489	Grimes, John B.			320	Jan.11,1840	
15	Husted, Lott			320	Mar.14,1839	
31	Hemphill, John			320	Mar.19,1839	
57	Holmes, William S.			320	May 2,1839	
61	Hamilton, James C.			320	May 2,1839	
113	Hayden, Millard W.			320	Jun.21,1839	
117	Harris, Arah			320	Jun.28,1839	
118	Hervey, Edward R.; Sr.			640	Jul. 4,1839	
119	Hervey, Robert E.			320	Jul. 4,1839	
120	Hervey, Edward R.; Jr.			320	Jul. 4,1839	
128	Harrington, Elias M.			640	Jul.18,1839	
129	Harrell, John			320	Jul.18,1839	
132	Harvey, Samuel H.			640	Jul.22,1839	
143	Harrington, John W.			320	Aug. 1,1839	
162	Hitchcock, Isaac W.			320	Sep. 5,1839	
182	Harrington, William			320	Sep.13,1839	
183	Hunter, Peter C.			320	Aug. 1,1839	
186	Higgins, Henry			640	Sep.16,1839	
198	Hanover, Hiram			320	Sep.28,1839	
205	Hitchcock, Matthew M.			320	Oct. 3,1839	
225	Higgins, Wm. H.			320	Dec. 5,1839	
266	Hogg, Joseph L.			320	Dec. 5,1839	
270	Harrell, James H.			320	Dec. 5,1839	
283	Happy, Umfra			320	Dec. 5,1839	
298	Hairston, Richard			640	Dec.12,1839	
385	Harris, Wm			640	Dec.20,1839	
406	Holmes, Willett			640	Dec.20,1839	
408	Harrell, John A.			640	Dec.20,1839	
422	Harris, Amanda C.			640	Dec.20,1839	
426	Hicks, Elbert			320	Dec.20,1839	
460	Harris, Mary R.			640	Dec.31,1839	
479	Hall, Wm. S.			320	Dec.31,1839	
227	Irvin, Jordan			320	Dec. 5,1839	
197	Johnson, Edward			320	Sep.28,1839	
208	Jackson, Riddick P.			640	Oct. 4,1839	
215	Jones, Allen			320	Dec. 5,1839	
290	Jones, James R.			320	Dec.11,1839	

No.	Name	Lgs.	Lbr.	Acres	Date	Remarks
393	Johnson, Greer			640	Dec.30,1839	
394	Johnson, Albert A.			320	Dec.30,1839	
395	Johnson, Rufus L.			320	Dec.30,1839	
504	Jones, Jefferson Y.			320	Jan.11,1840	
145	Killough, Isaac			640	Aug. 1,1839	
386	King, Enoch			640	Dec. 5,1839	
288	Knoop, John			320	Dec. 5,1839	
372	Kerr, Alfred B. F.			320	Dec.23,1839	
316	Kirk, Mary Ann			640	Dec.12,1839	
404	Kirk, Grandison			640	Dec.30,1839	
419	Kane, Richard T.			320	Dec.30,1839	
5	Labrack, Francis			640	Mar.14,1839	
33	Layne, George			640	Mar.19,1839	
53	Lytle, William			640	Apr. 4,1839	
70	Lott, Robert			320	May 2,1839	
101	Lockridge, William			640	May 2,1839	
153	Lyall, William H.			640	Sep. 5,1839	
216	Love, Allen			640	Dec. 5,1839	
291	Layne, Robert			320	Dec.11,1839	
217	Love, Young E.			320	Dec. 5,1839	
218	Love, James			320	Dec. 5,1839	
330	Lindsey, Buford B.			640	Dec.12,1839	
401	Langston, John W.			320	Dec.30,1839	
420	Lott, John, Jr.			320	Dec.30,1839	
421	Lott, Hiram			320	Dec.30,1839	
435	Lester, Elias			320	Dec.30,1839	
483	Lindsey, Alfred J.			320	Dec.30,1839	
514	Lamb, Mundy			640	Jan.11,1840	
4	Mabry, Evans			640	Mar.14,1839	
10	Moore, Martin			320	Mar.14,1839	
40	Moore, Alfred			640	Mar.20,1839	
83	Merriweather, A. G.			320	May 2,1839	
247	Meador, Daniel			640	Dec. 5,1839	
263	Mancha, Juan			320	Dec. 5,1839	
264	Mairs, W. H.			320	Dec. 5,1839	
269	Marshall, Charles			320	Dec. 5,1839	
279	Mills, John T.			320	Dec. 5,1839	
284	McCoy, Henry C.			320	Dec. 5,1839	
353	McEwen, Nancy H.			640	Dec.23,1839	
369	Miller, Robert F.			320	Dec.23,1839	
373	Mabin, Azariah			320	Dec.23,1839	
383	Morgan, Levi			640	Dec.30,1839	
390	Middleton, Mary Ann			640	Dec.30,1839	
398	Middleton, Samuel W.			640	Dec.30,1839	
399	Moore, W. W.			640	Dec.30,1839	
402	Mann, William			640	Dec.30,1839	
410	Morgan, Mordecni			320	Dec.30,1839	
417	Marler, Capus			320	Dec.30,1839	
423	Mosley, Mason			640	Dec.30,1839	
429	March, Wade H.			320	Dec.30,1839	

No.	Name	Lgs.	Lbr.	Acres	Date	Remarks
430	Marler, Thomas			640	Dec.30,1839	
438	Millbanks, John			320	Dec.30,1839	
439	Merick, William			320	Dec.30,1839	
453	Moore, George E.			640	Dec.31,1839	
454	Mariner, Charles			320	Dec.31,1839	
466	Millican, James			320	Dec.31,1839	
471	Mitchell, John			320	Dec.31,1839	
482	Morrow, Samuel			640	Jan.11,1840	
484	Martin, Isaiah			640	Jan.11,1840	
493	Mitchell, William			320	Jan.11,1840	
506	Marshall, William			320	Jan.11,1840	
71	McClusky, George B.			640	Mar. 9,1839	
131	McFarland, John C.			640	Jul.19,1839	
211	McCown, William			320	Oct. 4,1839	
212	McCaleb, Hiram			320	Oct,12,1839	
232	McPhail, Hugh			320	Dec. 5,1839	
256	McNeesse, Joy			640	Dec. 5,1839	
257	McNeesse, John			640	Dec. 5,1839	
258	McNeesse, Edward			320	Dec. 5,1839	
278	McLauren, Hugh			320	Dec. 5,1839	
311	McAdory, Robert			640	Dec.12,1839	
314	McConnell, James			320	Dec.12,1839	
341	McCaleb, William B.			320	Dec. 5,1839	
416	McGill, John E.			320	Dec.30,1839	
467	McDade, Alexander			640	Dec.31,1839	
468	McDade, John A.			320	Dec.31,1839	
103	Noble, Ann H. P.			640	May 23,1839	
209	Narcisse, Louis			320	Oct. 4,1839	
313	Newson, Nathan M.			320	Dec.12,1839	
396	Newman, Wm. T.			320	Dec.30,1839	
451	Nelson, Robert B.			320	Dec.31,1839	
347	Oldham, Moses			640	Dec. 5,1839	
3	Postern, Jeremiah			320	Mar.14,1839	
32	Patterson, Samuel			320	Mar.19,1839	
74	Pipkin, Stewart W.			320	May 2,1839	
131	Pitts, Isaac			320	Aug. 1,1839	
136	Payne, William H.			640	Aug. 1,1839	
137	Pacioak, Andrew			320	Aug. 1,1839	
189	Porter, Dempsey			320	Sep.18,1839	
219	Patterson, William			640	Dec. 5,1839	
226	Pierce, Horatio E.			320	Dec. 5,1839	
231	Pierce, Earle			320	Dec. 5,1839	
233	Punderson, Austin			640	Dec. 5,1839	
254	Price, Wm. C.			640	Dec. 5,1839	
255	Price, James M.			640	Dec. 5,1839	
265	Parrott, Handy M.			320	Dec. 5,1839	
287	Pace, William			640	Dec. 5,1839	
310	Pertte, F. G.			320	Dec. 5,1839	
382	Ponk, Moses			320	Dec.23,1839	
485	Payne, John			320	Jan.11,1840	

No.	Name	Lgs.	Lbr.	Acres	Date	Remarks
9	Rucker, Benjamin F.			320	Mar.14,1839	
47	Rutlidge, Thomas P.			320	Mar.19,1839	
69	Rice, Alpheus P.			320	Mar.19,1839	
168	Rice, Joseph			320	Sep. 5,1839	
179	Root, John B.			640	Sep.12,1839	
196	Rucker, Thomas J. R.			320	Sep.19,1839	
260	Rich, Isaac			640	Dec. 5,1839	
261	Rich, James A.			320	Dec. 5,1839	
262	Reddin, Isaac			320	Dec. 5,1839	
280	Reid, William H. J.			320	Dec. 5,1839	
310	Roberts, Thomas			320	Dec.12,1839	
334	Rouen, John			640	Dec.12,1839	
352	Rice, Joseph			320	Dec.21,1839	
414	Rhodes, John			320	Dec.30,1839	
424	Ringgold, Thomas			320	Dec.30,1839	
436	Rice, Saban			640	Dec.30,1839	
465	Rogers, Joseph H.			320	Dec.31,1839	
470	Ridens, John			320	Dec.31,1839	
478	Rogers, John H.			640	Dec.31,1839	
488	Ratliff, James			640	Jan.11,1840	
501	Roberts, Ingram S.			320	Jan.11,1840	
515	Reems, John			320	Jan.11,1840	
2	Sypert, Thomas			320	Mar.14,1839	
48	Sneed, George K.			320	Mar.20,1839	
59	Spencer, Stephen			320	May 2,1839	
65	Stiene, John			320	May 2,1839	
98	Strain, Isaac M.			320	May 2,1839	
144	Shaw, Lot			640	Aug. 1,1839	
165	Seward, John H.			320	Sep. 5,1839	
246	Snell, James O.			320	Dec. 5,1839	
252	Snell, Carlton			320	Dec. 5,1839	
267	Skinner, Robert A.			320	Dec. 5,1839	
294	Stephenson, Benjamin			640	Dec.12,1839	
296	Sivier, Ebzama			320	Dec.12,1839	
306	Skinner, Jesse			320	Dec.12,1839	
308	Steger, William M.			320	Dec.12,1839	
312	Swisher, James M.			320	Dec.12,1839	
320	Strickland, Duke			320	Dec.12,1839	
344	Smith, John H.			320	Dec.12,1839	
346	Sneed, Israil			640	Dec. 5,1839	
348	Smith, James			320	Dec. 5,1839	
351	Sampson, Allen			320	Dec.21,1839	
366	Sullivan, Holland			320	Dec.23,1839	
367	Smith, Samuel			320	Dec.23,1839	
370	Sowell, Charles J.			320	Dec.23,1839	
371	Swiney, Laiken B. S.			320	Dec.23,1839	
376	Stokes, Gay			320	Dec.23,1839	
400	Smith, John T.			320	Dec.30,1839	
405	Strumpski, John			320	Dec.20,1839	
407	Strother, Alex			320	Dec.30,1839	
410	Sargant, Washington			320	Dec.30,1839	
452	Sturtevant, Francis E.			320	Dec.31,1839	

No.	Name	Lgs.	Lbr.	Acres	Date	Remarks
517	Saunders, Drury			640	Jan.11,1840	
6	Templeton, James E.			320	Mar.14,1839	
62	Taylor, Edward W.			640	May 2,1839	
63	Taylor, H. D.			320	May 2,1839	
155	Tom, Joseph			640	Sep. 5,1839	
157	Tom, James H.			320	Sep. 5,1839	
158	Tom, R. W.			320	Sep. 5,1839	
185	Tom, Alfred			320	Sep.16,1839	
249	Tompkins, Caleb			320	Dec. 8,1839	
275	Terrell, Malcomb B.			640	Dec. 5,1839	
303	Trimmier, Thomas			640	Dec.12,1839	
304	Tate, Isham			640	Dec.12,1839	
305	Trimmier, John			320	Dec.12,1839	
360	Tidwell, Dempsey			640	Dec.23,1839	
437	Trout, Christopher C.			320	Dec.30,1839	
473	Temple, Wm. B.			320	Dec.31,1839	
481	Thompson, James M.			640	Jan.11,1840	
486	Terry, Micajah			640	Jan.11,1840	
289	Upchurch, Albert			320	Dec. 5,1839	
123	Vaughan, John			640	Jul. 4,1839	
188	Vardeman, Jeremiah			320	Sep.16,1839	
223	Vick, Cullen			640	Dec. 5,1839	
11	Wheeler, Asa			640	Mar.14,1839	
12	Wheeler, Rodney; Dec'd.			320	Mar.14,1839	Asa Wheeler,Ad
41	Waties, Thomas			320	Mar.20,1839	
78	Wilkins, WEst			320	May 2,1839	
79	Woodiel, Thomas C.			640	May 2,1839	
81	Wood, Ann			640	May 2,1839	
82	Wood, Augustus H.			320	May 2,1839	
171	Wood, A. H.			320	Sep. 5,1839	
276	Watson, Pleasant C.			640	Dec. 5,1839	
277	Watson, John			320	Dec. 5,1839	
285	Wheeler, William			640	Dec. 5,1839	
295	Watson, Lindsey			320	Dec.12,1839	
302	Walter, Wm. C.			640	Dec.12,1839	
318	Woodward, Jacob			640	Dec.12,1839	
335	Wilkinson, James			640	Dec.21,1839	
336	Wilkinson, Livingston			640	Dec.21,1839	
337	Wilkinson, Warren G.			320	Dec.21,1839	
345	Walter, Thomas			320	Dec. 5,1839	
363	Woods, William			320	Dec.23,1839	
386	Waddill, Frederick B.			640	Dec.30,1839	
392	Wedgeworth, David B.			640	Dec.30,1839	
418	White, Thomas C.			320	Dec.30,1839	
449	White, Littleberry			320	Dec.31,1839	
495	Walker, Miles			320	Jan.11,1840	
496	Wilkinson, Joel			640	Jan.11,1840	
499	Williams, Jonathan			320	Jan.11,1840	
512	Ward, John			640	Jan.11,1840	

No.	Name	Lgs.	Lbr.	Acres	Date	Remarks
513	Ward, Stephen S.			640	Jan.11,1840	
519	Welsh, Joseph			320	Jan.11,1840	
502	Young, Theodore L.			320	Jan.11,1840	

INDEX

NAMES IN THE INTRODUCTION ARE NOT INCLUDED IN THIS INDEX.
(PLEASE CHECK FOR VARIANT SPELLINGS OF SURNAMES)

www.ingramcontent.com/pod-product-compliance
Lightning Source LLC
LaVergne TN
LVHW080019110826
845148LV00019B/986

* 9 7 8 0 7 8 8 4 8 5 9 8 5 *